The Concierge's Guide™ to Washington, DC

Other Books in This Series

The Concierge's Guide™ to Washington, DC

McDowell Bryson
Adele Ziminski

John Wiley & Sons, Inc.

New York • Chichester • Brisbane • Toronto • Singapore

Library of Congress Cataloging-in-Publication Data

Bryson, McDowell. 1938-
  The concierge's guide to Washington, D.C. / McDowell Bryson. Adele Ziminski.
    p.   cm.
  ISBN 0-471-52651-7
  1. Washington, (D.C.)—Description—Guide books.
  2. Washington, (D.C.)—Directories.   I. Ziminski, Adele.
  II. Title.
  F192.3.B78 1990
  917.5304′4—dc20   90-40993
                                                      CIP

Printed in the United States of America

91 92 10 9 8 7 6 5 4 3 2 1

Contents

Contents

Contents

Contents

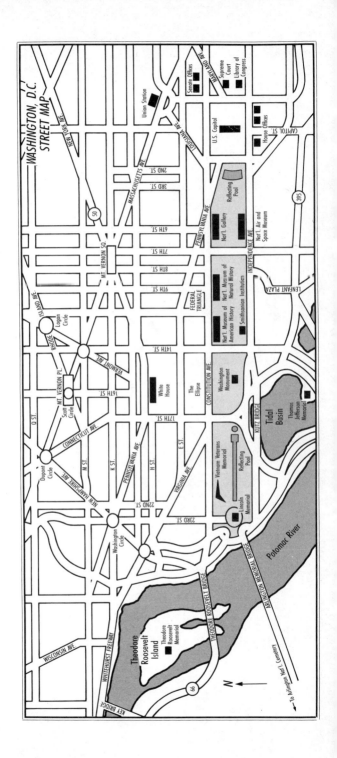

Metrorail System Map

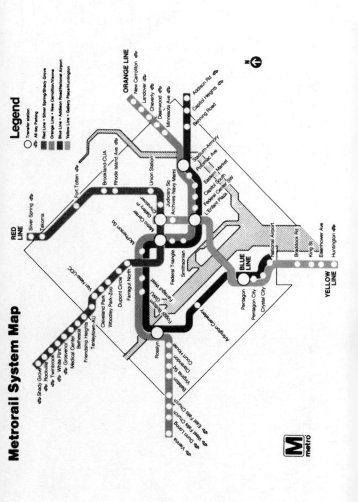

Legend

○ Transfer station
⇌ All day Parking

Red Line • Silver Spring/Shady Grove
Orange Line • New Carrollton/Vienna
Blue Line • Addison Road/National Airport
Yellow Line • Gallery Place/Huntington

ORANGE LINE

⇌ New Carrollton
⇌ Landover
⇌ Cheverly
⇌ Deanwood
Minnesota Ave ⇌

Addison Rd ⇌
Capitol Heights ⇌
Benning Road

Stadium-Armory
Potomac Ave
Eastern Market
Capitol South
Federal Center SW
L'Enfant Plaza

Archives-Navy Meml
Judiciary Sq
Gallery Pl
Metro Center
McPherson Sq

Union Station
Rhode Island Ave ⇌
Brookland-CUA
Fort Totten

⇌ Silver Spring
Takoma

RED LINE

⇌ Shady Grove
⇌ Rockville
⇌ Twinbrook
⇌ White Flint
⇌ Grosvenor
⇌ Medical Center
Bethesda
Friendship Heights
Tenleytown-AU
Van Ness-UDC
Cleveland Park
Woodley Park-Zoo
Dupont Circle
Farragut North

Federal Triangle
Smithsonian
Farragut West
Foggy Bottom-GWU

Rosslyn

⇌ Vienna
⇌ Dunn Loring
⇌ West Falls Church
⇌ East Falls Church
Ballston
Clarendon
Virginia Sq
Court House

Arlington Cemetery

Pentagon
Pentagon City
Crystal City
National Airport

BLUE LINE

Braddock Rd
King St
Eisenhower Ave
Huntington

YELLOW LINE

N

Ⓜ metro

INTRODUCTION

This book was written for the millions of people who visit Washington every year, as well as for the millions who live here year-round. It contains answers to the questions that we, as concierges in major hotels, have been asked over and over again. In fact, it is an expanded version of our own "Little Black Book," organized in the concise and immediately accessible manner that brings the major tool of concierges—information—to your fingertips.

Because of our unique position as arbiters and dispensers of service to so many guests, we know you have no time to be inundated with excess information, so we have deliberately excluded out-of-the-way places and obscure "finds." Our experience has shown that most visitors, be they savvy cosmopolites, busy executives, or harried parents with small children in tow, have limited time and want to visit the places famous around the world as representing historic Washington. On the other hand, since Washington is famous around the world for the diversity of its offerings, we've included a variety of listings to reflect this quality as well. Thus, you'll find here not only expansive (and somewhat opinionated) listings of the city's major hotels, restaurants, museums, department stores, night clubs, and comedy clubs, as you'd well expect, but also a number of surprises, such as:

- Helicopter and balloon rides
- A Congressional directory
- The best places to have an "English tea"
- Singles bars, piano bars, sports bars, and gay bars
- Tennis courts, theater tickets, tobacconists, and tipping advice

To provide you with the same easy, fingertip accessibility that we as concierges have come to depend upon, we've organized the book alphabetically. Most entries appear at least twice, on their own and under a broader category. For example, if you wanted to see Washington's most visited monument, the Vietnam Veterans Memorial, and just need the address or telephone number, you'll find it listed under V. But it's also listed under S for SIGHTSEEING, with a complete description for those who are planning their own sightseeing tour and are uncertain as to what to visit. As another example, the Folger Shakespeare Library, which contains the world's largest collection of works by and about the Immortal Bard, is listed under F, but is also listed as an alphabetical subentry under S for SIGHTSEEING and under L for LIBRARIES. Want to get your hair cut by the barber to the presidents? Or at either the House of Representatives Barber Shop or the Senate Barber Shop? Look under H for HAIRCUTS or under B for BARBER SHOPS.

Unless otherwise noted, all telephone area codes are 202; and to make getting around easier, we've noted cross streets, whenever possible, in parentheses after the address. Prices and times are the most current available, but, of course, are always subject to change. We suggest that you always call and double-check before making your plans.

We've found our book easy to use and think you will too. Enjoy our nation's capital and don't forget to make use of the concierges at your hotel—they're there to help you.

A

A & A Fine Wines & Spirits   337-3161
2201 Wisconsin Avenue, N.W.

A-1 Quality Limousine   575-2040
1234 Massachusetts Avenue, N.W., Suite 119

A-Allied Rentals   1-301-229-5400
6825 Reed Street, Bethesda, Maryland

A.T. Jones & Sons   1-301-748-7087
708 North Howard Street, Baltimore, Maryland

AA Secretarial Services   466-3702
1522 K Street, N.W.

AAA Road Service   222-5000

Access for the Handicapped   966-5500

Adam A. Weschler & Son   628-1281
905 E Street, N.W.

Adams Davidson Galleries   965-3800
3233 P Street, N.W.

ADAMS MORGAN

Stretching along Columbia Road between 18th Street and
Kalorama Park, N.W., Adams Morgan is sometimes called
Washington's "United Nations," although this multi-
ethnic neighborhood has a distinctly Hispanic/Latin
flavor. Restaurants abound, serving foods from around
the world. Specialty shops and galleries, ethnic grocery
stores, street vendors, and colorful ethnic festivals, such
as "Adams Morgan Day" (early September), attract visitors and Washingtonians alike.

Adas Israel Synagogue   362-4433
3rd and G Streets, N.W.

Addison/Ripley Gallery, Ltd.   328-2332
9 Hillyer Court, N.W.

Adirondacks   682-1840
50 Massachusetts Avenue, N.E.

Admiral Limousine Service   554-1000
1243 1st Street, S.E.

Adventures Aloft   1-301-881-6262
Rockville, Maryland

Aer Lingus	**1-800-223-6567**
Aero Peru	**1-800-255-7378**

AEROBICS CLASSES

Exercise has become a major part of our lives, and we don't want to give it up when we travel. Staying fit on the road is a constant battle. While most major hotels now have some sort of facilities, it is still handy to know of a few independently owned places where one can work out the kinks. Very few will allow attendance on a one-time basis. We have listed establishments where it's possible either to sign up for a series of classes or just take individual ones.

Body Design by Gilda   **363-4801**
4801 Wisconsin Avenue, N.W.
Founded by Gilda Marx, this store offers not only exercise wear, but a full range of classes, from low impact aerobics to strenuous workouts. The store has a suspended floor, as well as a boutique. Available to both men and women, Gilda's offers various levels of classes to suit your needs.
> Monday–Friday 7:00 A.M.–7:00 P.M.
> Saturday–Sunday 9:00 A.M.–5:00 P.M.

Diana's Exercise Studio   **429-9393**
1122 Connecticut Avenue, N.W.
Diana's shows its awareness of our problem by offering a special 10-visit plan for travelers. It's also possible to attend individual classes, but be sure to call for a reservation—space is limited. They also offer some of the special things to pamper: massage, manicure, pedicure, skin care, a steam room, and a sauna make life a little more bearable.
> Monday–Friday 7:00 A.M.–9:00 P.M.
> Saturday 9:30 A.M.–1:00 P.M.

Aerolineas Argentinas	**1-800-327-0276**
Afghanistan (Embassy of)	**234-3770**
2341 Wyoming Avenue, N.W.	
After Hours	**1-301-654-2929**
4612 East-West Highway, Bethesda, Maryland	
After Hours	**1-703-522-6455**
2715 Wilson Boulevard, Arlington, Virginia	
Air Canada	**1-800-422-6232**
Air Jamaica	**1-800-523-5585**
Air New Zealand	**1-800-262-1234**
Air Taxi Charter Service	**892-2650**
Stuart Aviation, National Airport	
Aircraft Charter Specialist	**486-0086**

AIRPLANE CHARTER SERVICES

For those of you who need a charter, these are some of the best and most reliable.

Aircraft Charter Specialists   486-0086
                                        1-800-327-1966

Specializes in personal and executive charters. Available 24-hours a day, every day. World-wide service.

Gibson Aviation, Inc.   1-301-948-5300
7901 Queen Air Drive, Gaithersburg, Maryland
Features Learjets, Bell Jetranger helicopters, and Beechcraft. 24-hour service available

U.S. Jet Aviation   892-6200
Washington National Airport
Jets, turboprops, and helicopters are available. They also provide air ambulance service. Open 24-hours a day.

AIRLINE SHUTTLES

Pan Am   845-8000
National Airport
   Departures to New York, every hour on the half hour.
   Reservations are not required.
   Monday–Friday 6:30 A.M.–9:30 P.M.
   Saturday 7:30 A.M.–8:30 P.M.
   Sunday 8:30 A.M.–9:30 P.M.

Trump Shuttle, The   1-800-247-8786
National Airport
   Departures to New York, every hour on the hour.
   Reservations are not required.
   Monday–Friday 7:00 A.M.–9:00 P.M.
   Saturday 8:00 A.M.–9:00 P.M.
   Sunday 9:00 A.M.–9:00 P.M.

AIRLINES

Aer Lingus	1-800-223-6567
All Nippon Airways (ANA)	1-800-235-9262
Dulles International Airport	661-6800
Aerolineas Argentinas	1-800-327-0276
Aero Peru	1-800-255-7378
	293-4122
Air Canada	1-800-422-6232
Air Jamaica	1-800-523-5585
Air New Zealand	1-800-262-1234
Alaska Airlines	1-800-426-0333
Alitalia Airlines	1-800-223-5730
	331-1841

Allegheny Commuter	1-800-428-4253
National Airport	892-7381
American West	1-800-247-5692
American Airlines	393-2345
Avianca	1-800-284-2622
Braniff	1-800-272-6433
British Airways	1-800-247-9297
	471-4520
BWIA	1-800-327-7401
China Airlines	833-1760
Continental	1-800-525-0280
	478-9700
Delta	769-3720
Eastern	1-800-327-8376
	393-4000
Finnair	1-800-223-5700
	659-8233
Iberia	1-800-221-9741
	1-800-772-4642
Icelandair	1-800-223-5500
Japan Airlines	1-800-525-3663
	223-3310
KLM	1-800-777-5553
Korean Air	1-800-223-1155
Lan Chile	1-800-225-5526
Lufthansa	1-800-645-3880
	296-5604
Midway Airlines	1-800-621-5700
Midwest Express	1-800-452-2022
Northwest	1-800-225-2525
International Flights	737-7190
Olympic	1-800-223-1226
	659-2511
Pan Am	1-800-421-5330
	845-8000
Philippine Airlines	1-800-435-9725
Piedmont	620-0400
Royal Jordanian	1-800-223-0470
Scandinavian	1-800-221-2350
	833-2424
Singapore	1-800-742-3333
	466-3747

Swissair	1-800-221-4750
	296-5380
TACA	234-7006
Transworld Airlines (TWA)	1-800-221-2000
	727-7400
International Flights	737-7404
United Airlines	1-800-631-1500
	893-3400
U.S. Air	783-4500
Viasa Venezuelan	1-800-221-2150

AIRPORTS

The Washington area is served by three major airports: Baltimore–Washington International, Washington Dulles International, and Washington National.

Baltimore–Washington International Airport

Located approximately 45 minutes from downtown Washington, BWI offers rail and limousine service. It is currently served by 14 domestic and international airlines.

General Information	1-301-859-7111
Ground Transportation Desk	1-301-859-3000
Amtrak BWI Station	1-301-674-1167/674-1170
Police (Airport)	1-301-859-7040

Dulles International Airport

Chantilly, Virginia

Most international passengers land here, 26 miles west of the city. Limousine and motorcoach services are available to downtown Washington.

General Information	1-703-471-7838
Ground Transportation Desk:	
Washington Flyer	1-703-685-1400
Taxi Service	1-703-471-5555
Lost & Found	1-703-471-4114
Police	1-703-471-4114
Travelers Aid	1-703-661-8636
Language Assistance	1-703-661-8747
Customs	1-703-566-8511
U.S. Department of Agriculture	1-703-661-8263

Washington National Airport

The only airport served by the modern Metro subway system, National is located across the Potomac River from downtown Washington. It handles domestic flights only.

| General Information | 685-8000 |

Ground Transportation: Washington Flyer	**685-1400**
Lost & Found	**685-8034/685-8227**
Metrorail-Metro Bus Information	**637-7000**
Police	**685-8034**
Travelers Aid	**684-3472**

AIRPORTS, TRANSPORTATION TO/FROM

Airport Connection (Buses)   **685-1400**

Buses shuttle between the Baltimore–Washington International Airport and two downtown hotels–The Capitol Hilton and The Washington Hilton.

> Fares (one way) Adults $12.00
> Children (under 6) Free

Washington Flyer (Buses)

Runs to five city locations: The Capitol Hilton, The Washington Hilton, The Sheraton-Carlton, The Shoreham, and The J.W. Marriott Hotel.

> Fares (to any of the five locations)
> National Airport: $5.00 one way; $9.00 round trip
> Dulles $11.00 one way, $19.00 round trip
> Children under 6 ride free
> Taxi Fares:
> Baltimore–Washington $40.00
> Dulles $30.00
> Washington National $7.00

Airport Connection (Buses)	**685-1400**
Alaska Airlines	**1-800-426-0333**

ALEXANDRIA, VIRGINIA

See listing under Old Town

Alexandria Hospital   **1-703-379-3000**
4320 Seminary Road, Alexandria, Virginia

Algeria (Embassy of)   **382-5300**
2137 Wyoming Avenue, N.W.

Algonkian Park   **1-703-450-4655**
1600 Potomac View Road, Sterling, Virginia

Alitalia   **1-800-223-5730**

All Dolled Up (Repairs)   **546-0330**
203 10th Street, N.E.

All Nippon Airways (ANA)   **1-800-235-9262**

Allegheny Commuter   **1-800-428-4253**

Allegro   **638-2626**
The Sheraton Carlton, 923 16th Street, N.W.

Allstate Repair 3423 Minnesota Avenue, S.E.	**582-8444**
Ambulance	**911**
American Airlines	**393-2345**
American Coach Lines	**393-1616**
American Hand, The 2906 M Street, N.W.	**965-3273**
American Institute of Architects **Bookstore** 1735 New York Avenue, N.W.	**626-7474**
American West	**1-800-247-5692**
Ampersand Books & Records 118 King Street, Alexandria, Virginia	**1-703-549-0840**
AMTRAK Union Station Lost & Found	 **484-7540** **484-7540**
Anacostia Museum 1901 Fort Place, S.E. (Pearson/Bruce Pls.)	**287-3369**
Anderson House 2118 Massachusetts Avenue, N.W. (21st/22nd Sts.)	**785-0540**
Andre Bellini White Flint Mall, Rockville, Maryland	**1-301-231-9144**
Animal Bites	**576-6664**
Animal Inn 15820 Redland Road, Rockville, Maryland	**1-301-926-9000**
Ann Taylor 1720 K Street, N.W.	**466-3544**

ANNAPOLIS, MARYLAND

Annapolis was the capital of the United States from November 1783 to August 1784. In its historic State House, Congress ratified the Treaty of Paris, officially ending the Revolution.

Today, visitors come to Annapolis to visit the harbor, buy boats, wander through this charming college and naval town, and enjoy its historic district. A tour of the United States Naval Academy offers an interesting glimpse into the life of a midshipman. Just 30 miles east of Washington, DC via Route #50, Annapolis makes a delightful day's or overnight outing. The Annapolis Tourism Council (6 Deck Street, 1-301-268-7676) offers complete information.

Annapolis Boat Rentals, Inc.   **1-301-261-1947**
601 Sixth Street, Annapolis, Maryland

Annapolis Sailing Yacht   **1-800-638-5139**

Annastasia   **333-2500**
3204 M Street, N.W., Georgetown

Annex   **293-0064**
1413 22nd Street, N.W.

ANNUAL EVENTS

Dates for some of these events vary from year to year. To obtain exact dates, call the phone number listed, or contact the Washington Convention Bureau at 789-7000.

January

Congress opens (first week)

Martin Luther King, Jr.'s Birthday
(third Monday)   **755-1005**
Performances of music, dance, and drama by outstanding professional artists commemorate the life of the slain civil rights leader.

Robert E. Lee's Birthday
(January 26th)   **549-0205**

Washington Antiques Show
(Early January)   **234-0700**
At the Shoreham Hotel. Profits go to charity.

February

Chinese New Year
10,000 spectators come to watch as lions and dragon dancers make their way through Chinatown's colorful streets, accompanied by firecrackers and drums. For the Chinese, the festival symbolizes a time to close accounts, pay debts, clean house, honor ancestors, prepare exotic foods, and thank the gods for a prosperous year.

Abraham Lincoln's Birthday
(February 12th)
An elaborate wreath-laying ceremony and reading of the Gettysburg Address at the Lincoln Memorial.

Washington's Birthday
(February 22nd)

Washington's Birthday Parade
Alexandria's favorite son is honored at the nation's largest George Washington's Birthday parade down Washington (where else?) Street in Old Town, Alexandria.

Washington International Boat Show   789-1600

Boating enthusiasts flock to view the latest in pleasure craft and equipment.

World of Wheels Custom Auto Show   371-4200

March

Cherry Blossom Festival (late March/early April)   426-6700

Washington's cherry trees have become the symbol of spring for the entire country. When they bloom, in late March or early April, hundreds of thousands of people are drawn to the capital to see the 3,000 trees of 12 varieties that glorify the Tidal Basin. The trees were a gift from Japan in 1912, and they remind us each year of our many and varied ties to that country. Although the "Greenhouse Effect" has made it increasingly difficult for meteorologists to predict when the blossoms will appear, Festival planners have settled on the first week of April for the celebratory pageants, parades, concerts, and marathon. Be prepared for massive traffic jams, crowds, and the heartbreaking beauty of fragile, delicate blossoms that a strong wind might scatter.

Johann Sebastian Bach's Birthday (March 21st)   363-2202

Chevy Chase Presbyterian Church is the host for 16 organists who play eight hours of organ music in Bach's honor.

St. Patrick's Day Parade (March 17th)

Smithsonian Kite Festival   357-3030

Kite makers and flyers of all ages gather at the Washington Monument grounds to compete for prizes and trophies.

April

Cherry Blossom Festival (late March/early April)   426-6700

Easter Sunrise Services   1-703-697-2131

Sunrise service at Arlington National Cemetery's Memorial Amphitheatre.

Easter Egg Roll   456-2323

Children age 8 and under, accompanied by an adult, gather on the south lawn of the White House for this traditional Easter Egg Roll. Eggs are provided.

Georgetown Garden Tour (late April)   333-4953

A chance to see the remarkable private gardens of this lovely, historic neighborhood. The fee for the walking tour includes tea, and proceeds benefit the Georgetown Children's House.

11

Georgetown House Tour (late April)   338-1796
Unless you're a friend of the family, this is the only way you'll see the interior of these beautiful homes. Admission includes high tea at historic St. John's Georgetown Parish Church.

Gross National Parade   686-3215
This zany, unorthodox parade benefits the Police Boys and Girls Clubs of DC. Over 100,000 turn out annually to see this parade parody, sponsored by WMAL Radio. The route begins at M and Eighteenth Streets at 2:00 P.M. and goes to M Street and Wisconsin Avenue.

Jefferson's Birthday (April 13th)   426-6700
Ceremonies at the Jefferson Memorial at noon.

Old Town Alexandria House Tour   1-703-838-4200
An opportunity to tour Old Town Alexandria's most elegant homes and gardens.

Shakespeare's Birthday   544-7077
Saturday closest to April 23rd, Folger Shakespeare Library.

Washington Craft Show   357-2700

White House Spring Garden Tour   456-2200
The gardens are open to the public for two days between 2:00 P.M. and 5:00 P.M. Call for exact dates.

Spring Design for Living Show   798-1600

White House News Photographers
    Association Show   287-5000

May

Asian Pacific American Heritage
    Festival   223-5500
All of Washington's Asian communities honor America's first Japanese settlement and the completion of the transcontinental railroad, constructed largely by Chinese workers. The Sylvan Theater, on the south side of the Washington Monument, explodes with colorful cultural displays, dragon dances, martial arts exhibitions, craft booths, and wonderful ethnic foods.

Greek Spring Festival   829-2910
Saints Constantine and Helen Greek Orthodox Church at 4115 Sixteenth Street, N.W., celebrates spring with Greek food, music, dances, games, clowns, and arts and crafts.

Memorial Day
    Services at the Tomb of the
        Unknown Soldier   692-0931
    Services at the Vietnam Veterans
        Memorial   426-6700

| Washington Cathedral Outdoor Fair | **537-6200** |
| Jazz Festival | **1-703-838-4844** |

Old Town, Alexandria celebrates with big band music performed by local groups. The U.S. Navy Commodores open the program, which runs from noon to 6:00 P.M.

June

**Outdoor stages open: Wolftrap,
    Merriweather Post Pavillion,
    Carter Baron Amphitheater**

Potomac River Festival   **387-8292**
DC's river heritage is celebrated with free entertainment, tall ships, fireworks, arts and crafts, boat rides, water events, and ethnic foods.

**Smithsonian's Annual Folk Life
    Festival**   **357-2700**
More than one million visitors attend this major, grassroots celebration. Performances and demonstrations range from Appalachian fiddling to native American dancing, and from quilting to coal mining. All events are free.

July

Independence Day (July 4th)   **426-6700**
The nation's capital celebrates the Fourth of July in grand style, beginning at 12:30 P.M. with a National Independence Day Parade that follows a route down Constitution Avenue past many of the historic monuments on the Mall. A variety of free entertainment is available all day at the Sylvan Theater on the grounds of the Washington Monument. In the evening, the National Symphony Orchestra performs a free concert on the steps of the Capitol. Celebrations end with a fabulous fireworks display over the Washington Monument.

Bastille Day (July 14th)   **452-1132**
Adele, a graduate of the Illinois Institute of Juggling with a diploma to prove it, especially enjoys this one: Dominique's Restaurant sponsors an annual race in which waiters carry champagne glasses on trays and later demonstrate their juggling ability to win a trip to Paris. The race begins at Twentieth and Pennsylvania Avenue, N.W., at Noon.

Civil War Living History Weekend   **1-703-838-4848**
Soldiers in Civil War uniforms reenact the 1864 battle and perform drills in unit competitions at Fort Ward Museum and Park in Alexandria.

Virginia Scottish Games   1-703-838-4200
Alexandria celebrates its Scottish heritage with one of the largest Scottish festivals in the United States. It features traditional Highland dancing, bagpiping, national professional heptathlon, and fiddling competitions.

Hispanic-American Cultural Festival   265-2659
Washington's large Latino community in the Adams Morgan and Mt. Pleasant neighborhoods celebrates with a series of special events, including plays, music, dance, arts and crafts, and food kiosks.

August

August Tavern Days   1-703-549-0205
Gadsby's Tavern in Old Town, Alexandria, recreates colonial life via food, music, and entertainment.

1812 Overture   696-3399
A patriotic concert at the Sylvan Theater on the grounds of the Washington Monument performed by the U.S. Army Band assisted by the Salute Gun Platoon of the Third U.S. Infantry. Love those cannons! Call for exact date.

September

Adams Morgan Day   462-5113
Thousands of Washingtonians and visitors attend this annual event to celebrate the hispanic heritage of the Adams Morgan neighborhood.

Labor Day Concert (first Monday)   785-8100
It's farewell to summer when the National Symphony plays this concert on the grounds of the Capitol.

Rock Creek Park Day (last Saturday)   426-6832
Environmental and recreational organizations offer a variety of exhibits and demonstrations to celebrate the birthday of Washington's largest park. Naturally, there are special activities for children, as well as arts and crafts.

Washington National Cathedral Day   537-6247
This is the only time that visitors are allowed to ascend to the top of the tower to see the carillon as well as the spectacular view. A tour of the cathedral, and performances by dancers, choirs, and puppeteers add to the general festivities.

Washington Redskins   546-2222
Football season opens early September. RFK Stadium.

**Old Town Alexandria's Tour of
Homes**   1-703-838-4200
Tour some of the privately owned, historic homes in quaint Old Town. The proceeds benefit Alexandria Hospital.

October

Columbus Day (second Monday)   638-0220
Wreath laying ceremony at the Columbus Memorial, Union Station

Supreme Court opens (first Monday)   479-3000

Washington International Horse
         Show   1-301-840-0281
One of the country's most important equestrian events, held at the Capital Center in Largo, Maryland

White House Fall Garden Tour
         (mid-October)   426-6700
A chance to see the splendid gardens of the White House including the famous Rose Gardens and the South Lawn. Music by a military band accompanies the tours.

November

Marine Corps Marathon
         (early November)   1-703-690-3431
This event, which attracts thousands of world-class runners, begins at the Iwo Jima Statue. Runners pass some of Washington's most famous monuments.

Veterans Day (November 11th)   475-0843
This solemn commemoration of the signing of the armistice ending World War I commences with a service in the Memorial Amphitheatre at Arlington National Cemetery and includes the laying of a wreath (by the President or another high-ranking official) at the Tomb of the Unknown Soldier. Observances at the Vietnam Veterans Memorial include wreath laying and the playing of *Taps*.

Washington Bullets (late November)   622-3865
Capital Centre, Landover, Maryland

Alexandria Antiques Show   1-703-838-4200
The Office of Historic Alexandria and the Historic Alexandria Foundation co-sponsor this show and sale at the Old Colony Inn.

December

Christmas Candlelight Tour
         (second weekend)   1-703-838-4200
Visit historic Ramsay House, Gadsby's Tavern Museum, the Lee-Fendall House, and the Carlyle House in Old Town Alexandria. Music, colonial dancing, and light refreshments are included in the tour.

Christmas Tree Lighting
(mid-December) 224-3069
The magnificent Christmas tree on the west side of the Capitol is lighted each year the day before the Pageant of Peace begins. Military bands perform in concert.

A Christmas Carol 347-4833
Charles Dickens's beloved holiday classic returns to enthusiastic crowds year after year at historic Ford's Theatre. Adele knows every word by heart and recommends bringing along at least four hankies.

National Christmas Tree
Lighting/Pageant of Peace 485-9666
In a special holiday celebration with seasonal music and caroling, the giant National Christmas Tree near the White House is lighted by the President. For the next few weeks through New Year's Day, the Ellipse grounds are the site of nightly choral performances, a Nativity scene, a burning Yule log, and a spectacular display of lighted Christmas trees representing each state and territory in the U.S.A.

Pearl Harbor Day (December 7th) 285-2600
At the Iwo Jima Memorial.

Scottish Christmas Walk
(early December) 1-703-549-SCOT
Old Town Alexandria salutes its Scottish heritage with a parade, highland dancers, house tours, and children's events.

Trees of Christmas 357-2700
The annual holiday display at the Smithsonian's National Museum of American History. A spectacular array of trees in all shapes and sizes are decorated with different themes each year. This is one of Washington's most popular holiday treats.

White House Christmas Candlelight
Tour (late December) 456-2200
Evening tours of the White House, aglow with holiday decorations and candlelight, begin at 6:00 P.M. Tours are extremely popular, so it's best to show up early.

New Year's Eve Celebration
(December 31st) 289-4224
It's one gigantic block party at the Old Post Office Pavilion, 12th Street and Pennsylvania Avenue, N.W. At Midnight, the U.S. Postal Service Love Stamp is lowered from the Pavilion's Clock Tower to ring in the new year.

ANTIQUES

What could be more natural in this historic area than a strong interest in antiques? And, judging from the number of shops to be found, the demand is there.

Bobbie's Antiques & Interiors   **1-301-949-5552**
3760 Howard Avenue, Kensington, Maryland
  Monday–Saturday 10:00 A.M.–5:30 P.M.
  Sunday Noon–5:30 P.M.

Eighteenth- and nineteenth- century Americana. Owner Thomas Kruez has an obvious interest in old gas and electric light fixtures and has restored a comprehensive collection of them.

Bruton Antiques   **1-301-564-1226**
4125 Howard Avenue, Kensington, Maryland
  Monday–Sunday 1:00 A.M.–6:00 P.M.

A good place to know about if your interest is in antiques from Wales, Ireland, Scotland, and England. Since the owner lives in Wales, he easily keeps his store supplied with interesting furniture and decorative items.

Burke's Peerage, Ltd.   **1-703-549-5155**
128 South Royal Street, Alexandria, Virginia
  Tuesday–Saturday 10:00 A.M.–5:00 P.M.

The owner has lived in England, so it's only natural that he specialize in English antiques. There is a concentration on the Regency period, as well as those wonderful garden ornaments that make landscaping so worthwhile. The quality of the pieces may compensate for the high prices.

Cherishables   **785-4087**
1608 20th Street, N.W.
  Monday–Saturday 11:00 A.M.–6:00 P.M.

Eighteenth and Nineteenth century quilts and folk art. Prices seem unusually high.

C & M Antiques/Eagle Antiques   **1-703-548-9882**
311 Cameron Street,   **1-703-549-7611**
Alexandria, Virginia
  Monday–Saturday 11:00 A.M.–5:00 P.M.
  Sunday Noon–5:00 P.M.

China, quilts, old glass, silver, clocks, and some paintings make up the stock of this reasonably priced shop. It's on the second floor of the old Norford Inn and is a good place to browse for those small items. We always find the kitchen items fascinating. Those old molds, churns, pots, and pans remind us of our grandmothers—it wasn't too long ago that these things were in daily use.

Cranberry Box 1-301-946-7464
3742 Howard Avenue, Kensington, Maryland

Dark Horse Antiques 1-301-942-0016
3784 Howard Avenue, Kensington, Maryland
  Saturday 11:00 A.M.–5:30 P.M.
  Sunday Noon–5:30 P.M.

Oak antiques are combined with new furniture in this shop.

Donna Lee's Collectibles 1-703-548-5830
206 Queen Street, Alexandria, Virginia
  Monday–Sunday 11:00 A.M.–4:00 P.M.

The only antique store we've heard of that specializes in the memorabilia of African Americans. The owner, Donna Lee Wilson, has collected quite a variety of rag dolls, china figures, books and many other items produced by, for, and about African Americans.

Doug's Forget Me Nots 1-301-942-0016
3784 Howard Avenue, 1-301-649-2072
Kensington, Maryland
  Saturday 11:00 A.M.–5:30 P.M.
  Sunday Noon–5:30 P.M.

Doug Stuart specializes in Fiestaware, Hall, Roseville, and Harlequin china. All of that cheap stuff that was given away as premiums in the 1930s and 1940s has become highly sought after by collectors.

Edward G. Haddad II 1-301-946-1400
3774 Howard Avenue, Kensington, Maryland
  Monday–Saturday 10:30 A.M.–5:00 P.M.
  Sunday Noon–5:00 P.M.

French and English furniture from the late nineteenth century, American Victorian, art deco, and art nouveau pieces—all of extremely high quality. No credit cards.

Ethridge Ltd. 1-703-548-7722
220 South Washington Street, Alexandria, Virginia
  Wednesday–Saturday 11:30 A.M.–5:00 P.M.
  Also open by appointment.

Their area of interest takes in a big chunk of time. They handle the best of the seventeenth-, eighteenth-, and nineteenth-century English and American furniture (except beds), and it's all in perfect condition. Everything seems to be a major piece. A first class shop, it's the kind of place that we really enjoy visiting. No credit cards.

European Imports 1-301-946-1400
3774 Howard Avenue, Kensington, Maryland
  Tuesday–Sunday 10:00 A.M.–5:00 P.M.

This is a warehouse full of furniture. Primarily armoires, wardrobes, chests, chairs, desks, and tables of assorted sizes.

Franco Antiques 332-0210
2601 Connecticut Avenue, N.W.
Monday–Saturday 10:00 A.M.–6:30 P.M.
Sunday Noon–5:00 P.M.
European, Oriental, and American antiques take the
form of jewelry, furniture, paintings, and their signature
crystal chandeliers.

Georgian Shell Interiors/Antiques,
Inc. 1-301-933-4464
10419 Fawcett Street, Kensington, Maryland
Wednesday–Sunday 10:00 A.M.–5:00 P.M.
Hours also by appointment.
Furniture from the 1920s and 1930s as well as some
stained glass. They also handle reproductions.

Gonzales Antiques 234-3336
2313 Calvert Street, N.W.
Monday–Friday 9:30 A.M.–6:30 P.M.
Saturday 10:00 A.M.–5:00 P.M.
In addition to furniture from France, England, and Italy,
they stock unusual ornamental items and china.

Heller Antiques, Ltd. 654-0218
5454 Wisconsin Avenue, N.W.
Monday–Saturday 10:00 A.M.–5:30 P.M.
Antique (as well as contemporary) jewelry and silver are
the mainstays at Heller Antiques. Silver flatware, trays, tea
sets, coffee services, and lots of little odds and ends.

James B. Barnes Gallery 1-703-548-8008
222 South Washington Street, Alexandria, Virginia
Tuesday–Friday 10:00 A.M.–6:00 P.M.
Saturday 10:00 A.M.–5:00 P.M.
Maps, prints, and various sorts of documents are the attraction here. They are also qualified to do museum quality
conservation and framing.

Jill & Co., Antiques 1-301-946-7464
3744 Howard Avenue, Kensington, Maryland

Joanne's Antique Alley 1-301-933-6939
3746 Howard Avenue, Kensington, Maryland
Monday–Saturday 10:00 A.M.–5:30 P.M.
Sunday Noon–5:30 P.M.
You can find mahogany and walnut furniture here, but
Joanne Alley's real interest is in glassware.

Just For You Antiques 1-301-933-5067
3730 Howard Avenue, Kensington, Maryland
Monday–Saturday 10:00 A.M.–5:30 P.M.
Sunday Noon–5:30 P.M.

A very small store where Janet Gilden sells her favorite glass and china pieces.

Krupsaw's Antique Shop   **1-301-654-5658**
7825 Old Georgetown Road, Bethesda, Maryland
    Monday–Friday 9:30 A.M.–5:00 P.M.
    Saturday 10:00 A.M.–4:00 P.M.

A mixture of collectables, some antique and some not. Most of the antiques are nineteenth-century English. They also carry a lot of paperweights and other small items that make perfect gifts.

Lenore & Daughters   **1-703-836-3356**
130 South Royal Street, Alexandria, Virginia
    Monday–Saturday 10:00 A.M.–5:00 P.M.
    Sunday 1:00 P.M.–5:00 P.M.

Lenore Binzer has built up a good collection of silver flatware, porcelain, and glass. She avoids furniture and keeps her prices low. Prints and engravings are also part of the stock of small, easily handled items.

Lloyd's Row   **1-703-549-7517**
119 South Henry Street, Alexandria, Virginia
    Tuesday–Saturday 11:00 A.M.–5:00 P.M.

This is actually owner R.J. Mraz's home. The entire townhouse is his shop, and he presents his collection of fine English and American eighteenth-century furniture very tastefully. Due to the quality of his stock, the prices can be quite high—but they're worth it.

Lost & Found   **1-301-946-8666**
3734 Howard Avenue, Kensington, Maryland
    Monday–Saturday 11:00 A.M.–5:00 P.M.
    Sunday Noon–5:00 P.M.
A little of everything—except furniture.

Marston Luce   **775-9460**
1314 21st Street, N.W.
    Monday–Saturday 11:00 A.M.–6:00 P.M.

Nineteenth-century country furniture makes up the nucleus of their stock. Much of it is painted and in less than perfect shape. Country people really use their furniture.

Micheline's Antiques   **1-703-836-1893**
1600 King Street   **1-703-256-0950**
Alexandria, Virginia
    Tuesday–Friday 11:00 A.M.–4:00 P.M.
    Saturday 11:00 A.M.–5:00 P.M.
    Also open by appointment. No credit cards.

French country antiques from the Normandy region. Art deco clocks, armoires, and even a selection of traditional fabrics will make your mouth water. They do all of their own buying in France.

Nautical & Scientific Shop   1-301-942-0636
3760 Howard Avenue (upstairs), Kensington, Maryland
   Saturday–Sunday Noon–5:00 P.M.
   Hours also by appointment.

Check this out. A wide selection of nautical and scientific instruments—just like the name says. A wonderful place to find presents or just to browse.

Onslow Square   1-301-530-9393
4131 Howard Avenue, Kensington, Maryland
   Monday–Sunday 11:00 A.M.–6:00 P.M.

A medium-sized warehouse filled with eighteenth- and nineteenth-century English antiques.

Phyllis Van Auken Antiques   1-301-933-3772
10425 Fawcett Street, Kensington, Maryland
   Monday–Friday 10:30 A.M.–4:30 P.M.
   Saturday 10:00 A.M.–5:00 P.M.
   Sunday Noon–5:00 P.M.

One of the best shops in Kensington. A limited collection of small eighteenth- and nineteenth-century furniture complements fine but small-scale accessories. Quite expensive.

Plain Jane's   1-703-548-2457
222 North Lee Street, Alexandria, Virginia
   Monday 11:00 A.M.–6:00 P.M.
   Tuesday, Wednesday, Thursday,
     and Saturday 10:00 A.M.–6:00 P.M.
   Friday 10:00 A.M.–9:00 P.M.
   Sunday Noon–6:00 P.M.

Primarily English and French furniture made of mahogany. A fine selection of crystal chandeliers and wall-mounted light fixtures also grace this small shop.

Seidner Antiques   775-8212
1333 New Hampshire Avenue, N.W.
   Monday–Saturday 11:00 A.M.–6:00 P.M.

One of the really fine shops. Continental furniture ranging from the sixteenth to the nineteenth centuries is of excellent quality. Prices are high, but it's still hard to resist some of the choice items in this highly personal collection.

Silverman Galleries, Inc.   1-703-836-5363
110 North Asaph Street, Alexandria, Virginia
   Tuesday–Saturday 11:00 A.M.–5:00 P.M.

Eighteenth- and nineteenth-century jewelry, clocks, silver, as well as porcelain and china are among the decorative arts represented here. Since they have their own jeweler, one is assured that the clocks actually work.

Sparrows   **1-301-530-0175**
4115 Howard Avenue, Kensington, Maryland
    Monday–Saturday 10:00 A.M.–5:00 P.M.
French furniture for the well heeled. Also art deco and art nouveau.

Studio Antiques, Inc.   **1-703-548-5188**
628 North Washington Street, Alexandria, Virginia
    Tuesday–Saturday 10:00 A.M.–5:00 P.M.
    Sunday Noon–5:00 P.M.
Well worth a visit. A large part of their business is with art galleries since they specialize in nineteenth-century European and American paintings. They also handle high-quality furniture and Oriental decorative arts.

Trocadero Asian Art   **234-5656**
1501 Connecticut Avenue, N.W.
    Tuesday–Saturday 10:30 A.M.–6:00 P.M.
One of the best places to shop for choice oriental selections. Their ceramics, carved furniture, and chests show unusual quality.

Warehouse Antiques   **1-703-548-2150**
218 North Lee Street, Alexandria, Virginia

Antoinette's Heirloom Jewelry   **347-8110**
The Willard Hotel, 1400 F Street, N.W.

Anton Gallery   **328-0828**
2108 R Street, N.W.

Anton's 1201 Club   **783-1201**
1201 Pennsylvania Avenue, N.W.

Anton's Loyal Opposition   **546-4545**
400 1st Street, S.E.

Appalachian Spring   **337-5780**
1415 Wisconsin Avenue, N.W.

Arena Stage   **488-3300**
6th and M Streets, S.W.

Argentina (Embassy of)   **939-6400**
1600 New Hampshire Avenue, N.W.

Arlington Hospital   **1-703-558-5000**
1701 N. George Mason Drive, Alexandria, Virginia

ARLINGTON NATIONAL CEMETERY

Arlington, Virginia   **1-703-692-0931**
    Open daily:
    October–March 8:00 A.M.–5:00 P.M.
    April–September 8:00 A.M.–7:00 P.M.
    Metro: Arlington Cemetery

Across the Potomac River into Virginia via Memorial Bridge, these peaceful acres were once the estate of the Custis family. General Robert E. Lee, our most famous confederate leader, married Mary Ann Randolph Custis (daughter of George Washington's adopted son, George Washington Parke Custis) in 1831, and they lived here until Union troops overran the mansion during the Civil War and forced the family out. Later, the federal government seized the land for unpaid taxes, but a Supreme Court decision returned the house to Lee's son, George Washington Custis Lee, in 1883. The Custis-Lee mansion, as it is now known, is open to the public. Right in front of it is the tomb of Pierre Charles L'Enfant, the original designer and city planner of Washington.

Thousands of simple markers honor the dead of numerous wars, a solemn sight that causes one to reflect on the rights most dear to all of us. Among the many prominent people buried here are, of course, the Kennedys—J.F.K and his brother Robert share a hillside with a wonderful view of Washington. Generals Omar Bradley, George Marshall, and John Pershing are here, as is boxing great Joe Louis. But the most moving memorial is the perpetual honor guard at the Tomb of the Unknown Soldier. The changing of the guard is a simple yet stirring ceremony that has taken place every half hour for many years.

The best and most comfortable way to tour the cemetery is by Tourmobile. It is the only conveyance allowed on the grounds and will shuttle you back and forth from the Mall area in the city as well as taking you to all of the most interesting places in the cemetery.

Armed Forces Medical Museum   **576-2348**
Walter Reed Army Medical Center, 6825 16th Street, N.W.

ART GALLERIES

Washington is a city interested in supporting its young artists. Most of the galleries show contemporary work, and the following list reflects that. We have commented only on the ones which handle something else. All of the galleries listed are among the most interesting and are worth a visit.

Adams Davidson Galleries   **965-3800**
3233 P Street, N.W.
Nineteenth- and twentieth-century painting and sculpture.

Addison/Ripley Gallery Ltd.   **328-2332**
9 Hillyer Court, N.W.

Anton Gallery   328-0828
2108 R Street, N.W.

Baumgarten Galleries   232-6320
2016 R Street, N.W.
Contemporary American and European painting and sculpture.

B.R. Kornblatt Gallery   638-7657
406 7th Street, N.W.
Post-1945 work by big name artists.

David Adamson Gallery   628-0257
406 7th Street, N.W.
Graphics, paintings, and drawings.

Fendrick Gallery   338-4544
3059 M Street, N.W.
Contemporary work by well-known artists.

Carega Foxley Leach Gallery   337-3661
3214 O Street, N.W.

Franz Bader Gallery   659-5515
1701 Pennsylvania Avenue, N.W.

Gallery K   234-0339
2010 R Street, N.W.

Gallery 10   232-3326
1519 Connecticut Avenue, N.W.

Hom Gallery   466-4076
103 O Street, N.W.
Big name nineteenth- and twentieth-century artists.

Jane Haslem   232-4644
2025 Hillyer Place, N.W.

Jones Troyer Fitzpatrick Gallery   328-7189
1614 20th Street, N.W.
Contemporary artists and photographers.

Kathleen Ewing Gallery   328-0955
1609 Connecticut Avenue, N.W., Suite 200
Photography by local artists.

Kimberly Gallery of Art   223-6346
One Westin Center, 2445 M Street, N.W.
Contemporary Latin American artists.

Marsha Mateyka Gallery   328-0088
2012 R Street, N.W.
Contemporary art—some by major artists.

Martin Gallery   232-2009
1609 Connecticut Avenue, N.W., Suite 200
Nineteenth- and twentieth century photography.

McIntosh/Drysdale Gallery   **783-5190**
406 7th Street, N.W.

Middendorf Gallery   **462-2009**
2009 Columbia Road, N.W.
Nineteenth- and twentieth-century painting, sculpture, and photography.

Osuna Gallery   **296-1963**
406 7th Street, N.W.
Nineteenth- and twentieth-century art and old masters.

Studio Gallery   **232-8734**
2108 R Street, N.W.

Tartt Gallery   **332-5652**
2017 Q Street, N.W.
Contemporary painting and sculpture, photography, and "contemporary folk art."

Wallace Wentworth Gallery   **387-7152**
2006 R Street, N.W.
Twentieth century American and European art.

Winston Gallery   **333-5414**
1204 31st Street, N.W.

Zenith Gallery   **783-2963**
413 7th Street, N.W.
Contemporary painting, sculpture, and crafts.

Arthur A. Adler   **628-0131**
1101 Connecticut Avenue, N.W.

Arthur M. Sackler Collection of Asian
    & Near Eastern Art   **357-2700**
The Smithsonian Institution, The Quadrangle

Arts & Industries Building   **357-1300**
Smithsonian Institution, 900 Jefferson Drive, S.W.

Arts Club of Washington   **331-7282**
2017 I Street, N.W.

ATMs. *See* **MONEY MACHINES.**

Au Pied de Cochon   **333-5440**
1335 Wisconsin Avenue, N.W.

AUCTIONS

If you read any newspapers or magazines, you will be aware of the enormous amount of activity in the auction world today. Prices for everything have soared to heights undreamed of a few years ago. The auction houses vie with the stock market as the place where the moneyed giants meet to do battle. With the influx of international money into the arena, the pace of bidding and the excitement have out-done fiction. Millions of dollars for antiques, jewelry, and paintings are commonplace. This is where the action is. Try to go to either of the places listed below on a day when important collections are being auctioned. The newspapers list when and what so you can make your plans. Note that there are "viewing days" prior to the actual auctions so that you can go and get a close-up view of the items to be sold.

Adam A. Weschler & Son 905 E Street, N.W.	628-1281
C.G. Sloan & Co., Inc. 919 E Street, N.W.	628-1468

AUDIOVISUAL EQUIPMENT
See RENTAL, AUDIOVISUAL

Audubon Naturalist Book Shop 1621 Wisconsin Avenue, N.W.	337-6062
8940 Jones Mill Road, Che vy Chase, Maryland	1-301-652-3606
Australia (Embassy of) 1601 Massachusetts Avenue, N.W.	797-3000
Austria (Embassy of) 2343 Massachusetts Avenue, N.W.	483-4474

AUTOMATIC TELLER MACHINES.
See **MONEY MACHINES.**

Aux Beaux Champs Four Seasons Hotel, 2800 Pennsylvania Avenue, N.W., Georgetown	342-0810
Avcom 919 12th Street, N.W.	638-1513
Avenel Farms Potomac, Maryland	1-301-469-3700
Avianca	1-800-284-2622
Avis	1-800-331-1212

B

B & B News Stand 2621 Connecticut Avenue, N.W.	234-0494 234-0497

B'nai B'rith Klutznick Museum   857-6583
1640 Rhode Island Avenue, N.W.

B. Dalton Bookseller
1331 Pennsylvania Avenue, N.W.   393-1468
Mazza Gallerie   362-7055

B.R. Kornblatt Gallery   638-7657
406 7th Street, N.W.

Babel Limousine Service   328-1297

BABYSITTERS

All hotels can arrange for babysitters and, whenever possible, we suggest that you use them. They are bonded, perfectly safe, and reliable. Since hotels use them constantly, they also have a track record. In the event you want to arrange things for yourself, try one of these:

Child's Play   785-0211
16th and K Streets, N.W.

Family & Nursing Care   1-301-588-8200
911 Silver Spring Avenue, Silver Spring, Maryland

Mother's Aides, Inc.   1-703-250-0700
Fairfax, Virginia

Sitters Unlimited   1-703-823-0888
205 Yoakum Parkway, #1505 Alexandria, Virginia.

Bacchus   785-0734
1827 Jefferson Place, N.W. (M/N Sts.)

Bachelor's Mill   544-1931
1104 8th Street, S.E.

Back Door Pub   546-5979
1104 8th Street, S.E.

Backstage Rental & Sales   775-1488
2101 P Street, N.W.

Badland's   296-0505
1415 22nd Street, N.W.

Bahamas (Embassy of)   944-3390
600 New Hampshire Avenue, N.W.

Bahrain (Embassy of)   342-0741
3502 International Drive, N.W.

Baker's Photo Supply, Inc.   362-9100
4433 Wisconsin Avenue, N.W.

Balloon Man, The   338-9000
1800 Wisconsin Avenue, N.W.

BALLOON RIDES

Ballooning has gained great popularity in recent years and there are a few places outside of Washington where one may enjoy this sport. Probably more for local residents than tourists on a tight schedule, we list a few of the better known places. Phone ahead for complete information and directions.

Adventures Aloft Rockville, Maryland	**1-301-881-6262**
Balloon-A-Tics 7713 Lake Drive, Manasas, Virginia	**1-703-361-4725**
Balloons Unlimited	**1-703-281-2300**
Balloon-A-Tics 7713 Lake Drive, Manasas, Virginia	**1-703-361-4725**

BALLOONS

Balloons are a booming business. They compare well to singing telegrams and surprise strip teases (now available for both men and women). Most of their business is done over the telephone via credit card. The companies listed below can deliver all kinds of strange and wonderful balloons for parties, special events, or just because.

Balloon Man, The 1800 Wisconsin Avenue, N.W.	**298-7080**
Balloons Over America 7720 Wisconsin Avenue, Bethesda, Maryland	**1-301-656-6020**
Wickel's World of Balloons	**449-7460**
Balloons Over America 7720 Wisconsin Avenue, Bethesda, Maryland	**1-301-656-6020**
Balloons Unlimited	**1-703-281-2300**
Bally of Switzerland 1022 Connecticut Avenue, N.W.	**429-0604**

BALTIMORE, MARYLAND

Located just 38 miles north of Washington, DC, Baltimore has recently undergone a dramatic renaissance. In a neighborhood formerly comprised of decaying warehouses and piers, the Inner Harbor complex attracts tourists and locals alike with fine dining, shops, and special events. The National Aquarium is a knockout—a five story marine display tank boasts more than 5,000 creatures. Other interesting attractions are the Baltimore Museum of Art, the B & O Railroad Museum, the U.S. Frigate Constellation, and Fort

McHenry National Monument and Historic Shrine. Fort McHenry successfully defended Baltimore against the British during the War of 1812. During the bombardment, Francis Scott Key was inspired to write his famous poem, "The Star Spangled Banner." Set to the tune of a drinking song, it became our national anthem in 1931.

Baltimore–Washington International
Airport   859-7111
P.O. Box 8766, BWI Airport   859-3000

Bamiyan   338-1896
3320 M Street, N.W. (33rd St.), Georgetown

Bangladesh (Embassy of)   342-8372
2201 Wisconsin Avenue, N.W.

BANK MACHINES

See **MONEY MACHINES**

Bar, The   393-1000
Capital Hilton Hotel, 16th and K Streets, N.W.

Barbados (Embassy of)   939-9200
2144 Wyoming Avenue, N.W.

BARBER SHOPS

See **HAIRCUTS**

Barman International   1-301-657-8844
7009 Wisconsin Avenue, Bethesda, Maryland

Barry Ephraim   628-6465
816 15th Street, N.W.

BARS

(*see also* GAY BARS, SINGLES BARS, and SPORTS BARS)
Bars are an exciting part of Washington's nightlife and power scene. They provide entertainment, relaxation, and the setting for major deals. The following are some of the best.

   Au Pied de Cochon   333-5440
   1335 Wisconsin Avenue, N.W.

   Basin Street Lounge, The   1-703-549-1141
   219 King Street, Alexandria, Virginia (Old Town)

   Boathouse Bar at Trader Vic's   347-7100
   The Capitol Hilton Hotel, 16th and K Streets, N.W.
   Is there anyone who doesn't know what a Trader Vic's bar is like? Watch out for those drinks with the umbrellas in them–they're lethal.

Brickskeller, The   293-1885
1523 22nd Street, N.W. (P/O Sts.)
The primary attraction is beer—over 500 brands. They also specialize in drinks which contain beer. Our stomachs shudder just writing about it.

Bullfeathers   543-5005
410 1st Street, S.E.

Cafe Lautrec   265-6436
2431 18th Street, N.W.
The decor makes use of reproductions of Toulouse Lautrec's artwork to develop a French bistro effect that seems to work—it's very comfortable. It has all of the ingredients that should spell success: outdoor cafe, live jazz, plenty of space, and most peculiarly, a tap dancer named John Forge. His performance takes place on the bar, so be warned.

Camelot   887-5966
1823 M Street, N.W.
Go-Go girls, if you're still into that sort of thing.

Champions   965-4005
1206 Wisconsin Avenue, N.W.
Probably the most macho place in town. It's one of the best singles bars, and everywhere you look there is sports equipment. The bar sports a fantastic collection of baseball cards. Liberated women may find it all a bit much.

Chicago Bar & Grill   463-8888
19th and Dupont Circle
We don't like bars that seat over 1,000 people. It has, of course, everything you might think of in the way of entertainment (except Go-Go dancers). If you like huge crowds, dance floors, video screens, something referred to as a "sports trivia message board" and the occassional live band, this may be for you. If you are a tourist with limited time, don't waste it here.

Childe Harold   483-6702
1610 20th Street, N.W.

Club Soda   244-3189
3433 Connecticut Avenue, N.W.
Really good '50s and '60s rock n' roll. The problem is that it's full of college students.

Clyde's   333-0294
3236 M Street, N.W.
Clyde's is one of the oldest of the saloons in Georgetown and also owns Old Ebbitt Grill near the White House. Lots of celebrities are to be found here, and on weekends it's packed.

Duddington's Underground
Sports Bar   544-3500
319 Pennsylvania Avenue, S.E.

If you're in the Capitol Hill area, this is a must. Jukebox, pinball, large screen TV, video games, noise, and a large and noisy crowd make this an ideal watering hole for some. Upstairs is a sports bar.

Fairfax Bar, The   293-2100
The Ritz Carlton Hotel
2100 Massachusetts Avenue, N.W.

One of the most expensive and elegant bars in town, it is primarily for the guests of the hotel and the occasional Washingtonian of taste. If you are looking for an active, noisy bar scene, this is not for you.

Hawk & Dove   543-3300
329 Pennsylvania Avenue, S.E.

Jenkins Hill   544-6600
223 Pennsylvania Avenue, S.E.

For weekends only. During the week it hosts locals and employees from the hill.

John Hay Room   638-2260
The Hay-Adams Hotel, 800 16th Street, N.W.

One of the most elegant places in town to unwind. We'd hardly call it a bar. It's a lovely, peaceful place where the pianist has been willing to play, on a quiet night, so that Adele could sing along and justify those thousands of dollars spent at Vassar and in Austria, training for an operatic career.

J. Paul's   333-3450
3218 M Street, N.W.

Another Georgetown bar with pretensions to a historic background—nothing special.

J.R.'s Bar & Grill   328-0091
1519 17th Street, N.W.

Nathan's   338-2000
3150 M Street, N.W., Georgetown

Do they really sell more champagne than any bar in the city?

Old Ebbitt Grill   347-4800
675 15th Street, N.W.

One of our favorite places for breakfast, the Old Ebbitt Grill started life as a saloon so it's far ahead of most of the competition. It has all the ingredients one is looking for in a bar: good drinks, good service, and no entertainment.

Paper Moon   965-6666
1073 31st Street, N.W.

Paul Mall   965-5353
3235 M Street, N.W.

The live music, which gets awards from local magazines, is the big draw. If you don't mind a packed floor, it's a good place to dance.

Rumors   466-7378
1900 M Street, N.W.

Seven nights of the week, this is a wild place. One of the hottest singles bars in the area, there is never a dull night.

Sign of the Whale   223-0608
1825 M Street, N.W.

If you're very young, you might like this mix. Beer and inexpensive food combine with lots of singles looking for other singles.

Sky Terrace, The   347-4499
The Hotel Washington, 15th Street and Pennsylvania Avenue, N.W.

This hotel has a great public relations person, who knows how to get the most out of the hotel's view of the White House and surrounding monuments. Frequently used for filming major movies, it's a good place for people-watching.

Stetson's   667-6295
1610 U Street, N.W.

Third Edition   333-3700
1218 Wisconsin Avenue, N.W.

Washington is a seat of power, so every place can claim to have an illustrious clientele. Although Third Edition also claims to have a gourmet menu, we wouldn't say this is a major draw. If you're going for the dancing upstairs, be prepared for a wait.

Tune Inn, The   543-2725
3311½ Pennsylvania Avenue, S.E.

One of the least glamourous bars around. Primarily a neighborhood bar, it sticks to the simple things that it does best: beer and sandwiches to a juke box accompaniment.

Basin Street Lounge, The   1-703-549-1141
219 King Street, Alexandria, Virginia

BATHROOMS

For tourists and residents alike, there is nothing as important as a public bathroom. Fortunately, Washington is a city geared to sightseers, and most of the public buildings have the necessary facilities. Keep in mind that most department stores and all hotels have bathrooms.

Baumgarten Galleries   232-6320
2016 R Street, N.W.

Bayou, The   333-2897
3135 K Street, N.W.

BEAUTY SALONS

Bogart, Inc.   (Hair Salon) 333-6550
1063 Wisconsin Avenue, N.W.
    Tuesday–Friday 10:00 A.M.–6:00 P.M.
    Thursday 10:00 A.M.–7:00 P.M.
    Saturday 9:00 A.M.–4:00 P.M.
Still one of the best, Bogart's prize winning hair designers have a loyal following. Shampoos and haircuts are the work of their staff; another company called "Chic" provides facials, waxing, and makeup lessons.

Elizabeth Arden   638-6212
1147 Connecticut Avenue, N.W.
    Monday–Saturday 8:30 A.M.–5:30 P.M.
Complete beauty care with the Elizabeth Arden reputation behind it. One of the most popular salons in most major cities. Be sure to call for an appointment.

Ilo   342-0350
1637 Wisconsin Avenue, N.W.
    Monday–Friday 10:00 A.M.–6:00 P.M.
    Thursday 10:00 A.M.–7:00 P.M.
    Saturday 9:00 A.M.–5:00 P.M.
Clients range across the spectrum from college students to well-known personalities. This is a busy shop that provides full service.

Okyo   342-2675
1519 Wisconsin Avenue, N.W.
    Monday–Friday 9:30 A.M.–6:00 P.M.
    Thursday 9:30 A.M.–7:30 P.M.
    Saturday 9:00 A.M.–6:00 P.M.
Bernard Portelli, the owner, brings all of his French charm to the operation of one of the city's best salons. Starting with a haircut on your first visit, you will gradually be introduced to all of the full service amenities he provides. Don't be surprised to see a lot of famous faces under those driers.

Robin Weir & Co.   861-0444
2134 P Street, N.W.
   Monday–Friday 9:30 A.M.–6:00 P.M.
   Thursday 9:30 A.M.–7:30 P.M.
   Saturday 9:00 A.M.–6:00 P.M.
One of the most desirable places to be seen in DC. Robin Weir has a reputation established during the last administration when many important people were clients–from Nancy Reagan on down. It's a big place and quite expensive. But remember, "You get what you pay for."

Salon Roi   234-2668
2602 Connecticut Avenue, N.W.
Salon Roi is quite happy to provide service for children as well as adults. Since they do both men and women, this could become a family outing.

Watergate Salon   333-3488
2532 Virginia Avenue, N.W.
   Monday–Friday 7:30 A.M.–6:30 P.M.
   Saturday 7:30 A.M.–5:00 P.M.
Like all of the Watergate service, this is top of the line. Every service you might want is available, including massages for the ladies. Early morning hours are a real plus.

Belgium (Embassy of)   333-6900
3330 Garfield Street, N.W.

Bellevue Hotel, The   638-0900
15 E Street, N.W.

Benin (Embassy of)   232-6656
2737 Cathedral Avenue, N.W.

Benson's Jewelers   628-1838
1319 F Street, N.W. (Second Floor)

Best Western Center City   682-5300
1201 13th Street, N.W.

Best Western Regency   546-9200
600 New York Avenue, N.E.

Bethesda Custom Tailors   1-301-656-2077
7836 Wisconsin Avenue, Bethesda, Maryland

Bethesda Marriott Hotel   1-301-897-9400
5151 Pooks Hill Road,
Bethesda, Maryland   1-800-228-9290

Bethune Museum & Archives   332-1233
1318 Vermont Avenue, N.W. (13th/14th Sts.)

Better Business Bureau   393-8000

BIB Couriers, Inc.   529-3966
817 Delafield Street, N.E.

Bick's Books   328-2356
2309 18th Street, N.W.

Bicycle Pro Shop   337-0311
3413 M Street, N.W.

BICYCLES
See **RENTALS, BICYCLE**

Big Wheel Bikes   638-3301
1004 Vermont Avenue, N.W.

Birchmere, The   1-703-549-5919
3901 Mt. Vernon Avenue, Alexandria, Virginia

Black & White   337-6660
1235 Wisconsin Avenue, N.W.

Blackistone, Inc.   347-1300
1427 H Street, N.W.

Blues Alley   337-4141
1073 Wisconsin Avenue, N.W. (rear)

BOATS
See **RENTALS, BOAT**

Bobbie's Antiques & Interiors   1-301-949-5552
3760 Howard Avenue, Kensington, Maryland

Body Design by Gilda   363-4801
4801 Wisconsin Avenue, N.W.

Bogart, Inc.   333-6550
1063 Wisconsin Avenue, N.W.

Bolivia (Embassy of)   483-4410
3014 Massachusetts Avenue, N.W.

Bombay Palace   331-0111
1835 K Street, N.W. (19th St.)

Booked Up   965-3244
1209 31st Street, N.W.

Books for Cooks   1-301-547-9066
301 South Light Street, Baltimore, Maryland

BOOKSTORES

American Institute of Architects   626-7474
1735 New York Avenue
   Monday–Friday 8:30 A.M.–5:00 P.M.
Everything one would expect to find in an architects'

bookstore plus a lot more. In addition to all of the wonderful books for adults about architecture and its history, there are special ones for children. They also stock travel guides and have a wide assortment of gift items such as T-shirts and games.

Ampersand Books & Records   1-703-549-0840
118 King Street, Alexandria, Virginia
   Monday–Thursday 10:00 A.M.–10:00 P.M.
   Friday–Saturday 10:00 A.M.–1:00 P.M.
   Sunday Noon–7:00 P.M.
Although small, this store has a good selection of the most recent releases.

Audubon Naturalist Book Shop   1-301-652-3606
8940 Jones Mill Road, Chevy Chase, Maryland
   Monday–Saturday 10:00 A.M.–5:00 P.M.
   Sunday (October–December & March–May)
   Noon–5:00 P.M.
Operated by the Audubon Naturalist Society, this is a mecca for those who seek the best books on birds and nature. They also carry a selection of wildlife feeders, binoculars, and gift items. Highly recommended.

B. Dalton Bookseller
Mazza Gallerie   362-7055
   Monday–Friday 10:00 A.M.–8:00 P.M.
   Saturday 1:00 A.M.–6:00 P.M.
   Sunday Noon–5:00 P.M.
One of the biggest of the national chains. With an inventory of 25,000 titles, you can count on them to have one of the best selections to be found. Their many locations make it easy to find a B. Dalton nearby.

The Shops at National Place   393-1468
1331 Pennsylvania Avenue, N.W.
   Monday–Saturday 10:00 A.M. –7:00 P.M.
   Sunday Noon–5:00 P.M.
Right next door to the J.W. Marriott Hotel, this is an ideal downtown location.

Bick's Books   328-2356
2309 18th Street, N.W.
   Monday–Thursday 10:00 A.M.–1:00 P.M.
   Friday–Saturday 10:00 A.M.–Midnight
   Sunday Noon–8:00 P.M.
While they have a wide assortment of books on the issues concern to African Americans and Hispanics, their primary focus is on the problems confronting women. There are also sections covering Eastern and Western philosophy and green politics.

Booked Up 965-3244

1209 31st Street, N.W., Georgetown
   Monday–Friday 11:00 A.M.–3:00 P.M.
   Thursday 11:00 A.M.–5:00 P.M.
   Saturday 10:00 A.M. –12:30 P.M.
   Closed Sunday

Rare books and first editions vie for space with more recent publications which appeal to the distinguished professionals who can afford this posh neighborhood. If you are wondering about the strange hours, the happy staff maintains that they accomplish all of the business they need within their own time frame. We have found this to be the sign of the highly specialized, quality shop. It's owned by Larry McMurtry, who wrote *The Lonesome Dove*.

Books For Cooks 1-301-547-9066

301 South Light Street, Baltimore, Maryland
   Monday–Saturday 10:00 A.M.–9:30 P.M.
   Sunday 10:00 A.M.–8:00 P.M.

Everything in the way of cookbooks, including those important books on diet and health. They will be glad to search for those hard-to-find books that you need, so don't hesitate to ask.

Bridge Street Books 965-5200

2814 Pennsylvania Avenue, N.W.
   Monday–Thursday 10:00 A.M.–7:00 P.M.
   Friday–Saturday 10:00 A.M.–10:00 P.M.
   Sunday 1:00 P.M.–6:00 P.M.

Books for the thinking reader. They seem to have all of the classics and things that we've all been promising ourselves to read. A particularly nice place to browse on a rainy afternoon.

Calliope Bookstore 364-0111

3424 Connecticut Avenue, N.W.
   Monday–Saturday 10:00 A.M.–1:00 P.M.
   Sunday Noon–9:00 P.M.

Current releases of the serious variety. Heavy in the humanities. Not much in the way of escape reading if you're looking for something light.

Chapters Literary Bookstore 861-1333

1613 I Street, N.W.
   Monday–Friday 10:00 A.M.–6:30 P.M.
   Saturday 1:00 A.M.–5:00 P.M.

The owners knew what they were doing when they named it. If you're looking for "literary" works, they're here. Small press editions, poetry, and all of the things that appeal to the literati.

Cheshire Cat Children's Book Store　　244-3956
5512 Connecticut Avenue, N.W.
　　Monday–Saturday 9:30 A.M.–5:30 P.M.
Former school teachers have developed this shop into a wonderful place for children. There is an area for the really young to play while parents and older children shop for their favorites.

Common Concerns　　463-6500
1347 Connecticut Avenue, N.W.
　　Monday–Saturday 10:00 A.M.–8:00 P.M.
　　Sunday Noon–6:00 P.M.
The name says it all. If you are one of the many who are interested in a particular cause, you are likely to find the relevant literature you want in this shop. They can also supply T-shirts with which to announce your interest to the world.

Crown Books　　659-2030
2020 K Street, N.W.
　　Monday–Friday 9:00 A.M.–8:00 P.M.
　　Saturday–Sunday 10:00 A.M.–6:00 P.M.
At this local chain everything is discounted. They have a complete selection of both hardcover and paperbacks, particularly the newest bestsellers we all look for. This is only one of their many locations.

1710 G Street, N.W.	**789-2277**
4400 Jenifer Street, N.W.	**966-8784**
1200 New Hampshire Avenue, N.W.	**822-8331**
3131 M Street, N.W.	**333-9433**
1275 K Street, N.W.	**289-7170**
1155 19th Street, N.W.	**659-4172**
3335 Connecticut Avenue, N.W.	**966-7232**
4301 Connecticut Avenue, N.W.	**966-2576**

Francis Scott Key Book Shop　　337-4144
1400 28th Street, N.W. (O St.), Georgetown
　　Monday–Sunday 9:30 A.M.–1:00 P.M.
Dedicated to showcasing local history. For over 50 years they've been selling books about the Civil War and all of those hard-to-find things that are so fascinating.

Franz Bader Bookstore　　337-5440
1911 I Street, N.W.
　　Tuesday–Saturday 10:00 A.M.–6:00 P.M.
One of the better art galleries is also a good source for books on the subject. Well worth a visit.

Gilpin House Book Shop　　1-703-549-1880
208 King Street, Alexandria, Virginia
　　Monday–Friday 10:00 A.M.–1:00 P.M.
　　Saturday 9:00 A.M.–1:00 P.M.
　　Sunday 8:30 A.M.–1:00 P.M.

A nice community bookshop that doubles as a newsstand. You can combine your trip to pick up the Sunday *Washington Post* or *The New York Times* with some serious browsing through the local history section.

Idle Time Books   232-4774
2410 18th Street, N.W.
    Monday–Sunday 11:00 A.M.–9:00 P.M.
With a wide assortment of used and out-of-print books, they offer something for everyone. Lots of places to sit and enjoy the atmosphere of this comfortable Adams Morgan shop.

International Learning Center   232-4111
1715 Connecticut Avenue, N.W.
    Monday–Saturday 10:00 A.M.–7:00 P.M.
Items that are of special interest to the many members of the diplomatic community. Heavy on books in foreign languages.

Kramerbooks & Afterwords Cafe   387-1400
1517 Connecticut Avenue, N.W.
    Monday–Thursday 7:30 A.M.–1:00 A.M.
    Weekends Open from 7:30 A.M. on Friday to 1:00 A.M. on Sunday night.
One of the better known places in DC, it combines an interesting bookstore and a restaurant. Right at Dupont Circle, it's a convenient place for a quick sandwich or burger while looking through the new releases. We can't think of anything nicer than living near a bookstore like this when it's 4:00 A.M. and you can't sleep.

Lambda Rising
1625 Connecticut Avenue, N.W.   462-6969
241 West Chase Street, Baltimore,
Maryland   1-301-234-0069
    Monday–Friday 10:00 A.M.–7:00 P.M.
    Saturday–Sunday 10:00 A.M.–Midnight
Off of Dupont Circle, the staff of Lambda Rising are some of the nicest and most helpful people in Washington. They all contributed to our information on the gay community. As the best of the gay bookshops, they are well qualified to advise anyone.

Although many of the volumes address the issues of importance to gays in today's society, the shop carries almost everything that one could ask for, regardless of personal preferences.

Lloyd Books, Ltd   333-8989
3145 Dumbarton Avenue, N.W.
    Monday–Saturday 10:00 A.M.–6:00 P.M.

Specialists in the travel book field. They have old, new, and those rare ones that are so hard to find. They also carry a wide assortment of maps and will special order any book your heart desires.

Map Store, Inc., The   628-2608
1636 I Street, N.W.
> Monday–Friday 9:00 A.M.–5:30 P.M.
> Saturday 10:00 A.M.–3:00 P.M.

A tiny little shop that is stuffed with globes, travel books, and, of course, maps. The only books they're missing are the ones we're still writing. The staff is friendly and very helpful.

Moonstone Bookcellars   659-2600
2145 Pennsylvania Avenue, N.W.
> Daily 11:00 A.M.–6:00 P.M.

Science fiction, fantasy, horror, suspense, mystery.

**National Map Gallery
     & Travel Center**   789-0100
Union Station (West Hall)
50 Massachusetts Avenue, N.E.
> Monday–Saturday 10:00 A.M.–9:00 P.M.
> Sunday Noon–6:00 P.M.

If it's a map, atlas, globe, or book about travel, it's here. Their stock is very extensive and includes relief maps, satellite images, and star maps. Don't miss a chance to visit this fascinating shop.

Olsson's Books & Records   338-9544
1239 Wisconsin Avenue, N.W.
> Monday–Thursday 10:00 A.M.–1:00 P.M.
> Friday–Saturday 10:00 A.M.–Midnight
> Sunday Noon–6:00 P.M.

One of Washington's most important chains–and they have an inventory to be proud of—from current best sellers to the classics. A big plus is the collection of tapes and records. Their many stores are sure to have almost anything you want. Hours vary slightly at the other stores.

1307 19th Street, N.W. (Dupont Circle)   **785-1133**
> Monday–Saturday 10:00 A.M.–9:00 P.M.
> Sunday Noon–6:00 P.M.

1200 F Street, N.W. (Metro Center)   **347-3686**
> Monday–Saturday 10:00 A.M.–7:00 P.M.
> Sunday Noon–6:00 P.M.

106 South Union Street (King St.),
Alexandria, Virginia   **1-703-684-0077**
> Monday–Thursday 10:00 A.M.–10:00 P.M.
> Friday–Saturday 10:00 A.M.–Midnight
> Sunday 11:00 A.M.–6:00 P.M.

7647 Old Georgetown Road,
Bethesda, Maryland   **1-301-652-3336**
    Monday–Saturday 10:00 A.M.–10:00 P.M.
    Sunday 11:00 A.M.–7:00 P.M.

One Good Tern   **820-8376**
1710 Fern Street, Alexandria, Virginia
    Monday, Wednesday, Friday 10:00 A.M.–6:00 P.M.
    Tuesday, Thursday 10:00 A.M.–8:00 P.M.
    Saturday 9:00 A.M.–6:00 P.M.
    Sunday Noon–5:00 P.M.
They call themselves a nature book store but they carry a
lot more than just a large selection of natural history books.
We like their travel and field guide section, too. Children
will enjoy books on nature subjects geared to their reading
levels.

Politics & Prose   **364-1919**
5015 Connecticut Ave, N.W.
    Monday–Saturday 10:00 A.M.–10:00 P.M.
    Sunday 11:00 A.M.–6:00 P.M.
What a great bookstore! A good place to browse and obviously a favorite with writers—they frequently have parties here to launch their latest books.

Pyramid Bookstore   **328-0190**
2849 Georgia Avenue, N.W.
    Monday–Friday 10:00 A.M.–7:00 P.M.
    Saturday 1:00 A.M.–7:00 P.M.
    Sunday Noon–5:00 P.M.
The books here are for and about people of African de-
scent. They cover a fascinating range of topics ranging from
African American history and literature to the questions
and issues of Islam.

Reiter's Scientific &
    Professional Books   **223-3327**
2021 K Street, N.W.
    Monday–Friday 9:00 A.M.–7:30 P.M.
    Saturday 9:30 A.M.–5:00 P.M.
    Sunday Noon–5:00 P.M.
Heavy reading for scientific professionals. All areas of
specialization seem to be covered and, if they don't have it,
they'll be glad to order it for you.

Revolution Books   **265-1969**
2438 18th Street, N.W.
    Monday–Friday Noon–7:00 P.M.
    Saturday 11:00 A.M.–7:00 P.M.
    Sunday Noon–5:00 P.M.
We thought this kind of bookstore was a thing of the past.

We must be getting old. It's for revolutionaries. If you are looking for material on a movement or on protests, it will be here. They also have a nice selection of books on the Third World.

Rogues Gallery Mystery Bookstore 1-301-986-5511
4934 Elm Street, Bethesda, Maryland
   Tuesday–Saturday 1:00 A.M.–7:00 P.M.
   Sunday 1:00 P.M.–5:00 P.M.
Everything in the way of mysteries. There are also games, puzzles, and even who-done-its for children.

Sidney Kramer Books, Inc. 293-2685
1825 I Street, N.W.
   Monday–Friday 9:00 A.M.–6:30 P.M.
   Saturday 10:00 A.M.–5:00 P.M.
While they carry some of everything, the real emphasis here is on economics and world studies. It's a highly specialized field and if it's yours, you must visit this store—they can be a major asset.

Travel Books Unlimited &
      Language Center 1-301-951-8533
4931 Cordell Avenue (Old Georgetown Rd./
Norfolk Ave.), Bethesda, Maryland
   Tuesday–Saturday 10:00 A.M.–9:00 P.M.
   Sunday Noon–5:00 P.M.
   Closed Monday
Six years ago, with 2,000 volumes, a lot of enthusiasm, and very little capital, Rochelle Jaffe started a small bookstore in Bethesda. Today, she has five full-time employees, 26,000 maps, 55,000 guidebooks, and a language center supplying material relating to 85 languages. The process of carefully selecting all of this material has made Rochelle one of the foremost experts in the travel field, and she is called upon by writers and publishers for help in creating some of the books that eventually end up on her shelves. She and her staff are a storehouse of information and, if you need real advice, she's the one to call.

Travel Merchandise Mart 371-6656
1425 K Street, N.W.
   Monday–Friday 9:00 A.M.–5:30 P.M.
Guidebooks and all of those little things that make for a comfortable trip. They have those indispensable voltage converters and luggage carts that can be so hard to find.

Trover Shops
Three locations featuring books, magazines, and a variety of cards, stationery, office supplies, and party goods. Handy places to know about.

227 Pennsylvania Avenue, S.E.   **543-8006**
   Monday–Friday 7:00 A.M.–9:00 P.M.
   Saturday 7:00 A.M.–7:00 P.M.
   Sunday 7:00 A.M.–3:00 P.M.
1031 Connecticut Avenue, N.W. (K St.)   **659-8138**
   Monday–Friday 8:00 A.M.–6:30 P.M.
   Saturday 9:00 A.M.–6:00 P.M.
800 15th Street, N.W. (H St.)   **347-2177**
   Monday–Friday 8:00 A.M.–6:00 P.M.

Waldenbooks   **393-1490**
1700 Pennsylvania Avenue, N.W.
   Monday–Friday 9:30 A.M.–6:00 P.M.
   Saturday 10:00 A.M.–6:00 P.M.

Not just another chain, Waldenbooks always has the ones we want most. All of the current best sellers in both hardback and soft cover.

Georgetown Park Mall, 3222 M Street, N.W.   **333-8033**
   Monday–Friday 10:00 A.M.–9:00 P.M.
   Saturday 10:00 A.M.–7:00 P.M.
   Sunday 10:00 A.M.–6:00 P.M.

Botswana (Embassy of)   **244-4990**
4301 Connecticut Avenue, N.W.

Bottom Line, The   **298-8488**
1716 I Street, N.W.

BOW TIES

Besides being able to read a map upside down, a concierge must possess the ability to tie a bow tie. Inevitably, on days when there is a big wedding in the hotel, the concierge will receive a frantic call in the late afternoon,

   "Does anybody down there know how to tie a bow tie?"

   "Come down to the desk and we'll take care of you."

Seating the guest in a low chair while wondering what sort of insurance the hotel carries against accidental strangulation, we strive to put the guest at ease with something like,

   "The most important thing is to remain totally relaxed."

The novice should allow at least a half hour's time for this operation. Relax. If you can tie a bow, you can tie a bow tie.

See the detailed instructions on pages 44–45.

The Art of Bow Tying

by

Ferrell Reed

Shown as you see it when you are looking at yourself in a mirror!

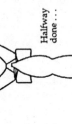

Just a simple overhand knot . . .

Make the front bow . . .

Halfway done . . . .

1.
Start with end in left hand extending 1" longer than end in right hand.

2.
Cross longer end (left) over shorter end (right) and pass it up through the loop at your neck so it is tied loosely at the throat.

3.
Fold lower hanging end up and to the right to form what will be the front of your bow tie, making sure the folded side is to your right.

4.
Hold this folded bow with your left hand and bring the other end down and over the bow.

44

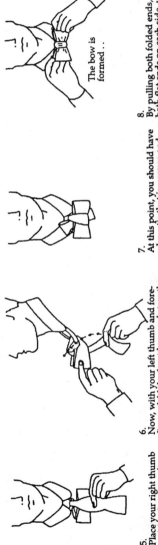

The bow is
formed . . .

5.
Place your right thumb and forefinger on the hanging end where it will be folded to form the back loop of your bow.

6.
Now, with your left thumb and forefinger, fold the front bow ends together, around the hanging end. By pulling the folded bow forward you will make a small passage behind it through which you can push the looped end of the back bow using your right forefinger.

7.
At this point, you should have a bow tie that is uneven and needs to be tightened.

8.
By pulling both folded ends, then both flat ends on each side, you can smooth out the bow and tighten the knot (like your shoelaces).

To untie, simply pull the flat ends . . .

45

Braniff	**1-800-272-6433**
Brass Rail	**371-6983**
476 K Street, N.W.	
Brazil (Embassy of)	**745-2700**
3006 Massachusetts Avenue, N.W.	
Brickskeller, The	**293-1885**
1523 22nd Street, N.W.	
Bridge Street Books	**965-5200**
2814 Pennsylvania Avenue, N.W.	
Britches of Georgetown	**338-3330**
1247 Wisconsin Avenue, N.W.	
British Airways	**1-800-247-9297**
Broker	**546-8300**
713 8th Street, S.E.	
Brooks Brothers	**659-4650**
1840 I Street, N.W.	
Bruton Antiques	**1-301-564-1226**
4125 Howard Avenue, Kensington, Maryland	
Budget Rent-a-Car	
Dulles Airport	**437-9373**
National Airport	**920-3360**
Wisconsin Avenue	**244-7437**
Budget Motor Inn	**529-3900**
1615 New York Avenue, N.E.	
Bulgaria (Embassy of)	**387-7969**
1621 22nd Street, N.W.	
Bullfeathers	**543-5005**
410 1st Street, S.E.	
Burberry's of London	**463-3000**
1155 Connecticut Avenue, N.W.	
Bureau of Engraving & Printing	**447-9709**
14th & C Streets, S.W.	
Burke's Peerage, Ltd.	**1-703-549-5155**
128 South Royal Street, Alexandria, Virginia	
Burma (Embassy of)	**332-9044**
2300 S Street, N.W.	
Burundi (Embassy of)	**342-2574**
2233 Wisconsin Avenue, N.W.	
Business & Professional Women's League	**291-4579**
3905 Georgia Avenue, N.W.	

BUS LINES

The bus system in Washington is not the best way for tourists to get around. Almost all of the sights you will want to see and all of the other major attractions are best served by the Metro— the subway. Rare exceptions are places in Georgetown and many of the best restaurants. We always take taxis. They're the worst taxis we have ever seen, but they will get you to that "out of the way" place safely and cheaply.

BWIA   **1-800-327-7401**

C

C & M Antiques/Eagle Antiques   **1-703-548-9882**
311 Cameron Street,   **1-703-549-7611**
Alexandria, Virginia

CHESAPEAKE & OHIO CANAL (C&O)   229-3614

One of the best preserved of the old American canals, this stretches 184½ miles from Georgetown to Cumberland, Maryland. Walking or biking along the old towpath provides a pleasant afternoon's excursion. From mid-April to mid-October, the canal boats Georgetown (653-5844) and the Canal Clipper (299-2026) operate.

C & O Canal Tours   **1-703-472-4376**
C.G. Sloan & Co., Inc.   **628-1468**
919 E Street, N.W.
Cafe Lautrec   **265-6436**
2431 18th Street, N.W.
Calliope Bookstore   **364-0111**
3424 Connecticut Avenue, N.W.
Camalier & Buckley   **347-7700**
1141 Connecticut Avenue, N.W.
Cambodian   **1-703-522-3832**
1727 Wilson Boulevard (Quinn St.), Arlington, Virginia
Camelot   **887-5966**
1823 M Street, N.W.

CAMERAS, REPAIR OF

See **REPAIRS, CAMERA**
Cameroon (Embassy of)   **265-8790**
2349 Massachusetts Avenue, N.W.

Canada (Embassy of) 2450 Massachusetts Avenue, N.W.	**483-5505**
Canterbury, The 1733 N Street, N.W.	**393-3000** **1-800-424-2950**
Cape Verde (Embassy of) 3415 Massachusetts Avenue, N.W.	**965-6820**
Capital Centre Capital Beltway (exits 15 & 17 east)	**350-3400**
Capital Children's Museum 800 3rd Street, N.E.	**543-8600**
Capital Hilton, The 16th and K Streets, N.W.	**393-1000** **1-800-HILTONS**
Capitol Cab	**546-2400**

CAPITOL HILL

The Capitol Hill area is one of the most thickly populated with sightseeing attractions. Both cultural and entertaining in nature, they will provide the entire family with a feeling for the history of our country. The following list is a guide to use as a walking tour of the area. Most of the places listed have been written about in the SIGHTSEEING section of this book. Places of lesser interest are included so you can be sure to see everything.

The Capitol

Spring Grotto

The Peace Monument

General Ulysses S. Grant Memorial

Library of Congress

Supreme Court

Sewall-Belmont House

Union Station

Capital Children's Museum

Union Market

Trinity College

Dance Place

**National Shrine of the Immaculate
    Conception**

The Catholic University of America

Franciscan Monastery

U.S. National Arboretum

Anacostia Park

Kenilworth Aquatic Gardens

Folger Shakespeare Library

Friendship Settlement

Christ Church, Washington Parish

Marine Corps Barracks

Washington Navy Yard

**Frederick Douglass National
Historic Site (Cedar Hill)**

Anacostia Museum

Congressional Cemetery

Capitol Hill Club	**484-4590**
300 1st Street, S.E.	
Capitol Reservations (for Hotels)	**1-800-VISIT-DC**
Capitol Yacht Club	**488-8110**
1000 Water Street, S.W.	
Capitol, The	**224-3121**
Pennsylvania Avenue and 1st Street, S.E.	
Caprice D'Amour	**783-2408**
2000 Pennsylvania Avenue, N.W.	
Carega Foxley Leach	**337-3661**
3214 O Street, N.W.	
Carlyle Suites, The	**234-3200**
1731 New Hampshire Avenue, N.W.	
Carnegie Deli	**1-703-790-5001**
Tyson's Corner Mall, 8517 Leesburg Pike Tyson's Corner, Virginia	
Central Africa Republic (Embassy of)	**483-7800**
1618 22nd Street, N.W.	
Central Delivery Service	**423-7117**
Central Liquor	**737-2800**
516–518 9th Street, N.W.	
Chad (Embassy of)	**462-4009**
2202 R Street, N.W.	
Champions	**965-4005**
1206 Wisconsin Avenue, N.W.	

Channel Inn   **554-2400**
650 Water Street, N.W.

Chapters Literary Bookstore   **861-1333**
1613 I Street, N.W.

Chardonnay   **232-7000**
Radisson Park Terrace Hotel,
1515 Rhode Island Avenue, N.W.

Charles Jourdan Boutique   **1-301-986-1460**
5506 Wisconsin Avenue, Chevy Chase, Maryland

CHARLOTTESVILLE, VIRGINIA

This is Thomas Jefferson's country, and his words are enough to encourage anyone to visit his homeland. In a letter to a friend, Jefferson described these mountains as "the Eden of the United States." Although it is only a 2½ hour drive from Washington, Charlottesville offers so much to the visitor we recommend staying over a night or two.

Jefferson's mountaintop estate, Monticello, continues to convey the personality and interests of its creator, who built and remodeled it over a period of forty years. His interest in horticulture has come alive with the painstaking recreation of his orchard, vineyard, and vegetable garden. Twenty-minute guided tours are given from 8:00 A.M. to 5:00 P.M. from March through October, and from 9:00 A.M. to 4:30 P.M. the rest of the year.

Jefferson also found time to conceive, write the charter, raise money, select the site, draw the plans, lay the cornerstone, supervise construction, select the faculty, serve as rector, and create the curriculum for the University of Virginia.

James Monroe, our nation's fifth President, moved to Albemarle to be near his good friend Thomas Jefferson. Monroe's 550 acre estate (which he named "Highland" and a later owner rechristened "Ash Lawn") recreates the atmosphere of a working farm, with strutting peacocks, spinning and weaving demonstrations, and gardens.

If time permits, a visit to Montpelier, the home of James Madison, gives yet another insight into the lives of the founders of our country.

Chaucer's   **296-0665**
Canterbury Hotel, 1733 N Street, N.W. (17th/18th Sts.)

Chelsea's   **298-8222**
1055 Thomas Jefferson Street, N.W.

Cherishables   **785-4087**
1608 20th Street, N.W.

CHERRY BLOSSOM FESTIVAL, THE

Washington's cherry trees have become the symbol of spring for the entire country. When they bloom, in late March or early April, hundreds of thousands of people are drawn to the capital to see the 3,000 trees of 12 varieties that glorify the Tidal Basin. A gift from Japan in 1912, they remind us each year of our many and varied ties to that country. Although the "Greenhouse Effect" has made it increasingly difficult for meteorologists to predict when the blossoms will appear, Festival planners have settled on the first week of April for the celebratory pageants, parades, concerts, and marathon. Be prepared for massive traffic jams, crowds, and the heartbreaking beauty of fragile, delicate blossoms that a strong wind might scatter.

Chesapeake House	**347-3600**
746 9th Street, N.W.	

Cheshire Cat Children's Book Store	**244-3956**
5512 Connecticut Avenue, N.W.	

CHEVY CHASE, MARYLAND

This town on the Maryland/DC border is a shopper's paradise—particularly the 5400–5500 blocks of Wisconsin Avenue. Best of all, it's easily accessible from downtown Washington. Just take the Metro to Friendship Heights, and you will exit directly into Mazza Gallerie. Anchored by Texas's famous Neiman Marcus, this ultra-high-fashion shopping center (*please* don't call it a mall) includes nearly 60 stores. Among others, you'll find Raleigh's, Ann Taylor, Benetton, Paul Harris, and Kron Chocolatier here. For a quick pick-me-up, your choices range from McDonald's to the Pleasant Peasant. You can then purchase a pair of running shoes at the Foot Locker and deceive yourself into thinking you'll work off the Peasant's sinful desserts.

On Wisconsin Avenue, Elizabeth Arden, Cartier, Gucci, and Saks Fifth Avenue await you. Both Lord & Taylor and Woodward & Lothrop are nearby.

Chicago Bar & Grill	**463-8888**
19th Street and Dupont Circle	

Child's Play	
16th and K Streets, N.W.	**785-0211**
The Shops at National Place	
1331 Pennsylvania Avenue, N.W.	**393-2382**

Childe Harold	**483-6702**
1610 20th Street, N.W.	

CHILDREN'S ACTIVITIES

Arts & Industries Building   357-2700
Jefferson Drive at 9th Street, N.W.   **Tours 357-3030**
    Daily 10:00 A.M.–5:30 P.M.
    Closed Christmas
    Metro Station: Smithsonian

It doesn't have the appeal of the National Air & Space Museum, it doesn't contain the Hope Diamond or other baubles, but to us this red-brick Victorian structure embodies the very spirit of "The Smithsonian." Originally built as the National Museum, it was finished in 1881 and was the site of the inaugural ball for James Garfield. Its real purpose, however, was to house all of the stuff left over from Philadelphia's Centennial Exhibition. Looking around, you'll understand why the Smithsonian has been labeled "the nation's attic." You can view a polyglot collection ranging from locomotives to totem poles. All of the Smithsonian's gift shops offer everything from books and bookmarks to expensive reproduction jewelry, but since this museum does not attract hordes of people, shopping here is a particular pleasure.

Bureau of Engraving & Printing   447-9709
14th and C Streets, S.W.
    Weekdays 8:30 A.M.–2:30 P.M.
    Metro Station: Smithsonian

Everyone loves touring this building where all the paper currency in the U.S. is made. After a short introductory film, you'll see the complicated intaglio process by which those lovely greenbacks are produced. Postage stamps, treasury notes, military certificates, and invitations to the White House are also printed here.

C & O Canal Barge Rides   **Information 472-4376**
30th and Jefferson Streets   **Reservations 653-5844**

Children will enjoy this unusual trip as much as adults. The canal is a narrow ditch that was used to transport both passengers and cargo before the days of the super highway. Drawn by mules, one moves at a leisurely pace from Georgetown to Great Falls, Maryland. Call the National Parks Service for full details.

Capitol, The   **Senate 224-3121**
Pennsylvania Avenue and   **House 225-3121**
1st Street, S.E.
    Daily 9:00 A.M.–3:45 A.M.
    Metro Station: Capitol South

Built on a hill that Pierre L'Enfant described as "a pedestal waiting for a monument," the Capitol is the first landmark that visitors to Washington search for on the horizon. This building once contained not only both houses of Congress, but the Supreme Court and Library of Congress as well.

Write to your Congressperson well in advance of your visit to request tickets to the morning congressional tour. Otherwise, take one of the free 35-minute guided tours that leave from the Rotunda every 15 minutes between 9:00 A.M. and 3:45 P.M.

Every President from Andrew Jackson through George Bush (except Reagan who changed tradition and was inaugurated on the West Front) has taken his oath of office on the East Front steps. It was here that Abraham Lincoln asked a divided nation to forge ahead "with malice toward none, with charity for all...." Franklin Delano Roosevelt reminded us that "the only thing we have to fear is fear itself." And John F. Kennedy challenged us to "Ask not what your country can do for you—ask what you can do for your country."

The huge (180 feet high and 97 feet across) Rotunda is the hub of the Capitol. Nine presidents have lain in state here. The House of Representatives met from 1807 to 1857 in what is now the National Statuary Hall. A curious acoustical effect enables one to hear what is whispered 45 feet away.

Capital Children's Museum, The   **543-8600**
800 3rd Street, N.E. (H Street)
    Daily 10:00 A.M.- 5:00 P.M.
    Closed Major Holidays
    Admission $5.00
    Metro Station: Union Station

Like similiar institutions which are springing up in other cities, this is not really a museum. It is a learning center where children can be exposed to techniques of learning which they perceive as play. There are things to play on, tactile things to feel, and sophisticated computers that talk and can be used for drawing.

Carousel, The
Right on the Mall, in front of the Arts & Industries Building, stands an old-fashioned carousel. You can't miss it and shouldn't. It's great fun for the younger children and it's a nice break between all of those museums.

FBI Building, The   **324-3447**
10th Street and Pennsylvania Avenue, N.W.
    Monday–Friday 9:00 A.M.–4:15
    Admission: Free.
    Metro Station: Federal Triangle or Gallery Place

Tourists don't flock here to admire the architectural wonders of this building—one of the ugliest in Washington. It's the firearms demonstration that packs 'em in. The well-informed and enthusiastic guides also explain the FBI's current work fighting organized crime, terrorism, espionage, and extortion. During the summer, about 5,000 people visit here daily, so you may have a long wait. If possible, write to your Senator or Congressperson well in advance of your trip and request passes for a VIP tour.

Ford's Theatre & Lincoln Museum

511 10th Street, N.W. (E/F Sts.)   **Box Office 347-4833**
   Daily 9:00AM–5:00 P.M.   **Museum 426-6927**
   Metro Station: Metro Center

Best known as the theater where Abraham Lincoln was assassinated as he watched a performance of "Our American Cousin," Ford's Theater has been beautifully restored and presents small-stage touring productions. The basement contains a small museum of mementos of both Lincoln and John Wilkes Booth.

Jefferson Memorial   426-6822 (or 6821)

14th Street and East Basin Drive, S.W.
   Daily 8:00 A.M.–Midnight
   Admission: Free
   The rotunda is open and lighted all night

One of Washington's most popular and most beautiful attractions, the Jefferson Memorial is located slightly off the beaten path. The interior of this simple classical structure is dominated by a 19-foot-high statue of Thomas Jefferson, an architect of words as well as buildings. In late March or early April when the cherry blossoms are blooming around the Tidal Basin, the whole effect is breathtaking.

Lincoln Memorial, The   426-6985

23rd Street off Constitution Ave, N.W.
   Admission: Free

Who can deny that this is one of the nation's outstanding memorials—and certainly a fitting one. Standing at the end of the reflecting pool, its classical Grecian design has been the background for some of the notable events that Lincoln would have championed. When denied the right to perform in the D.A.R. auditorium, Marion Anderson sang to a huge crowd from the steps. Years later, it was the site of the famous "I Have a Dream" speech made by the Reverand Martin Luther King, Jr.

After climbing the steep flight of steps, one is face to face with the huge statue of Abraham Lincoln by Daniel Chester French. Into the walls surrounding the brooding figure, are carved his Gettysburg and Second Inaugural Addresses.

Mount Vernon   **1-703-780-2000**
Southern end of George Washington Parkway
(16 miles south of downtown Washington)
    Daily March-October 9:00 A.M.–5:00 P.M.
    November-February 9:00 A.M.–4:00 P.M.
    Admission:
    Adults $5.00
    Children $2.00

Five hundred acres remain of George Washington's estate that once stretched most of the way to present-day Alexandria. Washington loved this house, renovating and expanding it throughout his life. Standing on the splendid verandah overlooking the Potomac, you'll understand why. Since 1860, the house and grounds have been owned and maintained by the Mount Vernon Ladies Association. It was meticulously restored in the early 1980s and provides a glimpse into the life of George Washington the private citizen. Of particular interest is the key to Paris's dreaded Bastille prison, presented to Washington by the Marquis de Lafayette, that hangs on the wall in the central hall. The gardens are splendidly maintained.

A unique way to visit the home of our first president is to take the *Spirit of Mount Vernon* (see separate listing), a cruise ship. In addition to being a most exciting way to get to the plantation, it is a chance to see Washington and the sights along the Potomac River from a new perspective. A narrator points out the various points of interest, and the two hours spent at Mount Vernon are adequate to see everything before the trip back to Washington. Children will love it.

National Air & Space Museum   **357-2700**
Smithsonian Institution
6th Street and Independence Avenue, S.W.
    Daily 10:00 A.M.–5:30 P.M.
    Closed Christmas
    Admission:Free
    Metro Station: Smithsonian on the Blue or Orange Lines

This is the most popular museum in the world, and there is not much we can say to improve upon that. If the combination of space exploration, rockets, astronomy, Lunar vehicles, space suits, missiles and spacecraft, Skylab, and the mystery of other planets doesn't get to you, we recommend the Work Horse Museum.

National Aquarium, The   **377-2825**
Department of Commerce Building
14th Street and Constitution Avenue, N.W.

Everyone loves an aquarium, and, while this is not one of the "great ones," it is a favorite with adults and children alike.

Tucked away in the basement of the Department of Commerce, it is the oldest public aquarium in the country, and features a wide variety of salt and fresh water specimens. The children seem to enjoy the "Touch Tank," that allows them to handle some of the hardier varieties of aquatic life. Adults don't mind watching them do it. Feeding time is prime time. Try to visit at 2:00 P.M. any day but Friday. Piranhas eat on Tuesday, Thursday, and Sunday. Sharks dine with equal gusto on Monday, Wednesday, and Saturday.

National Archives, The   523-3184
Constitution Avenue (7th/9th Sts., N.W.)
> Daily September 7th–March 10:00 A.M.–5:30 P.M.
> April–September 6th 10:00 A.M.–9:00 P.M.
> Admission: Free
> Metro Station: Archives on the Yellow Line; Smithsonian on the Blue or Orange Lines

A must for everyone. See the documents that are the cornerstones of our democracy. The Declaration of Independence, the Constitution, and the Bill of Rights are preserved here and are on view for all to see. But that's not all. The National Archives houses the 21-floor vault that stores millions of documents that are vital to the preservation of the history of our country. Treaties of all kinds, including some made with American Indian tribes, data relating to genealogical history, and the famous Civil War photographs of Matthew Brady, all share space with more recent items such as Franklin Roosevelt's recorded "Fireside Chats," and the propaganda messages broadcast by Tokyo Rose during World War II.

National Cathedral, The (Cathedral
Church of St. Peter & St. Paul)   537-6200
Wisconsin and Massachusetts Avenues., N.W.
(34th/Garfield)

Work on the sixth largest cathedral in the world, begun when President Theodore Roosevelt laid the cornerstone in 1907, is scheduled for completion on September 29, 1990.

Although it is the seat of the Episcopal Diocese of Washington, it has no local congregation and serves the entire nation as a house of prayer. The cathedral is built in fourteenth-century Gothic style, complete with flying butresses. The 57-acre grounds contain three gardens, four schools, the London Brass Rubbing Center, and a stone carver's shed where one can watch the carvers at work. In the crypt are the tombs of President Woodrow Wilson and his wife. Helen Keller is buried here as well.

**National Geographic
  Society/Explorers' Hall   857-7588**
M and 17th Streets, N.W.
  Monday-Saturday 9:00 A.M.–5:00 P.M.
  Sunday 10:00 A.M.–5:00 P.M.
  Admission: Free
  Metro Station: Farragut North or Dupont Circle on the
  Red Line
Every child is familiar with the National Geographic "specials" on TV and will feel right at home amongst the exhibits of equipment used on various expeditions. There is the world's largest free standing globe, artifacts from forgotten civilizations, and dioramas showing the development of man.

**National Museum of American
  History   357-2700**
Smithsonian Institution, 14th Street and Constitution Avenue, N.W.
  Daily 10:00 A.M.–5:30 P.M.
  Closed Christmas
  Admission: Free
  Metro Station: Smithsonian or Federal Triangle on
  Blue or Orange Lines
Both tourists and local residents find plenty here to interest and fascinate. With a mandate to deal with both scientific and cultural areas, it seems to have almost everything that relates to our history. To give you an idea: An enormous collection of models from the U.S. Patent Office, such as a Model T Ford from 1913, Alexander Graham Bell's first telephone, and Edison's light bulb. Things from the movies and TV, such as Judy Garland's famous ruby slippers and Archie Bunker's chair. McDowell's favorite is a locomotive, Adele enjoys the gowns of some of our First Ladies.

National Museum of Natural History   357-2700
Smithsonian Institution, 10th Street and Constitution Avenue, N.W.
  Daily 10:00 A.M.–5:30 P.M.
  Closed Christmas
  Admission: Free
  Metro Station: Smithsonian or Federal Triangle on the
  Blue or Orange Lines
Another wonderful experience and another reason why it takes so long to see the Washington museums. This is a huge collection, and you will probably have to choose be-

tween exhibits instead of seeing everything. From the time you are greeted by the giant elephant in the entrance hall, to your last lingering look at the Hope Diamond, you will be enthralled by marvelous collections. Children will enjoy the Insect Zoo, where they can actually fondle the little critters, and the Discovery Room, where there are all kinds of things with which they can interact.

Old Post Office Tower, The (Nancy Hanks Center)   523-5691
Pennsylvania Avenue between 11th and
12th Streets, N.W.
> Metro Station: Federal Triangle on the Blue or Orange
> Lines

At the turn of the century it was the largest government building in DC. Among its "firsts"—the first clock tower, the first steel framework, and the first electric power plant for lighting. It still has one of the largest uninterrupted open spaces in the city, now redesigned, with fast food and souvenir shops mixed in with toy and book stores. It is a haven for teenagers and young people. In 1983, the ten Congress Bells were installed in the 315 foot tower. A gift of the Ditchley Foundation of Great Britain, the bells are replicas of the ones in Westminster Abbey in London and weigh between 581 and 2953 pounds each. A complete peal, taking 3½ hours, is rung in honor of the opening and closing of Congress and on State occasions.

Peterson House   426-6830
516 10th Street, N.W.
> Daily 9:00 A.M.–5:00 P.M.
> Admission: Free
> Metro Station: Metro Center

Except for the fact that Lincoln died here, there is little to recommend this as a tourist attraction. He was taken here after being shot and thus established this building's place in history. Like most places where many people have experienced strong emotion, there is an aura of spirituality that seems to permeate the atmosphere. Combine it with a visit to Ford's Theater and Museum.

Washington Dolls' House & Toy Museum   1-301-244-0024
5236 44th Street, N.W. (Jenifer/Harrison Sts.),
Chevy Chase, Maryland
> Tuesday-Saturday 10:00 A.M.–5:00 P.M.
> Sunday Noon–5:00 P.M.
> Closed Monday
> Admission:

Adults: $3.00

Children: $1.00

Metro Station: Friendship Heights on the Red Line

Flora Gill Jacobs is recognized as the leading authority on the history of doll houses, and this is her museum. As she says, "It is dedicated to the proposition that doll's houses of the past comprise a study of the decorative arts in miniature, and that toys of the past reflect social history." There are so many things to see that we can't begin to list them—several hundred dolls are shown in the many interiors provided by the shops, houses, and rooms. If you are interested in rare dolls, they are here, too.

Don't miss the shops! There are two: One for collectors of dolls houses, miniature furniture, little stuff for decorating, and of course, dolls. The second shop is for people who like to build doll's houses and supplies everything necessary to do just that.

Washington Monument   426-6841

14th Street and Constitution Avenue, N.W.

Daily (Winter) 9:00 A.M.–4:30 P.M.

(Summer) 8:00 A.M.–Midnight

Admission: Free

Metro Station: Smithsonian on the Blue or Orange Lines

Located on the western part of the Mall, this is one of the easiest attractions to find. The needle-like shaft of the marble obelisk towers 555 feet, 5½ inches into the sky and seems to be visible from anyplace near the Mall. Built between 1848 and 1885, it opened to the public in 1886. At that time, it was the tallest structure in the world and is still the tallest structure of masonry. Everyone looking at the monument is immediately aware that there is a slight but definite change in the color of the exterior stone part way up. This is where construction was stopped in 1854 by the American Party (the Know Nothings). They objected to the donation of a block of marble by Pope Pius IX and not only stole the block but managed to sabotage contributions. Construction was unable to continue until 1876 when it was turned over to the Corps of Engineers for completion. They redesigned the proportions by altering the height and set the capstone of aluminum in place on December 6, 1884. Today, you can take a quick elevator ride to the top rather than walking up the 188 steps. The view from the top is spectacular.

White House, The   456-1414

1600 Pennsylvania Avenue, N.W.

Tuesday–Saturday 10:00 A.M.–Noon

Admission: Free

Metro Station: Farragut West or McPherson Square on
the Blue or Orange Lines

More than a million and a half visitors each year take
advantage of the opportunity to tour the world's only residence of a head of state that is open to the public free of
charge. This can lead to long lines, so we advise that you
contact your Senator or Congressperson far in advance of
your visit and request tickets for a VIP tour. These are conducted in the mornings before the regular tour hours and
include a few more rooms. Visitors on the regular tour
will see the East Room, familiar through televised press
conferences and concerts, dominated by Gilbert Stuart's
famous painting of George Washington. This was daringly saved by Dolley Madison just before the British set
fire to the White House in 1814. (Legend has it that she
also saved an extremely flattering portrait of herself that
now hangs in the Red Room.) In less formal days, Abigail
Adams hung her laundry here and Theodore Roosevelt's
children practiced their roller skating in this room. The
tour continues to the Green Room and the oval-shaped
Blue Room, used as a wedding chapel by Grover Cleveland in 1886 when he married Frances Folsom. The President brings Heads of State and VIPs here after welcoming
them on the South Lawn. The final stop is the State Dining
Room, which seats up to 140. The John Adams White
House Prayer, "I pray heaven to bestow the best of blessings on this house and all that shall hereafter inhabit it.
May none but honest and wise men ever rule under this
roof," written in a letter to his wife, is inscribed on the
marble mantlepiece. Although picture taking is forbidden
within the White House, when you emerge on the north
side under the great portico, you'll want to stop to take a
snapshot for posterity.

Children's Hospital	**745-5005**
111 Michigan Avenue, N.W.	
Chile (Embassy of)	**785-1746**
1736 Massachusetts Avenue, N.W.	
China Airlines	**833-1760**
China Inn	**842-0909**
631 H Street, N.W. (6th/7th Sts.)	
China Pearl	**328-7194**
2020 K Street, N.W. (20th/21st Sts.)	
China, People's Republic of (Embassy of)	**328-2500**
2300 Connecticut Avenue, N.W.	

CHINATOWN

Located roughly between H and K Streets, N.W., from 6th to 9th Streets, Washington's Chinatown is graced by the spectacular Friendship Archway, decorated in classical Chinese art of the Ming and Ch'ing Dynasties. Compared to its New York and San Francisco counterparts, it covers a small area. As one would expect, restaurants offering outstanding cuisine and value abound.

CHOCOLATE

Caprice D'Amour   783-2408
2000 Pennsylvania Avenue, N.W.
Fine imported Belgian chocolate and they deliver.

Chocolate Chocolate   338-3356
3222 M Street, N.W.
Swiss and Belgian imports plus their own line of goodies. Our favorites are the truffles, of course.

Chocolate Chocolate   466-2190
Washington Square
1050 Connecticut Avenue, N.W.

Kron Chocolatier   966-4946
Mazza Gallerie
5300 Wisconsin Avenue, N.W.
Not up to their old standards but still not to be ignored. If you're really into chocolate, ignore the novelty items and try the dried fruit dipped in you know what.

La Bonbonniere   333-6425
1724 H Street, N.W.
Probably the best Washington has to offer. Although French chocolate is not usually thought of as top of the line, anything in the food arena is dependent upon the person who does the cooking. Francois Cochin must be doing something right.

Neuchatel Chocolates   347-8570
The Willard Hotel, 1455 Pennsylvania Avenue, N.W., Suite 115
They sound better than they taste. At $30.00 a pound, expect perfection every time.

Chocolate Chocolate   338-3356
3222 M Street, N.W.

Chorus Line   965-7277
Georgetown Park Mall, 3222 M Street, N.W.

Christ Church (Episcopal)   547-9300
620 G Street, S.E. (6th/7th Streets)

**Christian Heurich
    Mansion/Columbia Historical
    Society**   **785-2068**
1307 New Hampshire Avenue, N.W. (19th/20th Sts.)

Chronicles   **293-6247**
2000 Pennsylvania Avenue, N.W.

**Church of Jesus Christ of the Latter
    Day Saints**   **1-301-587-0144**
9900 Stoneybrook Drive, Kensington, Maryland

Church of the Ascension of St. Agnes   **347-8161**
1217 Massachusetts Avenue, N.W. (12th Street)

Church of the Epiphany   **347-2635**
1317 G Street, N.W.

CHURCHES, SYNAGOGUES, and MOSQUES

The churches, synagogues, and mosques listed here are a small portion of the total number in Washington and the surrounding communities. If you are visiting the nation's capital as a tourist, you may want to take advantage of the opportunity to worship in the same places frequented by our presidents and other famous leaders. We have included the ones we felt had the most historic interest. They range from very simple to opulent, but they share a spirituality that has been important to us since the days of our founding fathers.

Adas Israel Synagogue   **362-4433**
3rd and G Streets, N.W.
Now the home of the Lillian and Albert Small Jewish Museum, this synagogue was built in 1876.

Christ Church (Episcopal)   **547-9300**
620 G Street, S.E. (6th/7th Sts.)
    Metro Station: Eastern Market
Probably the oldest church in the city. Thomas Jefferson, John Quincy Adams, and James Madison were members of the congregation.

Church of the Ascension of St. Agnes   **347-8161**
1217 Massachusetts Avenue, N.W. (12th St.)
    Metro Station: McPherson Square
The congregation of St. Agnes is well known for its interest in music and has developed quite a tradition. The church is a fitting background with its Victorian Gothic architecture and its elegant interior.

Church of the Epiphany (Episcopal)   **347-2635**
1317 G Street, N.W.

Metro Station: Metro Center

A beautiful church in the downtown area, this was originally attended by all of the best families in Washington.

Church of Jesus Christ of the Latter Day Saints (Mormon)   1-301-587-0144
9900 Stoneybrook Drive, Kensington, Maryland

Next to the National Cathedral this is the house of worship that generates the most awe. Built for the ages, everything about it is huge. The interior of the temple is open only to members of the Mormon Church.

First Baptist Church (Baptist)   387-2206
1328 16th Street, N.W. (O St.)

  Metro Station: Dupont Circle

One of our more religious politicians, President Carter, attended services here on a regular basis.

Franciscan Monastery (Roman Catholic)   526-6800
(the Commissariat of the Holy Land for the U.S.)

1400 Quincy Street, N.E.

Devoted to raising money to preserve shrines in the Holy Land, the Order of the Friars Minor maintains a beautiful place of worship. The gardens are exquisite, and the Italian Renaissance church is a delight. True to their mission, the Order has built a number of reproductions of the shrines they support—there are even catacombs.

Friends Meeting House (Quaker)   483-3310
2111 Florida Avenue, N.W.

  Metro Station: Dupont Circle

President Herbert Hoover and his wife worshipped in this simple structure built of stone. Like all of the Quaker churches, it reminds us of the basics of life and religious belief.

Grace Reformed Church   387-3131
1405 15th Street, N.W.

Teddy Roosevelt laid the cornerstone in 1903, and he and his family worshipped here. In more recent times, Presidents Nixon and Eisenhower attended services.

Islamic Mosque and Center   332-8343
2551 Massachusetts Avenue, N.W.

It is always a delight to see the beautiful architecture of a mosque, with its graceful minaret thrusting into the sky. This one is located in the midst of Embassy Row and is certainly at odds with its more staid neighbors.

Metropolitan AME Church (Methodist)   331-1426
1518 M Street, N.W.

Metro Stations: Farragut North and McPherson Square

Completed in 1881, this church played an important role in the Civil War era as a hiding place for escaping slaves. The national headquarters for the church, its membership has continued to play a leading role in the fight for civil rights for Black citizens.

National Cathedral   537-6200
(Cathedral Church of St. Peter & St. Paul)
Massachusetts and Wisconsin Avenues, N.W.

The sixth largest cathedral in the world is scheduled for completion just before this book is printed. September 29, 1990, ends the work begun when President Theodore Roosevelt laid the cornerstone in 1907. Although it is the seat of the Episcopal Diocese of Washington, it has no local congregation and serves the entire nation as a house of prayer. The cathedral is built in fourteenth-century Gothic style, complete with flying butresses. The 57-acre grounds contain three gardens, four schools, the London Brass Rubbing Center, and a stone carvers shed where one can watch the carvers at work. In the crypt are the tombs of President Woodrow Wilson and his wife. Helen Keller is buried here as well.

National Shrine of the Immaculate
Conception (Roman Catholic)   526-8300
4th Street and Michigan Avenue, N.E.

Pope Pius IX decreed that Mary should be the patron saint of the United States, and this huge church was built as a national shrine in her honor. Seating 6000 people, it is the largest catholic church in the western hemisphere and the seventh largest in the world. Pope John Paul II, the second pontiff to visit this country, led morning prayers here. Those of you who share our love of church bells, will be delighted to find that there is a 56-bell carillon in the Knights Tower. As any student of art history can tell you, the Catholic church has a long and important love of art. Art that depicts and honors the beliefs of the Church. In this church, it takes the form of mosaics; one of the most extensive collections in the world. Take one of the tours so that you can see them. The architecture is a combination of Byzantine and Romanesque, one of the most romantic forms of the building arts.

New York Avenue Presbyterian
Church (Presbyterian)   393-3700
1313 New York Avenue, N.W.

President Lincoln's pew remains a testament to his regular attendance at church services.

St. John's Church & Parish House
(Episcopal)   347-8766

16th and H Street, N.W.
    Metro Station: McPherson Square
Since it was finished in 1816, it has been visited by every president. Consequently called the Church of Presidents, it is very beautiful and well worth a visit.

St. Matthew's Cathedral
(Roman Catholic)   347-3215

1725 Rhode Island Avenue, N.W.
    Metro Station: Dupont Circle
This is the church where President Kennedy and his family worshipped and where his funeral Mass was said. Built in 1899, it is a study in contrasts—elaborate on the inside and quite simple on the exterior.

St. Sophia Cathedral
(Greek Orthodox)   333-4730

36th Street and Massachusetts Avenue, N.W.
Of recent construction (1956) this is the church of the largest Greek Orthodox congregation in the United States. In keeping with tradition, the architecture is Byzantine influenced and makes use of some remarkable mosiac work.

Washington Hebrew Congregation
(Reformed)   362-7100

Massachusetts Avenue & Macomb Street, N.W.
    This is the city's largest reformed congregation. It is also the oldest.

Washington National Cathedral
(*See* National Cathedral)

Ciao   296-6796
2000 Pennsylvania Avenue, N.W.

Cities   328-7194
2424 18th Street, N.W.

Claire Dratch   466-6500
1224 Connecticut Avenue, N.W.

Classy Chassis   829-7050
6505 Chillum Place, N.W.

CLOTHING, CHILDREN'S

Full of Beans   1-703-549-7920
Tavern Square Mall, 109 N. Pitt, Alexandria, Virginia

Kid's Closet, The
1226 Connecticut Ave. N.W.   429-9247
1919 K Street, N.W.   466-5589

Kids R Us
11818 Rockville Pike,
Rockville, Maryland   **1-301-770-0660**
3524 Jefferson Street,
Falls Church, Virginia   **1-703-820-0034**

Little Sprout, Inc.   **342-2273**
Georgetown Pike Mall, 3222 M Street N.W.

Monday's Child   **1-703-548-3505**
218 North Lee Street, Alexandria, Virginia

Why Not   **1-703-548-4420**
200 King Street, Alexandria, Virginia

CLOTHING, MEN'S

Arthur A. Adler   **628-0131**
1101 Connecticut Avenue, N.W.
Traditional, natural-shoulder clothing, with Southwick
and Norman Hilton among its top brands.

Britches of Georgetowne
1247 Wisconsin Avenue, N.W.   **338-3330**
1219 Connecticut Avenue N.W.   **347-8994**
One of the best men's stores in Washington, Britches is a
wonderful source for elegantly tailored suits and power
ties.

Brooks Brothers   **659-4650**
1840 L Street, N.W.
Traditional, conservative styling has always been the
Brooks Brothers trademark.

Jos. A. Bank   **466-2282**
3118 19th Street, N.W.
The Brooks Brothers look at slightly reduced prices.

Polo Shop (Ralph Lauren)   **463-7460**
1220 Connecticut Avenue, N.W.
His designs have become the symbol of a new classicism
in American clothing.

Raleighs   **785-7071**
1130 Connecticut Avenue, N.W.
A Washington standby offering a wide range of styles
and price ranges.

Steven-Windsor   **293-2770**
1730 K Street, N.W.
Big and tall men will find something suitable (pardon
the pun) here.

Syms   **1-703-241-8500**
1000 East Broad Street, Falls Church, Virginia
We've all seen those ads that claim, "An educated consumer is our best customer." If you know your merchandise and quality, you can find good bargains here.

CLOTHING, WOMEN'S

Ann Taylor   **466-3544**
1720 K Street, N.W.
Chic and contemporary.

Burberry's of London   **463-3000**
1155 Connecticut Avenue, N.W.
Everyone recognizes the signature Burberry plaid. Traditional, irreproachably styled, rather staid, and very expensive.

Claire Dratch   **466-6500**
1224 Connecticut Avenue, N.W.
Spectacular costume jewelry to accent their equally striking evening clothes and stunning casual wear.

Forgotten Woman, The   **363-0828**
Mazza Gallerie, 5300 Wisconsin Avenue, N.W.
Larger women have been forgotten up until now. This store proves that they can dress with flair.

Frankie Welch of Virginia   **1-703-549-0104**
305 Cameron Street, Alexandria, Virginia
Stylish and always "appropriate" clothing for business and evening wear.

Marie Claire   **466-2680**
1330 Connecticut Avenue, N.W.
The very latest in chic European imports.

Marie Coreen   **537-1667**
Mazza Gallerie
5300 Wisconsin Avenue, N.W.
The sort of shop that every woman dreams of—the last word in elegance and drop-dead glamour. Clothes will be altered or tailor-made to suit your fancy.

Rizik Brothers, Inc.   **223-4050**
1260 Connecticut Avenue, N.W.
Any woman who has traipsed from store to store trying to outfit her bridal party will appreciate Rizik's boast that it can clothe the entire group in either traditional or contemporary styles up to size 20.

Saint Laurent Rive Gauche　　　　　965-3555
600 New Hampshire Avenue, N.W.
When money is no object and looking ultra chic a neces-
sity, head straight for Saint Laurent.

Saks-Jandel　　　　　1-301-652-2250
5514 Wisconsin Avenue, Chevy Chase, Maryland
Designer fashions by Maud Frizon, Missoni, Claude
Montana, Ungaro, Givenchy, and many others.

Saks-Watergate　　　　　337-4200
2522 Virginia Avenue, N.W.
American and European designers are featured in this
cheerful boutique.

Valentino　　　　　333-8700
The Watergate, 600 New Hampshire Avenue NW
Valentino's deceptively simple designs and understated
elegance create timelessness.

Club Soda　　　　　244-3189
3433 Connecticut Avenue, N.W.

CLUBS, PRIVATE

Arts Club of Washington　　　　　331-7282
2017 I Street, N.W.

**Business & Professional Women's
　　League**　　　　　291-4579
3905 Georgia Avenue, N.W.

Capitol Yacht Club　　　　　488-8110
1000 Water Street, S.W.

Capitol Hill Club　　　　　484-4590
300 1st Street, S.E.

Congressional Club　　　　　332-1155
2001 New Hampshire Avenue, N.W.

Conservative Club, The　　　　　462-9702
1644 21st Street, N.W.

Cosmos Club　　　　　387-7783
2121 Massachusetts Avenue, N.W.

District Yacht Club　　　　　543-9788
1409 Water Street, S.E.

**General Federation of Women's
　　Clubs**　　　　　347-3168
1734 N Street, N.W.

Harvard Business School Club   **833-2686**
1522 K Street, N.W.

Harvard Club of Washington, DC   **833-2330**
1522 K Street, N.W.

League of Republican Women of DC   **296-2877**
1100 17th Street, N.W.

Les Amis Du Vin   **1-301-588-0980**
2302 Perkins Place, Silver Spring, Maryland

Metropolitan Club   **835-2500**
17th & H Streets, N.W.

National Association Executives Club   **223-1770**
1400 M Street, N.W.

**National Assoc. of Colored Women's
   Clubs**   **726-2044**
5808 16th Street, N.W.

**National Capital Area Federation of
   Garden Clubs**   **399-5958**
2402 R Street, N.E.

National Democratic Club   **543-2035**
30 Ivy Street, S.E.

National Economists Club   **293-2698**

National Lawyers Club   **638-3200**
1815 H Street, N.W.

Officers Club of Walter Reed   **726-8806**
6825 16th Street, N.W.

Pen Arts Headquarters   **785-1643**
1300 17th Street, N.W.

Potomac Appalachian Trail Club   **638-5306**
1718 N Street, N.W.

Potomac Boat Club   **333-9737**
3530 Water Street, N.W.

Rotary Club of Washington   **638-3555**
Washington Hotel, 15th Street and Pennsylvania
Avenue, N.W.

Texas State Society   **488-5869**
600 Maryland Avenue, S.W.

Touchdown Club   **223-1542**
2000 L Street, N.W.

USDA Travel Club, Inc.   **783-1972**
14th Street & Independence Avenue, S.W.

University Club, The   **862-8800**
1135 16th Street, N.W.

Washington Press Club Foundation	**393-0613**
National Press Building	
Women's National Democratic Club	**232-7363**
1526 New Hampshire Avenue, N.W.	
Yale Club of Washington, The	**244-7119**
4323 Cathedral Avenue, N.W.	

Clyde's	**333-0294**
3236 M Street, N.W.	

COFFEE/TEA

Coffee and tea are two of the staples of life. Those of you who insist on the very best will find it in places like the following:

Coffee Connection, The	**483-8050**
1627 Connecticut Avenue, N.W.	

They have a wide variety to select from, and the beans are always fresh because of the high turnover. However, their prices can be high .

Daily Grind, The	**265-3348**
1613 Connecticut Avenue, N.W.	

Right down the block from the Coffee Connection, the Daily Grind has almost as many choices to offer, and their prices may be better. They also have all of the usual coffee making equipment as well.

M.E. Swing Co., Inc.	**628-7601**
1013 E Street, N.W.	

A limited selection at reasonable prices. Both tea and coffee are available. If they have your brand, this can be a real find.

Coffee Connection, The	**483-8050**
1627 Connecticut Avenue, N.W.	
Collonade	**457-7000**
Westin Hotel, 24th & M Streets, N.W.	
Colonel Brooks' Tavern	**529-4002**
901 Monroe Street, N.E.	
Columbia (Embassy of)	**387-8338**
2118 Leroy Place, N.W.	
Columbia Hospital for Women	**293-6500**
2425 L Street, N.W.	
Comedy Cafe	**638-5653**
1520 K Street, N.W.	

COMEDY

These places have the best and funniest comedians in town.
Telephone for exact, up-to-date information on the acts and
make reservations in advance. If you are traveling by Metro
(subway), remember that trains stop running at midnight.

Comedy Cafe	**638-5653**
1520 K Street NW	
Comedy Stop	**342-7775**
34th and M Streets NW	
Garvin's Laugh Inn	**726-1334**
Cafe Maxime's, 1825 I Street NW	
Marquee Cabaret	**745-1023**
The Omni Shoreham Hotel, 2500 Calvert Street, N.W.	

Comedy Stop   **342-7775**
34th and M Streets, N.W.

Commando K-9 Detectives, Inc.   **1-301-868-7014**
7703 Woodyard Road, Clinton, Maryland

Common Concerns   **463-6500**
1347 Connecticut Avenue, N.W.

Compact Discovery   **1-301-587-1963**
8223 Georgia Avenue, Silver Spring, Maryland

Company Mouse, The   **1-301-654-1222**
4935 Elm Street, Bethesda, Maryland

Compton Jewelers   **393-2570**
1709 G Street, N.W.

Computer Rental Corp.   **347-1582**
666 11th Street, N.W.

COMPUTERS, RENTALS

See **RENTAL, COMPUTER**

Concert Hall, The   **254-3776**
John F. Kennedy Center, New Hampshire Ave., N.W.
and Rock Creek Parkway

CONCERT HALLS

Capital Centre	**1-301-350-3400**
Landover, Maryland	
Concert Hall, The	**254-3776**
John F. Kennedy Center, New Hampshire Ave., N.W.	
and Rock Creek Parkway	

DAR Constitution Hall	638-2661
18th and D Streets, N.W.	

Merriweather Post Pavilion	1-301-982-1800
off Route 29 in Columbia, Maryland	

Opera House	254-3770
The Kennedy Center	

RFK Stadium	546-3337
East Capitol Street and the Anacostia River	

Terrace Theater	254-9895
The Kennedy Center	

Warner Theater	626-1050
513 13th Street, N.W.	

Wolf Trap Farm Park's Filene Center	1-703-255-1860
Vienna, Virginia	

CONCIERGE SERVICES

As any businessperson will tell you, it isn't easy being on the road all the time. The strain of handling the details of actual travel arrangements combined with all the work one is supposed to be doing add enormously to the stress of one's job. The executives we've met who deal most succcessfully with travel problems have a secret weapon—the concierge. There is nothing mysterious about concierges. They are like any other tool you use—but you have to know how to use them. Like all tools, concierges come in various levels of quality and competence. The best way to learn how to use this tool is to just start using it.

Don't be shy or afraid to talk to your concierge. Remember that they are used to dealing with thousands of people just like you. Whether you are the CEO of a major company or a tourist from Topeka, the concierge has dealt with many people who are going to need exactly what you do. Also remember that because of the number of people they have seen, concierges can tell very quickly whether you are a tourist or a CEO and adjust their thinking accordingly. It's difficult to fool a concierge. Always take the direct approach.

When you have to travel, call the hotel in your destination city and ask for the concierge. Give him or her your basic data: name, date of arrival, credit card information, and ask the concierge to take care of the details of your visit. This is the time to tell him or her you are a tourist and don't know the city; or that you will find it necessary to entertain executives of another company. It gives the concierge a feeling for the level of service you will need and the amount of money you will spend to get it. If you are on a budget, say so; if money is not important, express that also. You don't have to mention money in so many words. If you say you want the best restaurant in town to entertain guests and limos to take you to and fro, the concierge will realize that money is no object.

The basic things that a concierge is called upon to arrange are few:

- Hotel reservations. At the concierge's hotel and at any others where you might stay during your trip—particularily if they are part of the same hotel chain. The concierge can call the concierges at the other hotels, alert them to your arrival and arrange for your needs to be taken care of. The fact that another concierge has called them establishes a challenge that they try very hard to meet.

- Limos to take you to and from the airport and to move you easily from one appointment to another. These are not necessarily a luxury item. In a city like Washington, getting from one place to another can take a great deal of time if you don't know how to use public transportation. The expense can be worth it. If you want the convience of a limo with less expense, ask the concierge to arrange for a radio car. Tell the concierge you want something cheaper than a limo and leave it up to him or her. There's nothing wrong with saving money.

- Reservations at restaurants, shows, theaters, and so forth. (Give the concierge as much leeway as possible with these because space availability is very fluid and he or she cannot be sure of getting your first choice.) When you are talking about tickets to a show, be sure to discuss a top price. It is important for concierges to know what they can spend on your behalf. If you really need tickets to a sold-out show, they can probably get them if they can spend several times the face price of the tickets. In Washington, it is not unusual to spend over a hundred dollars for theater tickets to a popular show. If you want to save money, let the concierge know far in advance so he or she can buy at the face price and still get the quality of ticket you desire.

- One of the greatest challenges traveling executives face involves correspondence from their offices. If you are expecting important mail, let the concierge know. Hotels receive thousands of pieces of mail a day, and yours needs special attention. Have your office mark it "Hold for arrival" and "Attention Concierge." When you arrive at the hotel, check with the concierge to pick up whatever might have arrived and to give instructions as to what to do with mail arriving after you leave.

Just by following these few suggestions, you will eliminate a lot of the basic problems of travel. If you stop at this level, you will have made your life a lot easier. But you can go further. How sophisticated you decide to be with your new tool is up to you. Your first challenge is to find a concierge with whom you feel a rapport. It's not as hard as you think. It's a lot like hiring a secretary—you want someone who is not only efficient but who knows what you really want no matter what you say. Once you find this paragon, be sure to give him or her as much information and feedback as you can. If they are any good at their job, they will record this information and use it to give you the service you require. Most of the first class concierges we have known prefer guests who have definite likes and dislikes. If a restaurant is not up to your standards, tell the concierge. If your limo service is not satisfactory, tell the concierge. Remember that the concierge is in constant contact with the owners of these companies and will relay complaints and praise to them. It helps everybody.

You may have friends or business associates for whom you would like to arrange a special welcome when they check into a hotel. There are many ways of doing this. You may call room service at the hotel and arrange for a fruit basket, bottle of champagne, or a wine and cheese tray. You may also call the concierge and tell him or her what you want. If the concierge thinks the room service amenities are not satisfactory, he or she has the additional option of ordering flowers or sending out for balloons and chocolate.

If you have gone this far, you have learned how to get the most out of your concierge. The nuances will follow naturally. We've had guests who would call us for all kinds of things they needed even when they weren't coming to stay in our hotels. We've had foreign guests call us from other hotels in our city because they preferred to deal with someone who knew them rather than a stranger. A good concierge welcomes and is flattered by this type of treatment. Taking care of a guest's needs leads to business, both current and future, for the hotel where the concierge works, and both the concierge and the hotel management realize this.

There are a few things not to do when dealing with a concierge. They are generally rather obvious.

1. Be direct with the concierge. If you want to know about a specific thing ask about that. Don't ask about the best Italian restaurants if you really want an opinion about a specific one. This may seem like a small thing to you, but the concierge has been through this many times each day.

2. Whatever you do, don't be a "no show." If the concierge has made reservations for you and you don't show up or cancel, he or she is in trouble. The restaurant or limo service holds concierges responsible, and it affects their ability to make reservations in the future. It is a simple thing to call the concierge and tell him or her to cancel. The concierge realizes that plans change and is happy to accommodate you.

3. Don't forget to tip the concierge. Aside from the fact that people in the service industry are not always well paid, the concierge has performed a service for you which has made your life easier and deserves to be recognized. You must realise that the whole point of tipping is to get better service and more of it. You're competing with many other people for service.

By now you must have realized that the concierge can help you with almost anything if you can verbalize it. Concierges are limited only by what is available and hotel policy. The simple rules are: don't be shy, be direct, and be appreciative. Remember that people have asked us about everything in this book.

Congo (Embassy of)   **726-5500**
4891 Colorado Avenue, N.W.

CONGRESSIONAL DIRECTORY
THE 102nd CONGRESS

Senate Leaders
Vice-President: Dan Quayle
Pres. Pro Temp: Robert C. Byrd
Majority Leader: George Mitchell
Majority Whip: Alan Cranston
Minority Leader: Robert Dole
Minority Whip: Alan K. Simpson

House of Representatives Leaders
Speaker: Thomas S. Foley
Majority Leader: Richard A. Gephardt

Majority Whip: William Gray
Minority Leader: Robert H. Michel
Minority Whip: Newt Gingrich

CONGRESSIONAL DIRECTORY—BY STATE
Congressional Telephone Number—224-3121

ALABAMA

Heflin, Howell (D)	Term–1997
Shelby, Richard C. (D)	Term–1993
Bevill, Tom (D)	4th District
Callahan, H.L. (R)	1st District
Dickinson, William (R)	2nd District
Erdreich, Ben (D)	6th District
Filippo, Ronnie G. (D)	5th District
Harris, Claude (D)	7th District
Nichols, Bill (D)	3rd District

ALASKA

Murkowski, Frank (R)	Term–1993
Stevens, Ted (R)	Term–1997
Young, Donald E. (R)	At Large

ARIZONA

De Concini, Dennis (D)	Term–1995
McCain, John (R)	Term–1993
Kolbe, Jim (R)	5th District
Kyl, Jon (R)	4th District
Rhodes, John III (R)	1st District
Stump, Bob (R)	3rd District
Udall, Morris (D)	2nd District

ARKANSAS

Bumpers, Dale (D)	Term–1993
Pryor, David (D)	Term–1989
Alexander, Bill (D)	1st District
Anthony, Beryl, Jr. (D)	4th District
Hammerschmidt, J. (R)	3rd District
Robinson, Tommy (D)	2nd District

CALIFORNIA

Cranston, Alan (D)	Term–1993
Wilson, Pete M. (R)	Term–1995
Anderson, Glenn M. (D)	32nd District
Bates, Jim (D)	44th District
Beilenson, Anthony (D)	23rd District
Berman, Howard L. (D)	26th District

Bosco, Douglas H. (D)	1st District
Boxer, Barbara (D)	6th District
Brown, George E. (D)	36th District
Campbell, Tom (R)	12th District
Condit, Gary (D)	15th District
Cox, Christopher (R)	40th District
Dannemeyer, William (R)	39th District
Dellums, Ronald V. (D)	8th District
Dixon, Julian (D)	28th District
Dooley, Calvin (D)	17th District
Doolittle, John (R)	14th District
Dornan, Robert K. (R)	38th District
Drier, Dave (R)	33rd District
Dymally, Mervyn (D)	31st District
Edwards, Don (D)	10th District
Fazio, Vic (D)	4th District
Gallegly, Elton (R)	21st District
Herger, Wally (R)	2nd District
Hunter, Duncan (R)	45th District
Lagomarsino, Robert (R)	19th District
Lantos, Tom (D)	11th District
Lehman, Richard (D)	18th District
Levine, Mel (D)	27th District
Lewis, Jerry (R)	35th District
Lowery, Bill (R)	41st District
Martinez, Matthew (D)	30th District
Matsui, Robert (D)	3rd District
McCandless, Al (R)	37th District
Miller, George (D)	7th District
Mineta, Norman (D)	13th District
Moorhead, Carlos (R)	22nd District
Packard, Ronald (R)	43rd District
Panetta, Leon (D)	16th District
Pelosi, Nancy (D)	5th District
Rohrabacher, Dana (R)	42nd District
Roybal, Edward R. (D)	25th District
Stark, Fortney (D)	9th District
Thomas, William (R)	20th District
Torres, Esteban (D)	34th District
Waters, Maxine (D)	29th District
Waxman, Henry (D)	24th District

COLORADO

Brown, Hank (R)	Term–1997
Wirth, Timothy (D)	Term–1993
Allard, Wayne (R)	4th District
Hefley, Joel (R)	5th District
Campbell, Ben (D)	3rd District

Schaefer, D.L. (R)	6th District
Schroeder, Patricia (D)	1st District
Skaggs, David (D)	2nd District

CONNECTICUT

Dodd, Christopher J. (?)	Term–1993
Lieberman, Joe (D)	Term–1995
Gejdenson, Sam (D)	2nd District
Johnson, Nancy L. (R)	6th District
Kennelly, Barbara B. (D)	1st District
Morrison, Bruce (D)	3rd District
Rowland, John G. (R)	5th District
Shays, Christopher (R)	4th District

DELAWARE

Biden, Joseph Jr. (D)	Term–1997
Roth, William V. Jr. (R)	Term–1995
Carper, Thomas R. (D)	At Large

DISTRICT OF COLUMBIA

Fauntroy, Walter E. (D)	

FLORIDA

Mack, Connie (R)	Term–1997
Graham, Bob (D)	Term–1993
Bennett, Charles E. (D)	3rd District
Bilirakis, Michael (R)	9th District
Fascell, Dante B. (D)	19th District
Gibbons, Sam (D)	7th District
Goss, Porter (R)	13th District
Hutto, Earl (D)	1st District
Ireland, Andy (D)	10th District
James, Craig T.(R)	4th District
Johnston, Harry (D)	14th District
Lehman, William (D)	17th District
Lewis, Tom (R)	12th District
McCullum, Bill (R)	5th District
Nelson, Bill (D)	11th District
Peterson, Pete (D)	2nd District
Ros-Lehtinen, I. (R)	18th District
Shaw, E. Clay, Jr. (R)	15th District
Smith, Larry (D)	16th District
Stearns, Cliff (R)	6th District
Young, C.W. (R)	8th District

GEORGIA

Nunn, Sam (D)	Term–1997
Fowler, Wyche, Jr. (D)	Term–1993

Barnard, Douglas, Jr. (D)	10th District
Darden, George (D)	7th District
Gingrich, Newt (R)	6th District
Hatcher, Charles (D)	2nd District
Jenkins, Ed. (D)	9th District
Jones, Ben (D)	4th District
LaRocco, Larry (D)	1st District
Lewis, John (D)	5th District
Ray, Richard (D)	3rd District
Rowland, J Roy (D)	8th District

HAWAII

Inouye, Daniel K. (D)	Term–1993
Matsunaga, Spark (D)	Term–1995
Abercrombie, Neil (D)	1st District
Akaka, Daniel K. (D)	2nd District

IDAHO

Craig, Larry E. (R)	Term–1997
Symms, Steven D. (R)	Term–1993
Craig, Larry E. (R)	1st District
Stallings, Rich (D)	2nd District

ILLINOIS

Dixon, Alan J. (D)	Term–1993
Simon, Paul (D)	Term–1997
Annunzio, Frank (D)	11th District
Bruce, Terry (D)	19th District
Collins, Cardiss (D)	7th District
Costello, Jerry(D)	21st District
Cox, John Jr. (D)	16th District
Crane, Phillip M. (R)	12th District
Durbin, Richard J. (D)	20th District
Evans, Lane (D)	17th District
Fawell, Harris W. (R)	13th District
Hastert, Dennis (R)	14th District
Hayes, Charles A. (D)	1st District
Hyde, Henry J. (R)	6th District
Lipinski, William (D)	5th District
Madigan, Edward R. (R)	15th District
Michel, Robert H. (R)	18th District
Porter, John (R)	10th District
Poshard, Glenn (D)	22nd District
Rosenkowski, Dan (D)	8th District
Russo, Martin (D)	3rd District
Sangmeister, George (D)	4th District
Savage, Gus (D)	2nd District
Yates, Sidney R. (D)	9th District

INDIANA

Coats, Dan (R)	Term–1993
Lugar, Richard G. (R)	Term–1995
Burton, Dan (R)	6th District
Coats, Dan (R)	4th District
Hamilton, Lee H. (D)	9th District
Jacobs, Andrew, Jr. (D)	10th District
Jontz, James (D)	5th District
McCloskey, Frank (D)	8th District
Myers, John T. (R)	7th District
Roemer, Tim (D)	3rd District
Sharp, Philip R. (D)	2nd District
Visclosky, Peter (D)	1st District

IOWA

Grassley, Charles E. (R)	Term–1993
Harkin, Tom (D)	Term–1997
Grandy, Fred (R)	6th District
Leach, James A.S. (R)	1st District
Lighfoot, J.R. (R)	5th District
Nagle, David (D)	3rd District
Smith, Neal (D)	4th District
Tauke, Thomas (R)	2nd District

KANSAS

Dole, Robert (R)	Term–1993
Kassebaum, Nancy (R)	Term–1997
Glickman, Dan (D)	4th District
Meyers, Jan (R)	3rd District
Roberts, Pat (R)	1st District
Slattery, Jim (D)	2nd District
Whittaker, Robert (R)	5th District

KENTUCKY

Ford, Wendell H. (D)	Term–1993
McConnell, A.M. (R)	Term–1997
Bunning, Jim (R)	4th District
Hopkins, Larry (R)	6th District
Hubbard, Carroll, Jr. (D)	1st District
Mazzoli, Romano L. (D)	3rd District
Natcher, William H. (D)	2nd District
Perkins, Carl D. (D)	7th District
Rogers, Harold (R)	5th District

LOUISIANA

Johnston, J. Bennett (D)	Term–1997
Breaux, John B. (D)	Term–1993

Boggs, Lindy Hill (D)	2nd District
Baker, Richard (R)	6th District
Hayes, James (D)	7th District
Holloway, Clyde C. (R)	8th District
Huckaby, Jerry (D)	5th District
Livingston, Bob (R)	1st District
McCrery, Jim (R)	4th District
Tauzin, Billy (D)	3rd District

MAINE

Cohen, William S. (R)	Term–1997
Mitchell, George (D)	Term–1995
Brennan, Joseph (D)	1st District
Snowe, Olympia (R)	2nd District

MARYLAND

Sarbanes, Paul S. (D)	Term–1995
Mikulski, Barbara (D)	Term–1993
Bentley, H. Delich (R)	2nd District
Byron, Beverly B. (D)	6th District
Cardin, Benjamin (D)	3rd District
Gilchrest, Wayne (R)	1st District
Hoyer, Stenyh (D)	5th District
McMillen, Tom (D)	4th District
Mfume, Kweisi (D)	7th District
Morelia, Constance (R)	8th District

MASSACHUSETTS

Kennedy, Edward M. (D)	Term–1993
Kerry, John (D)	Term–1997
Atkins, Chester G. (D)	5th District
Conte, Silvio O. (R)	1st District
Donnelly, Brian (D)	11th District
Early, Joseph (D)	3rd District
Frank, Barney (D)	4th District
Kennedy, Joseph (D)	8th District
Markey, Edward J. (D)	7th District
Mavroules, Nicholas (D)	6th District
Moakley, Joe (D)	9th District
Neal, Richard E. (D)	2nd District
Studds, Gerry E. (D)	10 District

MICHIGAN

Levin, Carl M. (D)	Term–1997
Riegle, Donald W. (D)	Term–1995
Bonior, David E. (D)	12th District
Broomfield, William S. (R)	18th District

Carr, Bob (D)	6th District
Conyers, John, Jr. (D)	1st District
Crockett, George (D)	13th District
Davis, Robert (R)	11th District
Dingell, John D. (D)	16th District
Ford, William D. (D)	15th District
Henry, Paul B. (R)	5th District
Hertel, Dennis (D)	14th District
Jagt Vander, Guy (R)	9th District
Kildee, Dale E. (D)	7th District
Levin, Sander (D)	17th District
Pursell, Carl C. (R)	2nd District
Schuette, Bill (R)	10th District
Traxler, Bob (D)	8th District
Upton, Fred (R)	4th District
Wolpe, Howard (D)	3rd District

MINNESOTA

Wellstone, Paul (D)	Term–1997
Durenberger, Dave (R)	Term–1993
Frenzel, Bill (R)	3rd District
Oberstar, James L. (D)	8th District
Penny, Timothy J. (D)	1st District
Peterson, Collin (D)	7th District
Sabo, Martin (D)	5th District
Sikorski, Gerry (D)	6th District
Vento, Bruce F. (D)	4th District
Weber, Vin (R)	2nd District

MISSISSIPPI

Cochran, Thad (R)	Term–1993
Lott, Trent (R)	Term–1995
Espy, Michael (D)	2nd District
Montgomery, G.V. (D)	3rd District
Parker, Mike (D)	4th District
Smith, Larkin I. (R)	5th District
Whitten, Jamie L. (D)	1st District

MISSOURI

Danforth, John C. (R)	Term–1995
Bond, Christopher (R)	Term–1993
Clay, William (D)	1st District
Coleman, Thomas (R)	6th District
Emerson, Bill (R)	8th District
Gephardt, Richard (D)	3rd District
Hancock, Melton D. (R)	7th District
Horn, Joan (D)	2nd District

Skelton, Ike (D)	4th District
Volkmer, Harold L. (D)	9th District
Wheat, Alan (D)	5th District

MONTANA

Baucus, Max (D)	Term–1997
Burns, Conrad (R)	Term–1995
Marlenee, Ron (R)	2nd District
Williams, Pat (D)	1st District

NEBRASKA

Exon, James J. (D)	Term–1997
Kerrey, Bob (D)	Term–1995
Bereuter, Douglas (R)	1st District
Hoagland, Peter (D)	2nd District
Smith, Virginia (R)	3rd District

NEVADA

Bryan, Richard (D)	Term–1995
Reid, Harry (D)	Term–1993
Bilbray, James (D)	1st District
Vucanovich, Barbara (R)	2nd District

NEW HAMPSHIRE

Smith, Robert C. (R)	Term–1997
Rudman, Warren (R)	Term–1993
Smith, Robert C. (R)	1st District
Swett, Douglas (D)	2nd District

NEW JERSEY

Bradley, Bill (D)	Term–1997
Lautenberg, Frank (D)	Term–1995
Courter, Jim (R)	12th District
Dwyer, Bernard (D)	6th District
	1st District
Gallo, Dean A. (R)	11th District
Guarini, Frank J. (D)	14th District
Hughes, William J. (D)	2nd District
Pallone, Frank (D)	3rd District
Payne, Donald (D)	10th District
Rinaldo, Matthew J. (R)	7th District
Roe, Robert A. (D)	8th District
Roukema, Marge (R)	5th District
Saxton, James H. (R)	13th District
Smith, Christopher (R)	4th District
Torricelli, Robert (D)	9th District

NEW MEXICO

Bingaman, Jeff (D)	Term–1995
Domenici, Pete V. (R)	Term–1993
Richardson, Bill (D)	3rd District
Schiff, Steven (R)	1st District
Skeen, Joseph R. (R)	2nd District

NEW YORK

Moynihan, Daniel P. (D)	Term–1995
D'Amato, Alfonse M. (R)	Term–1993
Ackerman, Gary (D)	7th District
Boehlert, Sherwood (R)	25th District
Downey, Thomas J. (D)	2nd District
Engel, Eliot (D)	19th District
Fish, Hamilton, Jr. (R)	21st District
Flake, Floyd (D)	6th District
	18th District
Gilman, Benjamin (R)	22nd District
Green, S. William (R)	15th District
Hochbrueckner, G. (D)	1st District
Horton, Frank (R)	29th District
Houghton, Amory (R)	34th District
La Falce, John J. (D)	32nd District
Lent, Norman F. (R)	4th District
Lowey, Nita (D)	20th District
Manton, Thomas J. (D)	9th District
Martin, David (R)	26th District
McGrath, R.J. (R)	5th District
McHugh, Matthew (D)	28th District
McNulty, Michael (D)	23rd District
	14th District
Mrazek, Robert J. (D)	3rd District
Nowak, Henry J. (D)	33rd District
Owens, Major R. (D)	12th District
Paxon, Bill (R)	31st District
Rangel, Charles B. (D)	16th District
Scheuer, James H. (D)	8th District
Schumer, Charles (D)	10th District
Slaughter, Louise (D)	30th District
Solarz, Stephen J. (D)	13th District
Solomon, Gerald (R)	24th District
Towns, Edolphus (D)	11th District
Walsh, James (R)	27th District
Weiss, Theodore S. (D)	17th District

NORTH CAROLINA

Helms, Jesse A. (R)	Term–1997
Sanford, Terry (D)	Term–1993
Ballenger, Cass (R)	10th District
Coble, Howard (R)	6th District
Clark, Jaime (D)	11th District
Hefner, W.G. (D)	8th District
Jones, Walter B. (D)	1st District
Lancaster, Martin (D)	3rd District
McMillan, Alex (R)	9th District
Neal, Stephen L. (D)	5th District
Price, David (D)	4th District
Rose, Charles III (D)	7th District
Valentine, I. Tim (D)	2nd District

NORTH DAKOTA

Burdick, Quentin N. (D)	Term–1995
Conrad, Kent (D)	Term–1993
Dorgan, Bryan (D)	At Large

OHIO

Glenn, John (D)	Term–1993
Metzenbaum, H. (D)	Term–1995
Applegate, Douglas (D)	18th District
De Wine, Michael (R)	7th District
Eckart, Dennis (D)	11th District
Feighan, Edward F. (D)	19th District
Gillmor, Paul E. (R)	5th District
Gradison, Willis, Jr. (R)	2nd District
Hall, Tony P. (D)	3rd District
Kaptur, Marcy (D)	9th District
Kasich, John R. (R)	12th District
Luken, Thomas A. (D)	1st District
Lekens, Donald E. (R)	8th District
McEwen, Bob (R)	6th District
Miller, Clarence E. (R)	10th District
Oakar, Mary Rose (D)	20th District
Oxley, Michael G. (R)	4th District
Pease, Donald J. (D)	13th District
Regula, Ralph S. (R)	16th District
Sawyer, Thomas (D)	14th District
Stokes, Louis (D)	21st District
Traficant, J.A., Jr. (R)	17th District
Wylie, Chalmers P. (R)	15th District

OKLAHOMA

Boren, David (D)	Term–1991

Nickles, Don (R)	Term–1993
Edwards, Mickey (R)	5th District
English, Glenn (D)	6th District
Inhofe, James (R)	1st District
McCurdy, David (D)	4th District
Synar, Mike (D)	2nd District
Watkins, Wes (D)	3rd District

OREGON

Hatfield, Mark O. (R)	Term–1997
Packwood, Bob (R)	Term–1993
AuCoin, Les (D)	1st District
DeFazio, Peter (D)	4th District
Kopetski, Mike (D)	5th District
Smith, Robert (R)	2nd District
Wyden, Ron (D)	3rd District

PENNSYLVANIA

Heinz, H. John III (R)	Term–1995
Specter, Arlen (R)	Term–1993
Borski, Robert A. (D)	3rd District
Clinger, William, Jr. (R)	23rd District
Coughlin, Lawrence (R)	13th District
Coyne, William (D)	14th District
Fogiletta, Thomas (D)	1st District
Gaydos, Joseph M. (D)	20th District
Gedas, George W. (R)	17th District
Goodling, William F. (R)	19th District
Gray, William H. III (D)	2nd District
Kanjorski, Paul E. (D)	11th District
Kolter, Joseph P. (D)	4th District
Kosmayer, Peter H. (D)	8th District
McDade, Joseph M. (R)	10th District
Murphy, Austin J. (D)	22nd District
Murtha, John P. (D)	12th District
Ridge, Thomas J. (R)	21st District
Ritter, Donald (R)	15th District
Schultze, Richard T. (R)	5th District
Shuster, Bud (R)	9th District
Walgren, Doug (D)	18th District
Walker, Robert S. (R)	16th District
Weldon, Curt (R)	7th District
Yatron, Gus (D)	6th District

RHODE ISLAND

Chafee, John H. (R)	Term–1995
Pell, Claiborne (D)	Term–1997

Machtley, Ronald (R)	1st District
Reed, Jack (D)	2nd District

SOUTH CAROLINA

Hollings, Ernest F. (D)	Term–1993
Thurmond, Strom (R)	Term–1997
Derrick, Butler (D)	3rd District
Patterson, Elizabeth (D)	4th District
Ravenel, Arthur (R)	1st District
Spence, Floyd (R)	2nd District
Spratt, John (D)	5th District
Tallon, Robin (D)	6th District

SOUTH DAKOTA

Pressler, Larry (R)	Term–1997
Daschle, Thomas (D)	Term–1993
Johnson, Timothy (D)	At Large

TENNESSEE

Gore, Albert, Jr. (D)	Term–1997
Sasser, James R. (D)	Term–1995
Clement, Bob (D)	5th District
Cooper, James (D)	4th District
Duncan, John, Jr. (R)	2nd District
Ford, Harold E. (D)	9th District
Gordon, Bart (D)	6th District
Lloyd, Marilyn (D)	3rd District
Quillen, James H. (R)	1st District
Sundquist, Don (R)	7th District
Tanner, John (D)	8th District

TEXAS

Bentsen, Lloyd (D)	Term–1995
Gramm, Phil (R)	Term–1997
Andrews, Mike (D)	25th District
Archer, Bill (R)	7th District
Armey, Richard (R)	26th District
Bartlett, Steve (R)	3rd District
Barton, Joe (R)	6th District
Brooks, Jack (D)	9th District
Bryant, John (D)	5th District
Bustamente, A.G. (D)	23rd District
Chapman, Jim (D)	1st District
Coleman, Ronald (D)	16th District
Combest, Larry (R)	19th District
de la Garza, E. (D)	15th District
DeLay, Tom (R)	22nd District

Fields, Jack (R)	8th District
Frost, Martin (D)	24th District
Gonzalez, Henry B. (D)	20th District
Hall, Ralph (D)	4th District
Laughlin, Greg (D)	14th District
Leath, Marvin (D)	11th District
Leland, Mickey (D)	18th District
Ortiz, Solomon P. (D)	27th District
Pickle, J.J. (D)	10th District
Sarpalius, Bill (D)	13th District
Smith, Lamar (R)	21st District
Stenholm, Charles (D)	17th District
Wilson, Charles (D)	2nd District
Wright, Jim (D)	12th District

UTAH

Garn, Jake (R)	Term–1993
Hatch, Orrin G. (R)	Term–1995
Hansen, James (R)	1st District
Orton, William (D)	3rd District
Owens, Wayne (D)	2nd District

VERMONT

Leahy, Patrick J. (D)	Term–1993
Jeffords, James M. (R)	Term–1995
Sander, Bernard (I)	At Large

VIRGINIA

Robb, Charles (D)	Term–1995
Warner, John W. (R)	Term–1997
Bateman, Herbert H. (R)	1st District
Bliley, Thomas (R)	3rd District
Boucher, Frederick C. (D)	9th District
Moran, James (D)	8th District
Olin, James R. (D)	6th District
Payne, Lewis F. (D)	5th District
Pickett, Owen (D)	2nd District
Sisisky, Norman (D)	4th District
Slaughter, D. French (R)	7th District
Wolf, Frank (R)	10th District

WASHINGTON

Gorton, Slade (R)	Term–1995
Adams, Brock (D)	Term–1993
Chandler, Rod (R)	8th District
Dicks, Norman D. (D)	6th District

Foley, Thomas S. (D)	5th District
McDermott, James (D)	7th District
Miller, John (R)	1st District
Morrison, Sid (R)	4th District
Swift, Al (D)	2nd District
Unsoeld, Jolene (D)	3rd District

WEST VIRGINIA

Byrd, Robert C. (D)	Term–1995
Rockefeller, J.D., IV (D)	Term–1997
Mollohan, Alan B. (D)	1st District
Rahall, Nick Joe, II (D)	4th District
Staggers, Harley O. (D)	2nd District
Wise, Robert, Jr. (D)	3rd District

WISCONSIN

Kasten, Robert W., Jr. (R)	Term–1993
Kohl, Herbert H. (D)	Term–1995
Aspin, Les (D)	1st District
Gunderson, S. (R)	3rd District
Kleczka, Gerald D. (D)	4th District
Klug, Scott (R)	2nd District
Moody, James (D)	5th District
Obey, David R. (D)	7th District
Petri, Thomas (R)	6th District
Roth, Tobias (R)	8th District
Sensenbrenner, James (R)	9th District

WYOMING

Simpson, Alan K. (R)	Term–1997
Wallop, Malcolm (R)	Term–1995
Cheney, Richard (R)	At Large

Congressional Club　　　　　　　　**332-1155**
2001 New Hampshire Avenue, N.W.

Congressional Photo Shoppe　　　　**543-3206**
209 Pennsylvania Avenue, S.E.

Conservative Club, The　　　　　　**462-9702**
1644 21st Street, N.W.

Constitution Gardens
Constitution Avenue (17th/23rd Sts., N.W.)

Continental Airlines　　　　**1-800-525-0280**

Corcoran Gallery of Art　　　　　　**638-3211**
17th Street and New York Avenue, N.W.

Cosmos Club, The　　　　　　　　　**387-7783**
2121 Massachusetts Avenue, N.W.

Costa Rica (Embassy of)   **234-2945**
1825 Connecticut Avenue, N.W.

COSTUMES
See **RENTAL, COSTUME**

Cranberry Box   **1-301-946-7464**
3742 Howard Avenue, Kensington, Maryland

Crisfield   **1-301-589-1306**
8012 Georgia Avenue, Silver Spring, Maryland

Crown Books   **659-2030**
2020 K Street, N.W.

Crowne Plaza Holiday Inn   **1-301-468-1100**
1750 Rockville, Rockville, Maryland   **1-800-638-5963**

Cruise Ship Dandy   **703-683-6076**
Prince Street, Alexandria, Virginia

CRUISES

Cruise Ship Dandy   **1-703-683-6076**
Prince Street, Alexandria, Virginia

Departing daily from Old Town Alexandria, these cruises vary in length from two and a half to three and a half hours. You dine while gliding past historic monuments and dance to a variety of musical styles. Reservations are necessary, of course.

Spirit of Mt. Vernon   **554-8000**
Pier 4 (6th/Water Sts., S.W.)

A wonderful way to visit Mt. Vernon. Sail the Potomac on a comfortable cruise ship and listen to the Captain as he describes the points of interest lining the riverbank. Many colonial homes were built along the river, and this is the way early visitors first saw them in the days when the Potomac was the major highway. You will also pass Old Town Alexandria and Ft. Washington. At Mt. Vernon, you will have a two hour visit to the house and grounds before a leisurely trip home.

Spirit of Washington   **554-8000**
Pier 4 (6th/Water Sts., S.W.)

Cruise International operates a fleet of cruise ships in all of the major cities of the United States. Some go to specific locations like the *Spirit of Mt. Vernon*, and some make up the famous "Broadway style entertainment," with singing waitresses and waiters. The latter normally cruise the harbors of the city in which they are located. In the case of the

Spirit of Washington, it duplicates the path of the *Spirit of Mt. Vernon* with the exception of the actual trip to the plantation. In addition to the music (two live bands), dancing, and live entertainment, the dining rooms also serve complete and elegant dinners. While not in the same league with Washington's best restaurants, the food is quite adequate and is served with a flair that makes it all worthwhile.

Crystal City Marriott   **1-703-521-5500**
1999 Jefferson Davis Highway   **1-800-446-6900**
Arlington, Virginia

Crystal Gateway Marriott   **1-703-920-3230**
1700 Jefferson Davis Highway, Arlington, Virginia

Cyprus (Embassy of)   **462-5772**
2211 R Street, N.W.

Czechoslovakia (Embassy of)   **363-6315**
3900 Linnean Avenue, N.W.

D

D.A.R. Library   **628-1776**
1776 D Street, N.W.

D.C. Armory Complex   **546-3337**
2001 E. Capitol Street, S.E.

D.C. Eagle   **347-6025**
639 New York Avenue, N.W.

Daily Grind, The   **265-3348**
1613 Connecticut Avenue, N.W.

Dakota   **265-6600**
1777 Columbia Road, N.W.

DANCING

Annastasia   **333-2500**
3204 M Street, N.W., Georgetown
A state-of-the-art lighting system, spacious bar, and DJ spinning Top 40 music have made this one of Georgetown's newest hot spots.
    Sunday–Thursday 5:00 P.M.–2:00 A.M.
    Friday & Saturday 5:00 P.M.–3:00 A.M.

Badlands   **296-0505**
1415 22nd Street, N.W.

Years have not diminished the appeal of this gay dance club in the Dupont Circle area.

Thursday 9:00 P.M.–2:00 A.M.
Friday–Saturday 9:00 P.M.–3:00 A.M.
Sunday 5:00 P.M.–2:00 A.M.

Chelsea's   298-8222
1055 Thomas Jefferson Street, N.W.

An Italian restaurant during the day, Chelsea's becomes a hot Latin spot at night. Salsa, calypso, and other Latin rhythms are provided by DJs on Wednesday, local bands the rest of the week.

Wednesday, Thursday, Sunday 11:00 P.M.–2:00 A.M.
Friday–Saturday 11:00 P.M.–3:00 A.M.

Dejà Vu   452-1966
2119 M Street, N.W.

Dance tunes from the '50s and '60s fill multiple rooms. On Thursday and Friday, complimentary hors d'oeuvres are served at Happy Hour.

Sunday–Wednesday 8:00 P.M.–2:00 A.M.
Thursday 4:00 P.M.–2:00 A.M.
Friday 4:00 P.M.–3:00 A.M.
Saturday 8:00 P.M.–3:00 A.M.

Fifth Column   393-3632
915 F Street, N.W.

This converted downtown bank is decorated with hanging sculptures and works by local artists. You can choose between progressive dance and good old-fashioned rock. Snacks ranging from hamburgers to caviar are available.

Wednesday, Thursday, Sunday 9:00 P.M.–2:00 A.M.
Friday–Saturday 9:00 P.M.–3:00 A.M.

Jonathan's   638-6800
1520 K Street, N.W.

DJ music of the '50s and '60s, marble-topped tables, hardwood floors, and a weekday happy hour from 4:00 P.M. to 7:00 P.M., create a warm atmosphere for mingling and dancing.

Daily 4:00 P.M.–2:00 A.M.

Kilmanjaro   328-3838
1724 California Avenue NW

On weekends, you can hear some of the top bands from Africa and the Caribbean in this sprawling Adams Morgan club. During the week the recorded music ranges from juju to reggae.

Daily Noon–4:00 A.M.

1063   342-7373
1063 Wisconsin Avenue, N.W. , Georgetown
This Georgetown bar makes some concessions to formality: no jeans, no sneakers, and no one under 21.
    Monday–Thursday 7:30 P.M.–1:30 A.M.
    Friday–Sunday 7:30 P.M.–2:30 A.M.

DAR Constitution Hall   638-2661
18th and D Streets, N.W.

Dar es Salam   342-1925
3056 M Street, N.W. (31st St.), Georgetown

DAR Headquarters & Museum   628-1776
1776 D Street, N.W.

Dark Horse Antiques   1-301-942-0016
3784 Howard Avenue, Kensington, Maryland

Days Inn Washington, DC   832-5800
2700 New York Avenue, N.E.

Deak-Perera   872-1427
1800 K Street, N.W.

Decatur House   673-4030
748 Jackson Place (H St., N.W./Lafayette Square)

Dejà Vu   452-1966
2119 M Street, N.W.

DELIVERY SERVICES

Delivery services are an essential part of today's daily life. If you don't have an account with one of these companies, you can still charge your delivery to one of your credit cards.
DHL Worldwide Express   1-800-225-5345
Call for information on overnight delivery in the U.S., or for overnight to three day delivery internationally.
Emery & Purolator Worldwide
    Courier   1-800-443-6379
Call for complete information on worldwide deliveries.
Federal Express   953-3333
Overnight delivery of documents or packages of up to 150 pounds within the United States, Canada, or Puerto Rico. This is the carrier most used by concierges who need immediate and guaranteed service.

Delta   769-3720

Denmark (Embassy of)   234-4300
3200 Whitehaven Street, N.W.

Dental Referral Service   686-0803

DEPARTMENT STORES

Garfinckel's   628-7730
1401 F Street, N.W. (14th St.)

The poshest of the downtown stores, Garfinckel's offers a full range of designer clothing, silver, crystal, china, and jewelry.

> Open daily 10:00 A.M.–6:00 P.M.
> Thursday 10:00 A.M.–8:00 P.M.
> Closed Sunday

Hecht's   628-6661
1201 G Street, N.W. (12th St.)

We loved shoping at this brand new Hecht's at Metro Center, just across the street from the Holiday Inn Crowne Plaza. They have everything—from housewares to brand name clothing.

> Monday–Saturday 10:00 A.M.–8:00 P.M.
> Sunday Noon–5:00 P.M.

Lord & Taylor   362-9600
5255 Western Avenue, N.W.

Located just behind the Mazza Gallary, Lord and Taylor is known nationwide.

Neiman Marcus   966-9700
Mazza Gallery, Wisconsin & Western Avenues, N.W.

Sure, we all call them "Needless Markup," but there's no denying that their merchandise is gorgeous. We wanted one of everything in the store.

Woodward & Lothrop   347-5300
1025 F Street, N.W. (11th Street)

Affectionately referred to as "Woodie's" by the locals, Woodward & Lothrop has provided a slightly conservative, full-service selection to Washingtonians for over a century.

> Monday–Saturday 10:00 A.M.–8:00 P.M.
> Sunday Noon–5:00 P.M.

DHL Worldwide Express   1-800-225-5345
115 East Reed Avenue, Alexandria, Virginia

Diamond Cab Co.   387-6200

Diana's Exercise Studio   429-9393
1122 Connecticut Avenue, N.W.

Diplomat Limousine Service   589-7620
1511 K Street, N.W.

District Yacht Club, The   543-9788
1409 Water Street, S.E.

Dive Shop   1-703-998-6140
1543 North Quaker Lane, Alexandria, Virginia

Doctor Referral	**466-2870**

Doll Shoppe, The (Repairs) **1-703-893-7272**
1696 Chain Bridge Road, McLean, Virginia

Dollar Rent A Car **1-800-421-6868**
National Airport **739-2255**
Dulles Airport **661-8577**

DOLLS

Dolls are a perennial favorite. These are a few of the best places to go to see dolls or to have your favorite repaired.

All Dolled Up (Repairs) **546-0330**
203 10th Street, N.E.

Company Mouse, The **1-301-654-1222**
4935 Elm Street, Bethesda, Maryland

Doll Shoppe, The (Repairs) **1-703-893-7272**
1696 Chain Bridge Road, McLean, Virginia

Miniatures From the Attic **1-703-237-0066**
2442 N. Harrison Street, Arlington, Virginia

Upstairs Doll House, The **1-301-645-9295**
Highway 925, South Waldorf, Maryland

Dominican Republic (Embassy of) **332-6280**
1715 22nd Street, N.W.

Dominique's **452-1126**
1900 Pennsylvania Avenue, N.W.

Donatello **333-1485**
2514 L Street, N.W. (Pennsylvania Ave.)

Donna Lee's Collectibles **1-703-548-5830**
206 Queen Street, Alexandria, Virginia

**Doudaklian Leathers Custom
  Designer** **293-0442**
2150 P Street, N.W.

Doug's Forget Me Nots **1-301-942-0016**
3784 Howard Avenue **1-301-649-2072**
Kensington, Maryland

Dover International, Ltd. **1-301-561-3500**
12826 Dover Road, Baltimore, Maryland

Downtown Motel **544-2000**
New York Avenue and 4th Street, N.E.

Draper W. Curtis Tobacconist, Inc. **638-2555**
507 11th Street, N.W.

DRUG STORES
See **PHARMACIES**

DRY CLEANING/LAUNDRY

Allstate Repair	**582-8444**
3423 Minnesota Avenue, S.E.	
24-hour emergency service available.	

Duangrat's　　　　　　　　　**1-703-820-5775**
5878 Leesburg Pike, Falls Church, Virginia

Dubliner, The　　　　　　　　**737-3773**
520 North Capitol Street, N.W.

**Duddington's Underground
　　　Sports Bar**　　　　　　　**544-3500**
319 Pennsylvania Avenue, N.W.

Dulles International Airport　**1-703-471-7838**
Chantilly, Virginia

Dumbarton Collections　　　　**342-3290**
1703 32nd Street, N.W.

Dumbarton Oaks　　　　　　　**342-3212**
31st & R Streets, N.W.

Dumbarton Oaks Gardens　　　**338-8278**
31st and R Streets, N.W. (garden entrance)

　　　　　　　　　　　　　　　342-3200

DUPONT CIRCLE

From the late nineteenth well into the twentieth century, Dupont Circle was Washington's fashionable residential area. Extending along Connecticut Avenue from N through T Streets, N.W., the still-Bohemian area is alive with numerous art galleries, bookstores, outdoor restaurants, elegant Victorian rowhouses, specialty shops and interesting people. This neighborhood also includes a variety of fascinating museums, such as the Textile Museum, the Phillips Collection, the Woodrow Wilson House, and the Barney Studio House Museum. Hotels range from the ever-so-slightly seedy Tabard Inn to the elegant Ritz Carlton, and you can eat anything from a slice of pizza at Pizza Hut to a gourmet's feast at Lucie in the Embassy Row Hotel.

Dupont Plaza Hotel　　　　　　**483-6000**
1500 New Hampshire Avenue, N.W.　**1-800-421-6662**

E

Earthworks Tobacco & Snuff   332-4323
1724 20th Street, N.W.

East Potomac Park Golf Course   554-7660
900 Ohio Drive

East Side   488-1205
1824 Half Street, S.W.

East Wind   1-703-836-1515
809 King Street (Washington St./Route 1),
Alexandria, Virginia

Eastern Airlines   1-800-327-8376

Easy Rentals, Inc.   342-9114
2121 Wisconsin Avenue, N.W.

Econo Lodge   832-3200
1600 New York Avenue, N.E.

Ecuador (Embassy of)   234-7200
2535 15th Street, N.W.

Eddie Bauer, Inc.   331-8009
1800 M Street, N.W.

Edward G. Haddad II   1-301-946-1400
3774 Howard Avenue, Kensington, Maryland

Egypt (Embassy of)   232-5400
2310 Decatur Place, N.W.

Eisenhower Theater, The   254-3670
John F. Kennedy Center, New Hampshire Avenue, N.W.
and Rock Creek Parkway

El Salvador (Embassy of)   265-3480
2308 California Street, N.W.

El Tamarindo   328-3660
1785 Florida Avenue, N.W. (18th/U Sts.)

Elizabeth Arden   638-6212
1147 Connecticut Avenue, N.W.

EMBASSIES

Afghanistan   234-3770
2341 Wyoming Avenue, N.W.
Algeria   328-5300
2137 Wyoming Avenue, N.W.
Argentina   939-6400
1600 New Hampshire Avenue, N.W.

Australia	**797-3000**
1601 Massachusetts Avenue, N.W.	
Austria	**483-4474**
2343 Massachusetts Avenue, N.W.	
Bahamas	**944-3390**
600 New Hampshire Avenue, N.W.	
Bahrain	**342-0741**
3502 International Drive, N.W.	
Bangladesh	**342-8372**
2201 Wisconsin Avenue, N.W.	
Barbados	**939-9200**
2144 Wyoming Avenue, N.W.	
Belgium	**333-6900**
3330 Garfield Street, N.W.	
Benin	**232-6656**
2737 Cathedral Avenue	
Bolivia	**483-4410**
3014 Massachusetts Avenue, N.W.	
Botswana	**244-4990**
4301 Connecticut Avenue, N.W.	
Brazil	**745-2700**
3006 Massachusetts Avenue, N.W.	
Bulgaria	**387-7969**
1621 22nd Street, N.W.	
Burma (Myanmer)	**332-9044**
2300 S Street, N.W.	
Burundi	**342-2574**
2233 Wisconsin Avenue, N.W.	
Cameroon	**265-8790**
2349 Massachusetts Avenue, N.W.	
Canada	**483-5505**
2450 Massachusetts Avenue, N.W.	
Cape Verde	**965-6820**
3415 Massachusetts Avenue, N.W.	
Central Africa Republic	**483-7800**
1618 22nd Street, N.W.	
Chad	**462-4009**
2202 R Street, N.W.	
Chile	**785-1746**
1736 Massachusetts Avenue, N.W.	
China, People's Republic of	**328-2500**
2300 Connecticut Avenue, N.W.	
Columbia	**387-8338**
2118 Leroy Place, N.W.	

Congo	**726-5500**
4891 Colorado Avenue, N.W.	
Costa Rica	**234-2945**
1825 Connecticut Avenue, N.W.	
Cyprus	**462-5772**
2211 R Street, N.W.	
Czechoslovakia	**363-6315**
3900 Linnean Avenue, N.W.	
Denmark	**234-4300**
3200 Whitehaven Street, N.W.	
Dominican Republic	**332-6280**
1715 22nd Street, N.W.	
Ecuador	**234-7200**
2535 15th Street, N.W.	
Egypt	**232-5400**
2310 Decatur Place, N.W.	
El Salvador	**265-3480**
2308 California Atreet, N.W.	
Ethiopia	**234-2281**
2134 Kalorama Road, N.W.	
Fiji	**337-8320**
2233 Wisconsin Avenue, N.W.	
Finland	**363-2430**
3216 New Mexico Avenue, N.W.	
France	**944-6000**
4104 Reservoir Road, N.W.	
Gabon	**797-1000**
2034 20th Street, N.W.	
German Democratic Republic (East)	**232-3134**
1717 Massachusetts Avenue, N.W.	
German Federal Republic (West)	**298-4000**
4645 Reservoir Road, N.W.	
Ghana	**462-0761**
2460 16th Street, N.W.	
Great Britain	**462-1340**
3100 Massachusetts Avenue, N.W.	
Greece	**667-3168**
2221 Massachusetts Avenue, N.W.	
Grenada	**265-2561**
1701 New Hampshire Avenue, N.W.	
Guatemala	**745-4952**
2220 R Street, N.W.	
Guinea	**483-9420**
2112 Leroy Place, N.W.	

Guyana 265-6900
2490 Tracy Place, N.W.

Haiti 332-4090
2311 Massachusetts Avenue, N.W.

Honduras 966-7700
4301 Connecticut Avenue, N.W.

Hungary 362-6730
3910 Shoemaker Street, N.W.

Iceland 265-6653
2022 Connecticut Avenue, N.W.

India 939-7000
2107 Massachusetts Avenue, N.W.

Indonesia 775-5200
2020 Massachusetts Avenue, N.W.

Iraq 483-7500
1801 P Street, N.W.

Ireland 462-3939
2234 Massachusetts Avenue, N.W.

Israel 364-5500
3514 International Drive, N.W.

Italy 328-5500
1601 Fuller Street, N.W.

Ivory Coast 483-2400
2424 Massachusetts Avenue, N.W.

Jamaica 452-0660
1850 K Street, N.W.

Japan 234-2266
2520 Massachusetts Avenue, N.W.

Jordan 966-2664
3504 International Drive, N.W.

Kenya 387-6101
2249 R Street, N.W.

Korea 939-5600
2320 Massachusetts Avenue, N.W.

Kuwait 966-0702
2940 Tilden Street, N.W.

Laos 332-6416
2222 S Street, N.W.

Latvia 726-8213
4325 17th Street, N.W.

Lebanon 939-6300
2560 28th Street, N.W.

Lesotho 797-5533
2511 Massachusetts Avenue, N.W.

Liberia	723-0437
5201 16th Street, N.W.	
Lithuania	234-5860
2622 16th Street, N.W.	
Luxembourg	265-4171
2200 Massachusetts Avenue, N.W.	
Madegascar	265-5525
2374 Massachusetts Avenue, N.W.	
Malawi	797-1007
2408 Massachusetts Avenue, N.W.	
Malaysia	328-2700
2401 Massachusetts Avenue, N.W.	
Mali	332-2249
2130 R Street, N.W.	
Maita	462-3611
2017 Connecticut Avenue, N.W.	
Mauritania	232-5700
2129 Leroy Place, N.W.	
Mauritius	244-1491
4301 Connecticut Avenue, N.W.	
Mexico	234-6000
2829 16th Street, N.W.	
Morocco	462-7979
1601 21st Street, N.W.	
Mozambique	293-7146
1990 M Street, N.W.	
Myanmar (Burma)	332-9044
2300 S Street, N.W.	
Nepal	667-4550
2131 Leroy Place, N.W.	
Netherlands	244-5300
4200 Linnean Avenue, N.W.	
New Zealand	328-4800
37 Observatory Circle, N.W.	
Nicaragua	387-4371
1627 New Hampshire, N.W.	
Niger	483-4224
2204 R Street, N.W.	
Nigeria	822-1500
2201 M Street, N.W.	
Norway	333-6000
2720 34th Street, N.W.	
Oman	387-1980
2342 Massachusetts Avenue, N.W.	

Pakistan   **939-6200**
2315 Massachusetts Avenue, N.W.

Panama   **483-1407**
2862 McGill Terrace, N.W.

Paraguay   **483-6960**
2400 Massachusetts Avenue, N.W.

Peru   **833-9860**
1700 Massachusetts Avenue, N.W.

Philippines   **483-1414**
1617 Massachusetts Avenue, N.W.

Poland   **234-3800**
2640 16th Street, N.W.

Portugal   **332-3007**
2310 Tracy Place, N.W.

Qator   **338-0111**
600 New Hampshire Avenue, N.W.

Romania   **232-4747**
1607 23rd Street, N.W.

Rwanda   **232-2882**
1714 New Hampshire Avenue, N.W.

San Marino   **223-3517**
1155 21st Street, N.W.

Saudi Arabia   **342-3800**
601 New Hampshire Avenue, N.W.

Senegal   **234-0540**
2112 Wyoming Avenue, N.W.

Sierra Leone   **939-9261**
1701 19th Street, N.W.

Singapore   **667-7555**
1824 R Street, N.W.

Somalia   **342-1575**
600 New Hampshire Avenue, N.W.

South Africa   **232-4400**
3051 Massachusetts Avenue, N.W.

Spain   **265-0190**
2700 15th Street, N.W.

Sri Lanka   **483-4025**
2148 Wyoming Avenue, N.W.

St. Lucia   **463-7378**
2100 M Street, N.W.

Sudan   **466-6280**
2210 Massachusetts Avenue, N.W.

Surinam   **244-7488**
4301 Connecticut Avenue, N.W.

Swaziland   **362-6683**
4301 Connecticut Avenue, N.W.

Sweden   **944-5600**
600 New Hampshire Avenue, N.W.

Switzerland   **745-7900**
2900 Cathedral Avenue, N.W.

Syria   **232-6313**
2215 Wyoming Avenue, N.W.

Tanzania   **939-6125**
2139 R Street, N.W.

Thailand   **483-7200**
2300 Kalorama Road, N.W.

Togo   **234-4212**
2208 Massachusetts Avenue, N.W.

Trinidad/Tobago   **467-6490**
1708 Massachusetts Avenue, N.W.

Tunisia   **862-1850**
1515 Massachusetts Avenue, N.W.

Turkey   **387-3200**
1606 23rd Street, N.W.

Uganda   **726-7100**
5909 16th Street, N.W.

United Arab Emirates   **338-6500**
600 New Hampshire Avenue, N.W.

Upper Volta   **332-5577**
2340 Massachusetts Avenue, N.W.

Uruguay   **331-1313**
1918 F Street, N.W.

U.S.S.R.   **628-7551**
1825 Phelps, N.W.

Vatican   **333-7121**
3339 Massachusetts Avenue, N.W.

Venezuela   **797-3800**
2445 Massachusetts Avenue, N.W.

Yemen   **965-4760**
600 New Hampshire Avenue, N.W.

Yugoslavia   **462-6566**
2410 California Avenue, N.W.

Zaire   **234-7690**
1800 New Hampshire Avenue, N.W.

Zambia   **265-9717**
2419 Massachusetts Avenue, N.W.

Zimbabwe   **332-7100**
2852 McGill Terrace, N.W.

Embassy Camera Center	483-7448
1709 Connecticut Avenue, N.W.	

Embassy Opticians	785-5700
1325 Connecticut Avenue, N.W.	

Embassy Opticians	544-6900
617 Pennsylvania Avenue, S.E.	

EMBASSY ROW

Metro Station: Dupont Circle

Diplomats from over 130 countries are concentrated in the Northwest quadrant in opulent houses built earlier this century for the fabulously rich. When you are feeling "museum-ed out" and desire a change of pace, take the Metro to Dupont Circle and stroll along Massachusetts Avenue past 2020 (the McLean Mansion, now the Indonesian Embassy) up as far as 3100—the British Embassy's stately country house. In mid-May, various embassies open their doors to the public to benefit Davis Memorial Goodwill industries. Call 1-202-636-4225 for details.

Embassy Row Hotel	265-1600
2015 Massachusetts Avenue, N.W.	1-800-424-2400

Embassy Square Suites Hotel	659-9000
2000 N Street, N.W.	1-800-424-2999

EMERGENCY TELEPHONE NUMBERS

AAA Road Service	222-5000
Access for the Handicapped	966-5500
Ambulance	911
Animal bites	576-6664
Better Business Bureau	393-8000
Capitol Reservations (for Hotels)	1-800-VISIT-DC
Congresspersons	224-3121
Dental Referral Service	686-0803
Doctor Referral	466-2870
FBI	324-3000
Fire	911
Harbor Police	727-4582
International Visitors Information Center	783-6540

Marriage License	879-2839
Maryland Poison Center	1-800-492-2414
Medical Referral Service for Doctors	872-0003
National Capital Poison Center	625-3333
Georgetown University Hospital	
Passport information	783-8200
Poison Control Center	625-3333
Police	911
Rape Crisis Center	333-7273
Sports Update (*Washington Post*)	223-8060
Time	844-2525
Tourist Information	737-8866
Traveler's Aid Society	347-0101
U.S. Capitol	224-3121
U.S. Coast Guard (Search & Rescue)	576-2520
U.S. Customs	566-8200
U.S. Park Police	426-6600
U.S. Passport Office	783-8200
U.S. Secret Service	634-5100
U.S. Supreme Court	479-3000
Visitor Information Center	789-7000
Visa Inquiries	663-1972
Washington Area Convention & Visitors Bureau	789-7000
Weather	936-1212
White House	456-1414

Emery & Purolator Worldwide Courier 1-800-443-6379
Energy Sciences 783-1099
The Shops at National Place,
1331 Pennsylvania Avenue, N.W.
English Grill 638-6600
Hay Adams Hotel, 1 Lafayette Square, N.W. (16th/H Sts.)
Enid A. Haupt Garden
Independence Avenue (Above the museum complex)
Enriqueta's 338-7772
2811 M Street, N.W. (28th/29th Sts.)
Enterprise Golf Course 1-301-249-2040
2802 Enterprise Road, Mitchellville, Maryland

Envoy Rentals   1-301-657-2304
2070 Chain Bridge Road, Bethesda, Maryland

Ethiopia (Embassy of)   234-2281
2134 Kalorama Road, N.W.

Ethridge, Ltd   1-703-548-7722
220 South Washington Street, Alexandria, Virginia

European Imports   1-301-946-1400
3774 Howard Avenue, Kensington, Maryland

Executive Security, Inc.   546-5800
3230 Pennsylvania Avenue, S.E.

EXERCISE EQUIPMENT
See **RENTAL, EXERCISE EQUIPMENT**

Expert Luggage & Shoe Repair   362-6681
3808 Northhampton, N.W.

F

Fairfax Bar   293-2100
The Ritz-Carlton Hotel, 2100 Massachusetts Avenue, N.W.

Family & Nursing Care   1-301-588-8200
911 Silver Spring Avenue, Silver Spring, Maryland

Fantasy Limousines   236-9363

FAO Schwartz
Mazza Gallerie, 5300 Wisconsin Avenue, N.W.   363-8455
Georgetown Park Mall, 3222 M Street, N.W.   342-2285

FBI   324-3000

FBI Building, The   324-3447
10th Street and Pennsylvania Avenue, N.W.

Federal Bar, The   429-1700
Vista International Hotel, 1400 M Street, N.W.

Federal Express   953-3333

Fendrick Gallery   338-4544
3059 M Street, N.W.

Fifth Column   393-3632
915 F Street, N.W.

Fiji (Embassy of)   337-8320
2233 Wisconsin Avenue, N.W.

Filomena's	**338-1800**
1063 Wisconsin Avenue, N.W., Georgetown	
Finland (Embassy of)	**363-2430**
3216 New Mexico Avenue, N.W.	
Finnair	**1-800-223-5700**
Fire	**911**
First Baptist Church	**387-2206**
1328 16th Street, N.W.	
Fish Wings & Tings	**234-0322**
2418 18th Street, N.W. (Columbia Rd.)	
Fletcher's Boathouse	**244-0461**
4940 Canal Road, N.W. (C & O Canal Towpath)	
Flights of Fancy	**783-2800**
The Shops at National Place, 1331 Pennsylvania Avenue, N.W.	

FLORISTS

In most parts of the country, flowers are sent for special occasions. In Washington, things are a little different. Washington is the power city. That colors and changes everything that happens. Florists don't just send flowers, they make a major contribution to the many indoor and outdoor parties that are continually happening. They are frequently expected to perform miracles and always expected to do a more spectacular job than everybody else. The following are among the most distinguished:

Blackistone, Inc.   **347-1300**
1427 H Street, N.W.
    Monday–Friday 9:00 A.M.–5:00 P.M.
    Saturday 9:00 A.M.–4:00 P.M.
Washingtonian magazine rates Blackistone as the best.

Greenworks, Inc.
The Willard Hotel, 1455 H Street, N.W.   **393-2142**
2015 Florida Avenue, N.W.   **265-3335**
    Monday–Saturday 9:00 A.M.–6:00 P.M.
    Sunday 1:00 A.M.–6:00 P.M.
A relative newcomer to the city, Greenworks likes to do those big spectacular floral arrangements, including the ones in the Willard.

Mark Turner Flowers   **547-2020**
7 8th Street, S.E.
    Monday–Saturday 9:00 A.M.–5:00 P.M.

Watergate Florist, Ltd.   337-2545
2548 Virginia Avenue, N.W.
Very friendly, very chic, very expensive.

Florsheim   223-0975
1218 Connecticut Avenue, N.W.

FOGGY BOTTOM

Once a marshy lowland docking area for trader clipper ships (the foggy "bottom" area of town), Foggy Bottom now encompasses the area between Pennsylvania and Virginia Avenues and from 22nd to 25th Streets, N.W. Adjacent to rowhouses dating back to the early nineteenth century, the State Department, the George Washington University, the Pan American Union, and the John F. Kennedy Center for the Performing Arts all find their home. Small boutiques, neighborhood cafes, intimate hotels, and fashionable shops at The Watergate complete the neighborhood.

Folger Shakespeare Library, The   544-7077
201 E. Capitol Street, S.E.

Folger Theater, The   546-4000
201 East Capitol Street, S.E.

Foong Lin   1-301-656-3427
7710 Norfold Avenue (Fairmont Ave.),
Bethesda, Maryland

FOOTBALL

The NFL Washington Redskins play their home games in the fifty-thousand seat Robert F. Kennedy Memorial Stadium at East Capitol and 22nd Streets, S.E. Call 547-9077 for ticket information.

Ford's Theatre & Lincoln Museum   426-6924
511 10th Street, N.W. (E/F Sts)

FOREIGN CURRENCY EXCHANGE

All of the airports serving Washington have currency exchange companies. The major banks in the downtown area have full service as have many of the hotels. If all else fails, the following companies are completely reliable.

Barman International   1-301-657-8844
7009 Wisconsin Avenue, Bethesda, Maryland

Deak-Perera	**872-1427**
1800 K Street, N.W.	
Ruesch International	**887-0990**
1140 19th Street, N.W.	
Forgotten Woman, The	**363-0828**
Mazza Gallery, 5300 Wisconsin Avenue, N.W.	

FORMAL WEAR

See **RENTAL, FORMAL WEAR, MEN'S**
See **RENTAL, FORMAL WEAR, WOMEN'S**

Fort Dupont Ice Arena	**581-0199**
3779 Ely Place, S.E. (Minnesota Ave.)	
Four Seasons Hotel	**342-0444**
2800 Pennsylvania Avenue, N.W.	**1-800-268-6282**
France (Embassy of)	**944-6000**
4104 Reservoir Road, N.W.	
Francis Scott Key Book Shop	**337-4144**
1400 28th Street, N.W. (O St.)	
Franciscan Monastery	**526-6800**
1400 Quincy Street, N.E.	
Franco Antiques	**332-0210**
2601 Connecticut Avenue, N.W.	
Frankie Welch of Virginia	**1-703-549-0104**
305 Cameron Street, Alexandria, Virginia	
Franz Bader Bookstore	**337-5440**
1911 I Street, N.W.	
Franz Bader Gallery	**659-5515**
1701 Pennsylvania Avenue, N.W.	
Fraternity House, The	**223-4917**
2122 P Street, N.W.	
Frederick Douglass National Historic Site	**426-5960**
1411 W Street, S.E. (14th/15th Sts.)	
Freer Gallery of Art, The	**357-2104**
The Smithsonian Institution, Jefferson Drive and 12th Street, S.W.	

FREE THINGS

Washington is a wonderful city for tourists. With rare exceptions, all of the sightseeing attractions and museums are free of charge.

Friendly Formals	842-5132
1220 L Street, N.W.	
Friendly Hospital for Animals	363-7300
4105 Brandywine Street, N.W.	
Friends	822-8909
2122 P Street, N.W.	
Friends Meeting House	483-3310
2111 Florida Avenue, N.W.	
Fuji	1-703-524-3666
77 North Glebe Road (Route 50), Arlington, Virginia	
Full Circle	1-703-683-4500
317 Cameron Street, Alexandria, Virginia	
Full of Beans	1-703-549-7920
Tavern Square Mall, 109 North Pitt, Alexandria, Virginia	
Fuller & D'Albert, Inc.	1-703-591-8000
3170 Campbell Drive, Fairfax, Virginia	

G

Gabon (Embassy of)	797-1000
2034 20th Street, N.W.	
Gaetano Gervasi	544-6772
621 Pennsylvania Avenue, S.E., (2nd Floor)	
Galileo	293-7191
2014 P Street, N.W. (20th/21st Sts.)	
Gallery 10	232-3326
1519 Connecticut Avenue, N.W.	
Gallery K	234-0339
2010 R Street, N.W.	

GARDENS

Dumbarton Oaks	338-8278
31st and R Streets, N.W. (garden entrance),	
Georgetown	342-3200

> Daily 2:00 P.M.–5:00 P.M.
> Closed Holidays
> Admission: Free
> Metro Station: None. Best transportation is a taxi.

Planned by Mrs. Robert Woods Bliss in conjunction with landscape gardener Beatrix Farrand, the formal gardens cupy about 16 acres. There are pools, terraces, and, of course, the rose garden. Walking along the paths of this nationally known garden is an incredible treat. In addition there are the 27 acres of natural woodland which are at their best in the spring.

Enid A. Haupt Garden
Independence Avenue at 10th Street, S.W.
> Daily 7:00 A.M.–5:45 P.M.(8:00 P.M.in the summer)
> Admission Free
> Metro Station: Smithsonian

This lovely garden is built over two subterranean museums: the Arthur M. Sackler Collection and the National Museum of African Art. On what is called the Quadrangle, between the Arts & Industries Building and the Freer Gallery of Art, the garden is a wonderful intermediary between the bustle of the city and the quiet of the museums. The Moongate Garden, near the Sackler, features two tall pink granite moongates, a pool, and cherry trees. The perfect introduction to a museum of oriental art. Just as appropriately, the Fountain Garden has a waterfall and some of those wonderful hawthorns that make us think of Africa and the hot desert countries.

U.S. Botanic GardenConservatory, The   225-8333
1st Street and Maryland Avenue, S.W.

As orchid fanciers, we couldn't pass this up. A greenhouse on the Mall by the Capitol for the purpose of "collecting, cultivating, and growing the various vegetable production of this and other countries for exhibition and display." In addition to our orchid favorites, there are palms, ferns, cacti, and other plants from tropical, subtropical, and desert habitats.

U. S. National Arboretum   475-4815
New York Avenue/Bladensburg Road and
M Street, N.E.

Primary concerns at the Arboretum are research on trees and shrubs and educating the public about them. Administered by the U.S. Department of Agriculture, this is a serious research center which shares with the public the beauty of the plants in its care. Occupying 444 acres, its major attractions are the National Bonsai Collection, a bicentennial gift of the Japanese government, the Morrison Azalea Garden, the oriental plantings in the Cryptomeria Valley of the Garden Club of America, the Gotelli Dwarf Conifer Collection, Fern Valley, the National Herb Garden, and the dogwood trees of the Women's National Farm and Garden Association. Parking spaces and picnic grounds are available.

Garfinkel Tobacconist, Inc.   638-1175
1585 I Street, N.W.

Garfinkel's   628-7730
1401 F Street, N.W.

Garvin's Laugh Inn   726-1334
Cafe Maxime's, 1825 I Street, N.W.

GAS STATIONS

There is nothing worse than needing a gas station except needing a bathroom. The following locations are of some of the convenient gas stations in downtown Washington.

Capitol Hill Chevron Service   543-9456
2nd Street and Massachusetts Avenue, N.E.
Open 24 hours.

Carl Exxon Service Centers   364-6365
22nd and M Streets, N.W.

Embassy Chevron Service Center   659-8560
22nd and P Streets, N.W.
Open 24 hours. In the heart of Embassy Row.

9th & H Gulf Northwest   842-3127
9th and H Streets, N.W.

Peoples # 3   387-2491
13th and N Streets, N.W.

L'Enfant Exxon Service Center   554-5120
970 D Street, S.W.

Watergate Exxon   338-7739
2708 Virginia Avenue, N.W. (27th St.)

Georgetown Amoco   337-9759
2715 Pennsylvania Avenue, N.W. (27th St.)
24 hour service.

Georgetown Texaco   338-3779
1576 Wisconsin Avenue, N.W.
24 hour service.

Capitol Hill Chevron Service   543-9456
2nd Street & Massachusetts Avenue, N.E.
24 hour service. One block from Union Station.

GAY BARS

One of the best ways to be current with the many happenings in the gay community is to pick up a copy of "The Washington Blade," which is available at Lambda Rising in Dupont Circle and many other locations.

Annex   293-0064
1413 22nd Street, N.W.
Leather, motorcycles, and country music.

Badlands   296-0505
1415 22nd Street, N.W.
One of the well-known spots, it is primarily for men.
There is dancing and they have the usual video show.

Bachelor's Mill   544-1931
1104 8th Street, S.E.
African American men enjoy dancing and mingling at
the Mill.

Back Door Pub   546-5979
1104 8th Street, S.E. (2nd Floor)
Upstairs over the Mill, it's a hideaway for African American men.

Brass Rail   371-6983
476 K Street, N.W.
Mainly African American men—dancing.

Chesapeake House   347-3600
746 9th Street, N.W.
Go-Go dancers. Caters primarily to men.

D.C. Eagle   347-6025
639 New York Avenue, N.W.
If you're into country/western and the leather scene,
park your bike outside and join the boys.

East Side   488-1205
1824 Half Street, S.W.

Fraternity House, The   223-4917
2122 P Street, N.W. (Rear)
Men gather here for the dancing on Thursday, Friday,
and Saturday after everything else is closed. Happy hour
4:00 P.M.–9:00 P.M. weekdays.

Friends   822-8909
2122 P Street, N.W.
A good place to go for dinner. Entertainment features the
Village People and such stars as LaDonna Mills. Later, you
can go around to the back to the Fraternity House.

Hill Haven   543-4242
516 8th Street, S.E.
For women who like dancing.

Hung Jury, The   785-8181
1819 H Street, N.W.
Suprise! It's for women—who like to dance.

J.R.'s 328-0090
1519 17th Street, N.W.
For both men and women, there is a restaurant and, of course, video entertainment.

L'il Sister 231-4213
237 2nd Avenue, N.W.
For women. There is a restaurant, which always makes for a nicer atmosphere, and dancing.

Lost & Found 488-1200
56 L Street, S.E.
A complete after-hours operation. For men, it has a restaurant, disco club, and dancing.

Mr. Henry's 546-8412
601 Pennsylvania Avenue, S.E.
For those of you who just want a restaurant, this may be it. No dancing or other distractions—other than the one you're with.

Phase One 544-6831
525 8th Street, S.E.
Dancing for women.

Remington's 543-3113
639 Pennsylvania Avenue, S.E.
Country music for the macho male. A chance to wear your new boots.

Rogue, The 371-2223
476 K Street, N.W.
Open only on weekends, this is a wild place. Men, either in drag or not, can dance or just watch the entertainment—don't miss the Mail Express (striptease) if it's happening.

Shooters 234-0975
3 Riggs Court, N.W.
Go-Go dancers—mainly for men.

Tracks 488-3320
1111 1st Street, S.E.
Tracks has something for everyone. Restaurant and disco with late hours, both men and women have a good time here.

Ziegfeld's 554-5141
1345 Half Street, S.E.
For women and men, many in drag, there is a restaurant and dancing. Also specially selected entertainment and different dancers each weekend.

General Federation of Women's Clubs 347-3168
1734 N Street, N.W.

Genji   **1-703-573-0112**
2816 Graham Road (Lee Hwy.), Falls Church, Virginia

George Washington Masonic
    National Memorial   **1-703-683-2007**
King Street and Callahan Drive, Alexandria, Virginia

George Washington University
    Hospital (Emergency Ward)   **676-3211**
901 23rd Street, N.W.

                                              994-1000

GEORGETOWN

Older than the District, Georgetown was established as a town with its own mayor in 1752 and was an important colonial port and trading center. It's become a prized residential area, with beautiful townhouses and tree-lined streets. Walking along its two main arteries (Wisconsin Avenue and M Street), lined with an assortment of international restaurants, expensive boutiques, and galleries, one immediately senses the independence that this area has always maintained from the rest of Washington. This isn't the District of Columbia, it's **Georgetown**. You will find neither a Metro stop nor a city lottery ticket here.

Georgetown Bar & Grill   **337-7777**
1310 Wisconsin Avenue, N.W., Georgetown

Georgetown Marbury House   **726-5000**
3000 M Street, N.W.   **368-5922**

Georgetown Park Mall
3222 M Street, N.W.

Georgetown Tobacco   **338-5100**
3144 Wisconsin Avenue, N.W.

Georgetown University Hospital
    (Emergency Ward)   **625-7151**
3800 Reservoir Road, N.W.   **342-2400**

Georgian Shell Interiors/Antiques,
    Inc.   **1-301-933-4464**
10419 Fawcett Street, Kensington, Maryland

Germaine's   **965-1185**
2400 Wisconsin Avenue, N.W. (Calvert St.), Georgetown

German (East) Dem. Rep. (Embassy of)   **232-3134**
1717 Massachusetts Avenue, N.W.

German (West) Fed. Rep. (Embassy of)   **298-4000**
4645 Reservoir Road, N.W.

Ghana (Embassy of)   462-0761
2460 16th Street, N.W.

Gibson Aviation, Inc.   1-301-948-5300
7901 Queen Air Drive, Gaithersburg, Maryland

Gilpin House Book Shop   1-703-549-1880
208 King Street, Alexandria, Virginia

Ginza   331-7991
1721 Connecticut Avenue, N.W.

Ginza's   833-1244
1009 21st Street, N.W. (K/L Sts.)

Goddard Space Flight Center (NASA)   1-301-286-8981
Soil Conservation Road, (Baltimore-Washington
Pkwy./Greenbelt Rd.), Greenbelt, Maryland

GOLF COURSES

Algonkian Park   1-703-450-4655
1600 Potomac View Road, Sterling, Virginia
One of the very best. It is a public course, wonderfully
laid out, and requires no reservations.

Avenel Farms   1-301-469-3700
Potomac, Maryland

East Potomac Park Golf Course   554-7660
900 Ohio Drive
Play within sight of some of the most beautiful monuments in the city. There are two 18-hole courses, a miniature
golf course, and a driving range.

Enterprise Golf Course   1-301-249-2040
2802 Enterprise Road
Mitchellville, Maryland
This is a beautiful, championship, 18-hole course. Par is
72 and the clubhouse is quite nice. No reservations are
needed.

Greendale Golf Course   1-703-971-6170
6700 Telegraph Road, Alexandria, Virginia

Langston Golf Course   397-8638
66th Street & Benning Road, N.E.

Northwest Park   1-301-598-6100
15701 Layhill Road, Wheaton, Maryland
Not for beginners, this one is a very difficult 27-hole
course.

Paint Branch Golf Course   1-301-935-0330
4690 University Boulevard, College Park, Maryland
No reservations are required for this 9-hole course.

Penderbrook Club   1-703-385-3700
3700 Golf Trail Lane, Fairfax, Virginia
A comfortable 18-hole course out in the woods.

Redgate Golf Course   1-301-340-2404
14500 Avery Road, Rockville, Maryland
Another difficult course that will appeal to skilled players. There are water hazards to add to the problems of negotiating the 18-holes.

Rock Creek Golf Course   723-9832
16th and Rittenhouse Streets, N.W.

Gonzales Antiques   234-3336
2313 Calvert Street, N.W.

GOURMET FOODS

Gourmet foods are a big business in Washington, as in most large cities. The combination of people who are gourmet cooks and people who live with deadlines and have no time to cook, has created a special market. The customers are demanding, and stores that can't provide quality soon drop by the wayside. We liked all of the following stores and have no qualms about suggesting that you try them. A couple were unique enough we had to say something special about them.

Ciao   296-6796
2000 Pennsylvania Avenue, N.W.

Helen's Too   483-4444
1811 18th Street, N.W.

Potomac Butter & Egg Co., Inc.   554-9200
220 E Street, S.W.
Their main function is to provide produce to the local hotels, supermarkets, and restaurants, but they also sell direct to the small consumer. Prices tend to be low.

Provisions   543-0694
218 7th Street, S.E.

Sutton Place Gourmet   363-5800
3201 New Mexico Avenue, N.W.
We feel this is the best the city offers. The selection is wide and of the finest quality. As snobbish New Yorkers, we would say it ranks with Balducci's, which is about as good as it gets.

Washington Park	**462-5566**
2331 Calvert Street, N.W.	
Grace Reformed Church	**387-3131**
1405 15th Street, N.W.	
Grand Hotel, The	**429-0100**
2350 M Street, N.W.	**1-800-848-0016**
Grand Hyatt, The	**582-1234**
1000 H Street, N.W.	
Gray Line	**479-5900**
Great Britain (Embassy of)	**462-1340**
3100 Massachusetts Avenue, N.W.	
Great Falls Boarding Kennels	**1-703-759-2620**
8920 Old Dominion Drive, McLean, Virginia	
Greater Laurel–Beltsville Hospital	**1-301-725-4300**
7100 Contee Road, Laurel, Maryland	
Greater Southeast Community	
Hospital	**574-6000**
1310 Southern Avenue, S.E.	
Greece (Embassy of)	**667-3168**
2221 Massachusetts Avenue, N.W.	
Greendale Golf Course	**1-703-971-6170**
6700 Telegraph Road, Alexandria, Virginia	
Greenworks, Inc.	
The Willard Hotel, 1455 H Street, N.W.	**393-2142**
2015 Florida Avenue, N.W.	**265-3335**
Grenada (Embassy of)	**265-2561**
1701 New Hampshire Avenue, N.W.	
Greyhound–Trailways Bus Lines	**565-2662**
Greyhound–Trailways Bus Center, 1005 First Street, N.E. (K/L Sts.)	
Guatemala (Embassy of)	**745-4952**
2220 R Street, N.W.	
Gucci	**965-1700**
600 New Hampshire Avenue, N.W.	
Guest Quarters Hotel	**785-2000**
801 New Hampshire Avenue, N.W.	**1-800-424-2900**
Guest Quarters Hotel	**333-8060**
2500 Pennsylvania Avenue, N.W.	**1-800-424-2900**
Guest Services, Inc.	**484-3475**
15th Street & Maine Avenue, S.W.	
Guinea (Embassy of)	**483-9420**
2112 Leroy Place, N.W.	

Gunston Hall 1-703-550-9220
10709 Gunston Road (Route 1), Lorton, Virginia

Guyana (Embassy of) 265-6900
2490 Tracy Place, N.W.

GYMS/HEALTH CLUBS
See **HEALTH CLUBS**

H

Hadley Memorial Hospital 574-5700
4601 Martin Luther King Jr. Avenue, S.W.

Hahn's 783-1080
14th & G Streets, N.W.

HAIRCUTS, MEN'S

Barber shops and haircuts are not normally featured in our books. In Washington, however, the situation is so interesting that we think you will be intrigued by it. It is possible to have a haircut in either the House of Representatives or the Senate barber shops. You will have to wait if a member of one of those august bodies drops in, however. They have precedence over outsiders. Call ahead for an appointment.

House Barber Shop
  (House of Representatives) 225-3559
  140 Cannon House Office Bldg., U.S. Capitol

House Barber Shop
  (House of Representatives) 225-7024
  B-323 Rayburn House Office Bldg., U.S. Capitol

Milton Pitts
  (Barber to the presidents) 333-3488
  The Sheraton Carlton Hotel, 16th & K Streets, N.W.
  Mr. Pitts, one of the most charming of men, has been clipping presidents since 1969 when he met President Nixon. Many of them have come to him at his shop in the Sheraton Carlton, one of the most distinguished hotels in Washington, and at other times he has made the trip to the White House. He has been cutting President Bush's hair for 16 years, as well as Gerald Ford, Jimmy Carter, and Ronald Reagan. His list includes other prominent men such as Vice President Rockefeller, Secretary of State James

Baker, Defense Secretary Richard Cheney, Henry Kissinger, Casper Weinberger, George Schultz, and many Congressmen and Senators. Mr. Pitts is a true "southern gentleman" and having him cut your hair is a luxurious experience not to be forgotten. Needless to say, he is a busy man and an appointment is necessary.

Pietro Hair Salon	628-3706
The Capitol Hilton Hotel	393-1000
1001 16th Street, N.W.	

Senate Barber Shop (U.S. Senate)	224-4560
B-68 Russell Senate Office Bldg., U.S. Capitol	

Haiti (Embassy of)	332-4090
2311 Massachusetts Avenue, N.W.	

Hampton National Historic Site	1-301-962-0688
535 Hampton Lane (Delaney Valley Rd.), Towson, Maryland	

Harbor Police	727-4582

Harvard Business School Club	833-2686
1522 K Street, N.W.	

Harvard Club of Washington, The	833-2330
1522 K Street, N.W.	

Hawk & Dove	543-3300
329 Pennsylvania Avenue, S.E.	

Hay-Adams	638-6600
One Lafayette Square	1-800-424-5054

HEALTH CLUBS/GYMS

All of us who travel would like a way to keep fit. Reviewing restaurants isn't all fun. Where does one take off all of the unwanted calories? It isn't easy to find health clubs that will take people on a no-membership basis. The one we found is The Watergate Health Club.

Watergate Health Club, The	298-4460
2650 Virginia Avenue, N.W.	

The Watergate provides a perfect health club. Best of all one can attend on a one time basis. Call for availability and costs.

Hecht's	628-6661
1201 G Street, N.W.	

Helen's Too	483-4444
1811 18th Street, N.W.	

HELICOPTER CHARTERS and TOURS

Dover International, Ltd.   1-301-561-3500
12826 Dover Road, Baltimore, Maryland
Aerial photography specialists.

Gibson Aviation, Inc.   1-301-948-5300
24-hour service featuring Bell Jetranger helicopters.

Stuart Aviation Service   1-703-892-2650
National Airport   1-800-225-0990
   In addition to special charters, Stuart operates daily flights to Atlantic City, Ocean City, and Williamsburg. Sightseeing tours are also available. You may take a short ride, the regular 30-minute tour, or charter as much time as you want. There are also the wonderful moonlight rides that let you see the city at its most glamourous.

U.S. Jet Aviation   892-6200
Washington National Airport

Heller Antiques, Ltd.   654-0218
5454 Wisconsin Avenue, N.W.

Henley Park Hotel, The   638-5200
926 Massachusetts Avenue, N.W.   222-8474

Herman's World of Sporting Goods   638-6434
800 E Street, N.W.

Hertz   1-800-654-3131

Hill Haven   543-4242
516 8th Street, S.E.

Hillwood Museum Gardens
4155 Linnean Avenue, N.W.

Hirshhorn Museum &
   Sculpture Garden   357-1461
The Smithsonian Institution, Independence Avenue and 8th Street, S.W.

Hisago   944-4181
305 K Street, N.W. (Washington Harbor)

Hoffritz   466-4382
1008 Connecticut Avenue, N.W.

Holiday Inn
550 C Street, S.W.   479-4000
Thomas Circle, N.W.   737-1200

Holiday Inn Crowne Plaza
   at Metro Center   737-2200
775 12th Street, N.W.

Holiday Inn Georgetown   338-4600
2101 Wisconsin Avenue, N.W.

Holy Cross Hospital of Silver Spring   1-301-565-0100
1500 Forest Glen Road, Silver Spring, Maryland

Hom Gallery 466-4076
103 O Street, N.W.

Honduras (Embassy of) 966-7700
4301 Connecticut Avenue, N.W.

HORSEBACK RIDING

Rock Creek Park Horse Center 362-0117
Military and Glover Roads, N.W.

HOSPITALS

Alexandria Hospital 1-703-379-3000
4320 Seminary Road, Alexandria, Virginia

Arlington Hospital 1-703-558-5000
1701 North George Mason Drive,
Alexandria, Virginia

Children's Hospital 745-5005
11 Michigan Avenue, N.W.

Columbia Hospital for Women 293-6500
2425 L Street, N.W.

George Washington University
Hospital 994-1000
Emergency Ward: 901 23rd Street, N.W. 676-3211

Georgetown University Hospital 342-2400
Emergency Ward: 3800 Reservoir Road, N.W. 625-7151

Greater Laurel–Beltsville Hospital 1-301-725-4300
7100 Contee Road, Laurel, Maryland

Greater Southeast Community
Hospital 574-6000
1310 Southern Avenue, S.E.

Hadley Memorial Hospital 574-5700
4601 Martin Luther King, Jr. Avenue, S.W.

Holy Cross Hospital of Silver Spring 1-301-565-0100
1500 Forest Glen Road, Silver Spring, Maryland

Howard County General Hospital 1-301-740-7890
5755 Cedar Lane, Columbia, Maryland

Howard University Hospital 745-6100
2041 Georgia Avenue, N.W.

Leland Memorial Hospital 1-301-699-2000
4409 East-West Highway, Riverdale, Maryland

Montgomery General Hospital 1-301-774-8882
18101 Prince Phillip Drive, Olney, Maryland

Prince George's Hospital Center   1-301-341-3300
3001 Hospital Drive, Cheverly, Maryland

Providence Hospital   269-7000
1150 Varnum Street, N.E.

Hotel Anthony   223-4320
1823 L Street, N.W.

  1-800-424-2970

HOTELS

Bellevue Hotel, The   638-0900
15 E Street, N.W.

Best Western Center City   682-5300
1201 13th Street, N.W.

Bethesda Marriott Hotel   1-301-897-9400
5151 Pooks Hill Road   1-800-228-9290
Bethesda, Maryland

Canterbury, The   393-3000
1733 N Street, N.W.   1-800-424-2950

Capital Hilton, The   393-1000
16th and K Streets, N.W.   **1-800-HILTONS**

Carlyle Suites, The   234-3200
1731 New Hampshire Avenue, N.W.

Crowne Plaza Holiday Inn   1-301-468-1100
1750 Rockville Pike   1-800-638-5963
Rockville, Maryland

Crystal City Marriott   1-703-521-5500
1999 Jefferson Davis Highway   1-800-446-6900
Arlington, Virginia

Crystal Gateway Marriott   1-703-920-3230
1700 Jefferson Davis Highway, Arlington, Virginia

Dupont Plaza Hotel   483-6000
1500 New Hampshire Avenue, N.W.   1-800-421-6662

Embassy Row Hotel   265-1600
2015 Massachusetts Avenue, N.W.   1-800-424-2400

Embassy Square Suites Hotel   659-9000
2000 N Street, N.W.   1-800-424-2999

Four Seasons Hotel   342-0444
2800 Pennsylvania Avenue, N.W.   1-800-268-6282

Georgetown Marbury House	**726-5000**
3000 M Street, N.W.	**368-5922**
Grand Hotel, The	**429-0100**
2350 M Street, N.W.	**1-800-848-0016**
Grand Hyatt, The	**582-1234**
1000 H Street, N.W.	
Guest Quarters Hotel	**785-2000**
801 New Hampshire Avenue, N.W.	**1-800-424-2900**
Guest Quarters Hotel	**333-8060**
2500 Pennsylvania Avenue, N.W.	**1-800-424-2900**
Hay-Adams	**638-6600**
One Lafayette Square	**1-800-424-5054**
Henley Park Hotel, The	**638-5200**
926 Massachusetts Avenue, N.W.	**222-8474**
Holiday Inn Crowne Plaza	**737-2200**
Metro Center, 755 12th Street, N.W.	
Holiday Inn Georgetown	**338-4600**
2101 Wisconsin Avenue, N.W.	
Hotel Anthony	**223-4320**
1823 L Street, N.W.	**1-800-424-2970**
Hotel Lombardy	**828-2600**
2019 I Street, N.W.	**1-800-424-5486**
Hotel Washington, The	**638-5900**
15th and Pennsylvania Avenue	**1-800-424-9540**
Hotel Wyndham Bristol	**955-6400**
2430 Pennsylvania Avenue, N.W.	**1-800-822-2430**
Hyatt Regency Bethesda	**1-301-657-1234**
1 Bethesda Metro Center	**1-800-228-9000**
Bethesda, Maryland	
Hyatt Regency on Capital Hill	**737-1234**
400 New Jersey Avenue, N.W.	**1-800-228-9000**
Jefferson, The	**347-2200**
1200 16th Street, N.W.	**1-800-368-5966**
J. W. Marriott Hotel	**626-6900**
1331 Pennsylvania Avenue, N.W.	**1-800-228-9290**
(at National Pl.)	

Key Bridge Marriott	1-703-524-6400
1401 Lee Highway	1-800-228-9290
Rosslyn, Virginia	

Madison Hotel, The	862-1600
15th and M Streets, N.W.	1-800-424-8577

Mayflower, The	347-3000
1127 Connecticut Avenue, N.W.	1-800-HOTELS-1

Morrison-Clark Hotel	898-1200
Massachusetts Avenue & 11th Street, N.W.	

Morrison House	838-8000
116 South Alfred Street	1-800-367-0800
Alexandria, Virginia	

Old Town Holiday Inn	1-703-549-6080
480 King Street	1-800-368-5047
Alexandria, Virginia	

Omni Georgetown Hotel, The	293-3100
2121 P Street, N.W.	1-800-THE-OMNI

Omni Shoreham Hotel	234-0700
2500 Calvert Street, N.W.	1-800-THE-OMNI

One Washington Circle	872-1680
1 Washington Circle	

Park Hyatt, The	789-1234
24th and M Streets	1-800-922-PARK

Phoenix Park Hotel	638-6900
520 North Capitol Street, N.W.	

Quality Hotel Capitol Hill	638-1616
415 New Jersey Avenue, N.W.	1-800-228-5151

Radisson Park Terrace	232-7000
1515 Rhode Island Avenue, N.W.	

Ramada Renaissance Techworld	898-9000
999 9th Street, N.W.	1-800-228-9898

Ritz-Carlton, The	835-2100
2100 Massachusetts Avenue, N.W.	1-800-424-8008

River Inn, The	337-7600
924 25th Street, N.W.	1-800-424-2741

Sheraton Carlton, The	638-2626
923 16th Street, N.W.	1-800-325-3535

Sheraton Crystal City Hotel	**1-703-486-1111**
1800 Jefferson Davis Highway	**1-800-325-3535**
Arlington, Virginia	

Sheraton Washington Hotel	**328-2000**
2660 Woodley Road, N.W.	**1-800-325-3535**

Tabard Inn, The	**785-1277**
1739 N Street, N.W.	

Vista International Hotel	**429-1700**
1400 M Street, N.W.	**1-800-HILTONS**

Washington Court Hotel	**628-2100**
525 New Jersey Avenue, N.W.	**1-800-325-3535**

Washington Hilton & Towers	**965-2300**
1919 Connecticut Avenue, N.W.	

Washington Hilton & Towers, The	**483-3000**
1919 Connecticut Avenue, N.W.	**1-800-HILTONS**

Watergate Hotel, The	**965-2300**
2650 Virginia Avenue, N.W.	**1-800-424-2736**

Westin Hotel, The	**429-2400**
2401 M Street, N.W.	**1-800-228-3000**

Willard, The	**628-9100**
1400 Pennsylvania Avenue, N.W.	
	1-800-327-0200

HOTELS, GRAND

Hay-Adams	**638-6600**
One Lafayette Square	**1-800-424-5054**

Singles: $155–325   Doubles: $155–350   Suites: $450–1550

This site was once the social center of Washington, when good friends John Hay (President Lincoln's private secretary and Theodore Roosevelt's Secretary of State) and historian Henry Adams (great grandson of John Adams) had homes here. Both buildings were razed in 1927, and the 200-room Hay-Adams House opened in 1928. Charles Lindbergh, Amelia Earhart, and Sinclair Lewis were among those to enjoy its Italian Renaissance luxury plus views of the White House and Lafayette Park. Like several other of Washington's "dowager" hotels, the Hay-Adams has benefited from extensive renovations and strives to make guests feel that they are staying at an exclusive private club. Stepping into the quiet bar, you'll see why it was Ollie North's choice for secret deal-making.

Hotel Washington, The   638-5900
15th and Pennsylvania Avenue, N.W.   **1-800-424-9540**
Singles: $133–173   Doubles: $147–187   Suites: $356–538

This National Landmark hotel's extensive renovation was completed early in 1988 and has restored the low-key elegance that has been the hallmark of the Hotel Washington since 1918. From May to October, the Sky Terrace and Two Continents restaurant share the roof—offering diners breathtaking views of the city. Many of the rooms overlook the White House or the Mall.

Jefferson, The   347-2200
1200 16th Street, N.W.   **1-800-368-5966**
Singles: $150–235   Doubles: $160–255   Suites: $275 & up

On our recent visit to the renowned Jefferson, we were delighted to be involved (as all visitors are) in the work of a *tromp l'oeil artist* who perfectly duplicates the look of pine paneling. Hard at work in the bar, restaurant, and lounge areas on the ground floor, he recreates the original atmosphere that made these areas so popular. The Chinese red, high-gloss walls are complimented by his *tromp l'oeil* wainscoating, making the bar and lounge, with its fireplace, particularly inviting for a quiet drink. The 100 rooms are highly individual—no two are decorated in the same fashion. The entrance and public areas, complete with chandeliers, fountains, and masses of flowers are elegant. CEOs comprise the bulk of their clientele, drawn here by the combination of elegance and high-tech efficiency (FAX machines and computers can be hooked up in the rooms).

Sheraton Carlton, The   638-2626
923 16th Street, N.W.   **1-800-325-3535**
Singles: $210–245   Doubles: $235–270   Suites: $310 & up

Service is our business, and we can judge within 15 seconds of entering a hotel lobby whether the management is on its toes. It is here. General Manager Michel Ducamp has created an atmosphere that combines warmth and professionalism in the ideal balance. From the moment the doorman opens the door of your taxi, to the warm "Welcome" uttered by the bellman (even when you're not carrying bags), the Sheraton Carlton's staff makes the visitor feel that this is his home. This isn't just a happy accident—the Sheraton Corporation spent millions renovating this property and a cool half million training its staff. Under the supervision of chief butler John Baker,

15 butlers keep computer profiles of their guests and stand ready twenty-four hours a day, seven days a week, to fulfill their every wish. On the lower level, renowned barber Milton Pitts—official barber to the presidents—offers a complete range of services from a trim to a pedicure. Michael Mayes, head concierge, accommodates the special needs of guests such as Barbara Mandrell, Audrey Hepburn, and Elizabeth Taylor. Lesser luminaries will be pleased to note that the Sheraton Carlton is only two blocks from the White House. Two Metro stations —Farragut North and McPherson Square—are close by. Afternoon tea is served in the lobby to the accompaniment of a harpist, and champagne flows freely at Sunday brunch.

Willard, The   628-9100
1400 Pennsylvania Avenue, N.W.   **1-800-327-0200**
Singles: $215–295   Doubles: $245–325   Suites: $425–2400

This magnificent building, designed by Henry Janeway Hardenbergh, whose other properties include the Plaza and Dakota apartments in New York, is rich in historical importance. In its heyday, it hosted Mark Twain, Jenny Lind, P.T. Barnum, the Duke of Windsor, Harry Houdini, and Mae West. Henry Clay mixed the first mint julep in Washington in the Round Robin Bar. And it was here that, outraged at the prices at the hotel newsstand, Thomas Marshall (Woodrow Wilson's Vice President) uttered the immortal words, "What this country needs is a good five cent cigar," a sentiment shared by McDowell. More recently, the Reverend Martin Luther King, Jr. wrote his "I have a dream" speech while he was a guest at The Willard. In 1968, The Willard closed. Its ornate doors and windows would remain boarded up for 15 years. Using old photographs, written memoirs, and taped interviews with former guests and employees, Tom Lee Ltd. handled the design elements that would restore the hotel to its turn-of-the-century elegance. Now managed by Inter-Continental hotels, The Willard reopened in 1986. Heads of state, Hollywood luminaries, politicians, and just plain folks in the mood to splurge have flocked back. As former concierges, we were particularly delighted that the original mahogany front desk has become the concierge desk—it's roomy, elegant, and well organized. Chef concierge Steven Bagley and his staff fulfill your every request. Even if your budget won't permit staying here, you owe it to yourself to wander through Peacock Alley for a glimpse of Washington's illustrious past.

HOTELS, LUXURY

Four Seasons Hotel   342-0444
2800 Pennsylvania Avenue, N.W.   **1-800-268-6282**
Singles: $205–235   Doubles: $235–265   Suites: From $425

Located just across the river in Georgetown, the Four Seasons emphasizes personal service.

J. W. Marriott Hotel   626-6900
1331 Pennsylvania Avenue, N.W.   **1-800-228-9290**
Singles: $224   Doubles: $244

This large (773 room) convention hotel profits from its prime location (just a few blocks from the White House, close to Metro Center and within an easy walk of the best of the Smithsonian) and easy access to the Shops at National Place. Although its size prevents it from offering true luxury service, the J.W. Marriott is still a credit to its namesake.

HOTELS, FIRST CLASS

Capital Hilton, The   393-1000
16th and K Streets, N.W.   **1-800-HILTONS**
Singles: $185–225   Doubles: $210–250   Suites: From $550

This lovely art deco building was recently renovated to the tune of $44 million. The location is terrific for both diplomats and tourists—only four blocks north of the White House, and two blocks from stops on three Metro lines. The rooms are among the most spacious in Washington, and both concierge services and complete business facilities are available. A branch of Trader Vic's adds to the fun of staying here.

Grand Hotel, The   429-0100
2350 M Street, N.W.   **1-800-848-0016**
Singles: $220   Doubles: $240

This elegant, small hotel (263 rooms) located near the Kennedy Center offers such niceties as all-marble bathrooms and in-room minibars. Entering the large, primarily marble lobby, one has the sensation of entering an exclusive, private club. Three restaurants, The Promenade Room, the Mayfair, and the Rose and Crown Pub, offer a variety for dining.

Grand Hyatt, The   582-1234
1000 H Street, N.W.
Singles: $169–189   Doubles: $194–214

Located just across the street from the Convention Center and within walking distance of the White House, Smithsonian Institution, FBI headquarters, and major department stores, the Grand Hyatt's signature atrium and cascading waterfall seem out-of-place in a business, rather than a resort, setting. Rooms are spacious and tastefully, if not imaginatively, decorated.

Holiday Inn Crowne Plaza   737-2200
   at Metro Center   1-800-HOLIDAY
775 12th Street, N.W.
Singles: $145–180   Doubles: $165–205

The Crowne Plaza name is applied to the upscale Holiday Inn hotels, and visitors here will be pleasantly surprised. David Woodward, the General Manager, is creating a force to be reckoned with. His background in the finest of English luxury hotels enables him to bring new pizzazz to the Crowne Plaza name. As he has pointed out, his most important ingredient is a friendly, American staff which can be trained to exacting standards. The location, directly above Metro Center, is a prized one—giving tourists immediate access to all the shopping and sightseeing Washington has to offer.

Hyatt Regency on Capitol Hill   737-1234
400 New Jersey Avenue, N.W.   1-800-228-9000
Singles: $185   Doubles: $210

The signature Hyatt atrium, fountain, and exotic vegetation, plus a variety of restaurants and a health club complete with indoor pool have combined to make this an extremely popular Capitol Hill spot.

Madison Hotel, The   862-1600
15th and M Streets, N.W.   1-800-424-8577
Singles: $235   Doubles: $234   Suites: $395–2500

Located just four blocks from the White House and across the street from the Washington Post, the Madison welcomes guests ranging from corporate executives to the King of Sweden. Antiques grace the lobby and guest rooms.

Mayflower, The   347-3000
1127 Connecticut Avenue, N.W.   1-800-HOTELS-1
Singles: $139   Doubles: $234

The enormous (721 rooms) Mayflower reminds us of New York's elegant Waldorf Astoria. Entering the lobby, which is constantly buzzing with activity, one always feels that something important is happening. It has been the site of several inaugural balls and is still a favored Washington residence for visiting dignitaries and celebrities.

Morrison House   1-703-838-8000
116 South Alfred Street   1-800-367-0800
Alexandria, Virginia
Singles: $135   Doubles: $150 to 190   Suites: $230–385

It looks like an authentic eighteenth-century inn, but the Morrison House was built less than 50 years ago. The beautifuly decorated rooms have four-poster beds and brass chandeliers. A short walk from the Old Town shopping district, it's a good choice not only for tourists, but for Washingtonians looking for a weekend getaway.

Park Hyatt, The   789-1234
24th and M Streets, N.W.   1-800-922-PARK
Singles: $245   Doubles: $245–1500   Suites: $260–1500

Beautiful art, spacious guest rooms, a restaurant of note, and a fashionable Georgetown location combine to make an elegant hotel.

Phoenix Park Hotel   638-6900
520 North Capitol Street, N.W.
Singles: $147-167   Doubles: $167-187   Suites: $275-425

A charming, small (84 room) hotel named after a famous Dublin park, the Phoenix Park welcomes travelers with warm Irish hospitality. Its two restaurants, Powerscourt (see complete description under RESTAURANTS) and the Dubliner pub offer a choice between elegant cuisine and pub food, complete with Celtic bands, sing-alongs, and Guiness on tap. It's close to the Mall and to wonderfully restored Union Station.

Ritz-Carlton, The   835-2100
2100 Massachusetts Avenue, N.W.   1-800-424-8008
Singles: From $190   Doubles: From $210   Suites: From $350

The Ritz-Carlton, a perennial favorite with the upper crust, is now undergoing a major renovation. Determined to accommodate their clientele, the management is keeping the hotel open during alterations. The new structure promises to be restored to its original splendor.

Washington Hilton & Towers   965-2300
1919 Connecticut Avenue, N.W.   1-800-424-2736
Singles: $186–206   Doubles: $206–226

Situated in the lively Dupont Circle neighborhood, this large (1,150 room) convention hotel offers almost every amenity. Boasting its own outdoor recreational and exercise areas, it is a favorite of both conventioneers and traveling businesspeople.

Washington Vista   429-1700
1400 M Street, N.W.   1-800-HILTONS
Singles: From $190   Doubles: From $205

Conveniently located in the downtown business district, the Washington Vista is typical of modern atrium-oriented hotels. There is one major exception, however. The tower in the center of the atrium houses a lounge and six suites designed by Givenchy. These terribly elegant rooms offer almost every luxury to the lucky guest.

Watergate Hotel, The   **965-2300**
2650 Virginia Avenue, N.W.   **1-800-424-2736**
Singles: $195–265   Doubles: $220–290   Suites: From $335

There's no denying that this name will forever be linked with the bungled "third-rate burglary" that took place in the adjoining office building, leading to Richard Nixon's resignation. It is also linked to the concept of luxury and houses numerous elegant shops as well as the Watergate Hotel, a luxurious 238-room establishment. Renovated in 1988, the hotel has a fine health club and exercise facilities. Jean-Louis, a restaurant of unpredictable quality, is also located on the premises.

Westin Hotel, The   **429-2400**
2401 M Street, N.W.   **1-800-228-3000**
Singles: $165-225   Doubles: $190-250   Suites from $250

Large rooms complete with minibars, an extremely friendly and helpful staff, a complete fitness center, plus a branch of Robin Weir's salon create a traveler's haven.

COMFORTABLE HOTELS

Washington is a popular destination for families. While the downtown hotel prices may leave parents gasping, suburban properties offer good value. The Metro has shortened transit times and increased comfort.

Bethesda Marriott Hotel   **1-301-897-9400**
5151 Pooks Hill Road   **1-800-228-9290**
Bethesda, Maryland
Singles: $160   Doubles: $180

Proximity to the Bethesda Naval Hospital and the National Institute of Health complex keep this Marriott humming. Children under 18 stay free, there's no charge for parking, and an indoor–outdoor swimming pool adds to guests' pleasure.

Canterbury, The   **393-3000**
1733 N Street, N.W.   **1-800-424-2950**
Singles: $135–175   Doubles: $155–195   Suites: $275–500

Tucked away on quiet N Street, N.W., not far from the lively Dupont Circle restaurants and clubs, the 99-room Canterbury caters to guests seeking European elegance at

American prices. Fully stocked wet bars in every room, turndown service, and Chaucer's restaurant are some of the features that draw repeat business.

Crowne Plaza Holiday Inn   **1-301-468-1100**
1750 Rockville Pike   **1-800-638-5963**
Rockville, Maryland
Singles: $123–150   Doubles: $138–165

It may not look like much from the outside, but an eight-story atrium complete with 20-foot waterfall welcomes guests to this unique suburban property. Children stay free, parking is free, and amenities include a swimming pool and health club. Downtown is easily accessible via the nearby Twinbrook Metro station.

Crystal City Marriott   **1-703-521-5500**
1999 Jefferson Davis Highway   **1-800-446-6900**
Arlington, Virginia
Singles: $155   Doubles: $175

Only two minutes from National Airport and connected to the Crystal City Metro complex, the Crystal City Marriott caters to conventioneers. Children under 18 stay free. Both they and the conventioneers enjoy the swimming pool.

Crystal Gateway Marriott   **1-703-920-3230**
1700 Jefferson Davis Highway, Arlington, Virginia
Singles: $180   Doubles: $200

Guests at this enormous (702 room) hotel enjoy use of a nearby racquet/health club, an on-site pool, sauna, whirlpool and jogging paths. Located one mile from the National Airport and 10 minutes from downtown via Metro, it's a favorite with business travelers and families alike.

Embassy Row Hotel   **265-1600**
2015 Massachusetts Avenue, N.W.   **1-800-424-2400**
Singles: $140–175   Doubles: $160–190

We expect this hotel to increase in popularity thanks to an extensive renovation program and the presence of Lucie, one of Washington's premier restaurants. Located just above Dupont Circle at the foot of Embassy Row, it combines easy access to the downtown attractions (via Metro) with the quiet charm of a residential neighborhood.

Georgetown Marbury House   **726-5000**
3000 M Street, N.W.   **368-5922**
Singles: $99–139   Doubles: From $149   Suites: From $159

A cozy, 164-room find in the heart of Georgetown.

Guest Quarters Hotel   **785-2000**
801 New Hampshire Avenue, N.W.   **1-800-424-2900**
Suites: $175

2500 Pennsylvania Avenue　　　　　**1-800-424-2900**
Suites: $175

The rooms at these all-suites hotels include separate living and dining areas, spacious baths and full kitchens. Personally, we enjoy <u>not</u> cooking when we're on the road but understand that others do not share this attitude.

Henley Park Hotel, The　　　　　　**638-5200**
926 Massachusetts Avenue, N.W.　　　**222-8474**
Singles: $115–195　　Doubles: $135–215　　Suites: $275–650

If it weren't located in a marginal neighborhood (you don't dare walk around after dark), it would be impossible to get reservations at this charming, tudor-style 96-room hotel.

Hotel Wyndham Bristol　　　　　　**955-6400**
2430 Pennsylvania Avenue, N.W.　　**1-800-822-2430**
Singles and Doubles: $155–195　　　Suites: From $215

Popular with performing artists because of its proximity to the Kennedy Center, the Wyndham Bristol has the air of a small, elegant, European hotel. It's located about equidistant from Georgetown and the central business district.

Hyatt Regency Bethesda　　　　**1-301-657-1234**
1 Bethesda Metro Center　　　　　**1-800-228-9000**
Bethesda, Maryland
Singles: $154　　　Doubles: $179

A terrific suburban location in the midst of Bethesda's office and retail district and easy access to Washington via the Metro are the attractions here. Children under 18 stay free.

Key Bridge Marriott　　　　　**1-703-524-6400**
1401 Lee Highway　　　　　　　**1-800-228-9290**
Rosslyn, Virginia
Singles: $159　　　Doubles: $179

Georgetown is just a short walk away, and the views of Washington are gorgeous. Children under 18 stay free.

Old Town Holiday Inn　　　　　**1-703-549-6080**
480 King Street　　　　　　　　**1-800-368-5047**
Alexandria, Virginia
Singles: $108–125　　Doubles: $114–140

Early American decor combines with those lovely modern amenities and a prime location right in the center of historic Old Town. Free shuttle bus service is offered to National Airport, where you can catch the Metro to downtown attractions. Children under 18 stay free.

Omni Georgetown Hotel, The　　　　**293-3100**
2121 P Street, N.W.　　　　　　**1-800-THE-OMNI**
Singles: $155–175　　Doubles: $175–195　　Suites: $200–475

Don't let the name fool you; the Omni Georgetown Hotel is actually just off Dupont Circle. This makes it much more convenient for guests who wish to use Washington's excellent Metro system. Businesspeople will appreciate the spacious rooms with work areas. Everyone appreciates the courtyard pool.

Omni Shoreham Hotel   **234-0700**
2500 Calvert Street, N.W.   **1-800-THE-OMNI**
Singles: $115–175   Doubles: $135–195   Suites: $300–850

Set on 11 picturesque acres in Rock Creek Park and within easy walking distance of the National Zoo, the Omni blends suburban charm with easy access to downtown via Metro.

One Washington Circle   **872-1680**
1 Washington Circle
Singles: $105–190   Doubles: $117–210

All-suites hotels have become increasingly popular, and One Washington Circle follows this trend. Georgetown, the Kennedy Center, and the downtown business area lie within easy walking distance. The hotel prides itself on providing high-quality service.

Radisson Park Terrace   **232-7000**
1515 Rhode Island Avenue, N.W.
Singles: $135   Doubles: $150   Suites: $175–195

On the opposite end of the scale, elegant, European-style small hotels are rising in popularity. The Radisson is located within the downtown business district, just six blocks from the White House and a quick Metro ride from Washington's wonderful museums. Diners can choose between Chardonnay with its dramatic setting and gourmet preparations or the Garden Terrace.

Ramada Renaissance Techworld   **898-9000**
999 9th Street, N.W.   **1-800-228-9898**
Singles: $135–155   Doubles: $155–175

Conventioneers will enjoy the Ramada's location at the Convention Center as well as the fitness center and pool. The hotel seeks to combine the best of modern technology with the gracious service that so often gets lost in large properties.

Sheraton Washington Hotel   **328-2000**
2660 Woodley Road, N.W.   **1-800-325-3535**
Singles: $165–215   Doubles: $195–245   Suites: $230–1800

With 1505 rooms, this hotel doesn't offer much in the way of personalized service. However, the thousands of conventioneers who flock here don't seem to mind. Children under 17 stay free and enjoy visiting the pandas at the nearby National Zoo.

HOTELS, INEXPENSIVE

Bellevue Hotel, The   638-0900
15 E Street, N.W.
Singles: $89.50–99.50   Doubles: $104.50–114.50

Located just two blocks from Union Station, the slightly tired Bellevue offers excellent value. The 140 rooms are large (some even have mini-refrigerators), and the staff is well trained. You can walk to the Capitol and all those marvelous Smithsonian museums on The Mall.

Best Western Center City   682-5300
1201 13th Street, N.W.
Singles: $85–105   Doubles: $95–115.

Located near the Convention Center, the Best Western Center City is distinguished by an extraordinarily friendly and helpful staff.

Carlyle Suites, The   234-3200
1731 New Hampshire Avenue, N.W.
Singles: $59–99   Doubles: $69–109

The convenience of suites with fully equipped kitchens, coin-operated laundry facilities, casual dining, and convenient access to the Metro make this very attractive for families.

Dupont Plaza Hotel   483-6000
1500 New Hampshire Avenue, N.W.   **1-800-421-6662**
Singles: $125–175   Doubles: $145–195

Just off Dupont Circle and near Embassy Row, the Dupont Plaza's comfortable rooms are all equipped with refrigerators and wet bars.

Embassy Square Suites Hotel   659-9000
2000 N Street, N.W.   **1-800-424-2999**
Singles: $149–169   One Bedroom $169–189
Two Bedroom: $209–239

Ideal for business travelers who need extra space for their paperwork plus room for meeting and entertaining clients.

Holiday Inn Georgetown   338-4600
2101 Wisconsin Avenue, N.W.
Singles: From $79   Doubles: To $150

Dependable Holiday Inn quality on the outskirts of fashionable Georgetown.

Hotel Anthony   223-4320
1823 L Street, N.W.   **1-800-424-2970**

Singles: $97–117   Doubles: $107–127

With only 99 suites, the staff of the intimate Hotel Anthony can devote itself to giving guests personalized service. Some suites are equipped with microwave ovens and coffee makers. It's a short walk to the White House and a slightly longer one to The Mall.

Hotel Lombardy	**828-2600**
2019 I Street, N.W.	**1-800-424-5486**

Singles: $90–140   Doubles: $110–125   Suites: $125–155

A delightful find located just a few blocks from the White House and convenient to the Farragut West Metro station. About 70% of the Hotel Lombardy's rooms have fully equipped kitchens. Modern amenities, including VCRs and laundry facilities on the lower level, combine with old-world charm. Weekend rates plunge to $89.

Morrison-Clark Inn	**898-1200**

Massachusetts Avenue & 11th Street, N.W.

Singles: $95–195   Doubles: $115–215

The Morrison-Clark, which boasts that it is Washington's only historic inn, is comprised of two grand townhouses plus a modern addition. Each of the 54 guest rooms is individually decorated with original artwork and authentic period furnishings. Although guests feel that they are stepping back into a previous century, the guest rooms feature such modern amenities as computer access data ports. Complimentary morning limousine service to the Central business district and Capitol Hill is offerred. Conveniently located near the Convention Center, Techworld, and the Metro Center, the Morrison-Clark combines efficiency with graciousness and Southern charm. Reserve well in advance.

Quality Hotel Capitol Hill	**638-1616**
415 New Jersey Avenue, N.W.	**1-800-228-5151**

Singles: $79–105   Doubles: $94–120   Suites: $200–315

Families will appreciate having free indoor parking; children 18 and under stay free; there's an indoor pool; and it's only two blocks from Union Station.

River Inn, The	**337-7600**
924 25th Street, N.W.	**1-800-424-2741**

Singles: $99–150   Doubles: $111–162

An all-suites hotel in the Foggy Bottom neighborhood, with Georgetown and the Kennedy Center nearby.

Sheraton Crystal City Hotel	**1-703-486-1111**
1800 Jefferson Davis Highway	**1-800-325-3535**
Arlington, Virginia	

Singles: $115–140   Doubles: $130–155

Situated at the Crystal City Metro stop. All rooms have mini-bars. Guests enjoy the outdoor rooftop pool and health club with sauna.

Tabard Inn, The   785-1277
1739 N Street, N.W.
Singles and Doubles: $53–$119

Named after the famous hostelry of Chaucer's *Canterbury Tales*, the Tabard Inn claims to be the oldest continuously operated hotel in Washington, D.C.—and it looks it. Those seeking something "quaint and charming" will not be disappointed, for the Tabard resembles a slightly ramshackle English inn. Not all rooms have private baths. There is a surprisingly good restaurant downstairs, with a terrace garden that make it a quiet haven in the lively Dupont Circle neighborhood.

Washington Court Hotel   628-2100
525 New Jersey Avenue, N.W.   **1-800-325-3535**
Singles: $160–220   Doubles: $185–245

The former Sheraton Grand Hotel's location on Capitol Hill offers convenient access to Union Station, the Smithsonian Museums and the National Gallery.

**House Barber Shop (House of
        Representatives)**   225-3559
140 Cannon House Office Building, U.S. Capitol

**House Barber Shop (House of
        Representatives)**   225-7024
B-323 Rayburn House Office Building, U.S. Capitol

Houston's   338-7760
1065 Wisconsin Avenue, N.W. (M St.)

Howard County General Hospital   1-301-740-7890
5755 Cedar Lane, Columbia, Maryland

Howard University Hospital   745-6100
2041 Georgia Avenue, N.W.

Hudson Country News   783-1720
The Shops at National Place, 1331 Pennsylvania
Avenue, N.W.

Hudson Trail Outfitters, Ltd.   393-1244
The Shops at National Place, 1331 Pennsylvania
Avenue, N.W.

Hunan Chinatown   783-5858
624 H Street (6th/7th Sts.)

Hung Jury, The   785-8181
1819 H Street, N.W.

Hungary (Embassy of)	**362-6730**
3910 Shoemaker Street, N.W.	
Hunt Club	**347-2200**
Jefferson Hotel, 1200 16th Street, N.W.	
Hyatt Regency Bethesda	**1-301-657-1234**
1 Bethesda Metro Center,	**1-800-228-9000**
Bethesda, Maryland	
Hyatt Regency on Capitol Hill	**737-1234**
400 New Jersey Avenue, N.W.	**1-800-228-9000**

I

I Ricchi	**835-0459**
1220 19th Street, N.W.	
Iberia	**1-800-221-9741**
Iceland (Embassy of)	**265-6653**
2022 Connecticut Avenue, N.W.	
Icelandair	**1-800-223-5500**

ICE SKATING

One doesn't think of Washington as being cold enough in the winter to produce lots of places for ice skating. Remember that although they think they are in the South, they're on the very northernmost edge of it. It gets plenty cold in this part of the country, and there are several fine rinks.

C & O Canal

A very scenic place to skate but remember to be sure of the thickness of the ice and the depth of the water under it. Call the National Park Service (458-9666) for information.

Fort Dupont Ice Arena   581-0199
3779 Ely Place, S.E. (Minnesota Ave.)
Open from Labor Day until the middle of April. Skate rental available.

National Sculpture Garden Ice Rink   347-9042
Across the Mall from the Hirshhorn Museum

Pershing Park   737-6938
15th Street and Pennsylvania Avenue, N.W.
Another outdoor rink. Skate rentals available.

Reflecting Pool, The
The Mall
Between the Lincoln Memorial & the Washington Monument. One of the most dramatic places to skate and certainly our choice. Beautiful views of the most famous of the monuments and buildings while you skate under the sky.

Idle Time Books	232-4774
2410 18th Street, N.W.	

Ignacy Kunin 265-5900
1725 Wisconsin Avenue, N.W.

Ilo 342-0350
1637 Wisconsin Avenue, N.W.

India (Embassy of) 939-7000
2107 Massachusetts Avenue, N.W.

Indonesia (Embassy of) 775-5200
2020 Massachusetts Avenue, N.W.

Inn at Little Washington 1-703-675-3800
Middle and Main Streets, Washington, Virginia

International Learning Center 232-4111
1715 Connecticut Avenue, N.W.

International Limousine Service, Inc 388-6800
2300 T Street, N.E.

**International Visitors Information
  Center** 783-6540

Iraq (Embassy of) 483-7500
1801 P Street, N.W.

Ireland (Embassy of) 462-3939
2234 Massachusetts Avenue, N.W.

Irving's Sport Shops 393-2626
10th and E Streets, N.W.

Islamic Mosque and Center 332-8343
2551 Massachusetts Avenue, N.W. (Belmont Rd.)

Israel (Embassy of) 364-5500
3514 International Drive, N.W.

Italy (Embassy of) 328-5500
1601 Fuller Street, N.W.

Ivory Coast (Embassy of) 483-2400
2424 Massachusetts Avenue, N.W.

Iwo Jima Memorial   **1-703-285-2598**
Arlington Boulevard and Meade Street,
Arlington, Virginia

J

J & D Inn	**832-1492**
1007 Rhode Island Avenue, N.E.	
J. Lynn & Co.	**223-0210**
1900 I Street, N.W.	
J. Paul's	**333-3450**
3218 M Street, N.W.	
J.E. Caldwell Co.	**466-6780**
1140 Connecticut Avenue, N.W.	
J.R.'s	**328-0090**
1519 17th Street, N.W.	
J.R.'s Bar & Grill	**328-0091**
1519 17th Street, N.W.	
J.W. Marriott Hotel at National Place	**626-6900**
1331 Pennsylvania Avenue, N.W.	**1-800-228-9290**
Jamaica (Embassy of)	**452-0660**
1850 K Street, N.W.	
James B. Barnes Gallery	**1-703-548-8008**
222 S. Washington Street, Alexandria, Virginia	
Japan (Embassy of)	**234-2266**
2520 Massachusetts Avenue, N.W.	
Japan Airlines	**1-800-525-3663**

JAZZ

While Washington is not particularly known for its nightlife, much good jazz can still be found here, if you know where to look.

 Blues Alley   **337-4141**
 1073 Wisconsin Avenue, N.W. (Rear)
 The biggest names in jazz (Dizzy Gillespie, Wynton Marsalis, Herbie Mann, Ramsay Lewis) entertain at this intimate supper club. Diners (who choose from regional New Orleans-style cuisine, steaks and seafood) are given preferential seating over those who come only for the show. Cover charges range from $10 to $25, depending on who's appearing.

Colonel Brooks' Tavern   529-4002
901 Monroe Street, N.E.
Every Tuesday night, this casual, reliable, neighborhood bar comes alive with the sound of Dixie and Jazz.

King of France Tavern   1-301-261-2206
Maryland Inn, 16 Church Circle, Annapolis,
Maryland
Guitarist Charlie Byrd's home base presents a mix of local and nationally known jazz musicians. Monday night's jam sessions led by house pianist Stef Scaffiari are well worth the one-hour drive from Washington.

One Step Down   331-8863
2517 Pennsylvania Avenue, N.W.
You never know what you'll encounter in this tiny, dark, and smokey room. Local groups perform during the week, and New York-based trios and quartets are weekend headliners—sometimes.

Philly's Finest   635-7790
1601 Rhode Island Avenue, N.E.
Crowds come here for straight-ahead jazz, performed by the likes of Houston Person, Etta Jones, and Washington's own Mary Jefferson.

219 Basin Street Lounge   1-703-549-1141
219 King Street , Alexandria, Virginia
Downstairs, barbecued shrimp and other Creole specialties may be enjoyed. Upstairs, traditional jazz. *Take note:* The music starts at 10:00 A.M. on Sunday, and by mid-afternoon, this is the hottest spot in town.

Jean-Louis   298-4488
The Watergate Hotel, 2650 Virginia Avenue, N.W.
(New Hampshire Ave.)

Jean-Pierre   466-2022
1835 K Street, N.W. (18th/19th)

Jefferson Memorial   426-6822
On the Tidal Basin near 15th Street, S.W.

Jefferson Restaurant, The   785-0500
The Jefferson Hotel, 16th and M Streets.N.W.

Jefferson Hotel, The   347-2200
1200 16th Street, N.W.   1-800-368-5966

Jenkins Hill   544-6600
223 Pennsylvania Avenue, S.E.

Jill & Co., Antiques   1-301-946-7464
3744 Howard Avenue, Kensington, Maryland

Joanne's Antique Alley   **1-301-933-6939**
3746 Howard Avenue, Kensington, Maryland

Jockey Club   **293-2100**
The Ritz-Carlton Hotel, 2100 Massachusetts Avenue,
N.W. (21st St.)

John Crouch Tobacconist   **1-703-548-2900**
128 King Street, Alexandria, Virginia

John Davy Toys   **1-703-683-0079**
301 Cameron Street, Alexandria, Virginia

**John F. Kennedy Center for the
    Performing Arts**   **254-3600**
New Hampshire Avenue, N.W. and Rock Creek Parkway

John Hay Room   **638-2260**
The Hay-Adams Hotel, 800 16th Street, N.W.

Jonathan's   **638-6800**
1520 K Street, N.W.

Jones Troyer Fitzpatrick Gallery   **328-7189**
1614 20th Street, N.W.

Jordan (Embassy of)   **966-2664**
3504 International Drive, N.W.

Jos. A. Bank Clothiers   **466-2282**
3118 19th Street, N.W.

Jos. A. Wilner & Co.   **223-0448**
1714 L Street, N.W.

Just For You Antiques   **1-301-933-5067**
3730 Howard Avenue, Kensington, Maryland

K

Kabul Caravan   **1-703-522-8394**
Colonial Shopping Center, 1725 Wilson Boulevard,
Arlington, Virginia

Kathleen Ewing Gallery   **328-0955**
1609 Connecticut Avenue, N.W., Suite 200

Kenilworth Aquatic Gardens   **426-6905**
Kenilworth Avenue & Douglas Street, N.E.

KENNELS

Most hotels will allow you to bring your animals as long as
you understand that they can't annoy the other guests or

eat the furniture. Guests must pay for hotel property that is damaged. Most of the pets we have met in hotels have been very well behaved and are a pleasure to see. All of the kennels serving the Washington area seem to be in the outlying areas, but most have pick-up and delivery services. By being out of town, they can provide better accommodations for your pets, so don't be put off by location.

Animal Inn   **1-301-926-9000**
15820 Redland Road, Rockville, Maryland

Great Falls Boarding Kennels   **1-703-759-2620**
8920 Old Dominion Drive, McLean, Virginia

Rivermist Kennels   **1-301-774-3100**
19515 New Hampshire Avenue, Brinklow, Maryland

Kenya (Embassy of)   **387-6101**
2249 R Street, N.W.

Key Bridge Marriott   **1-703-524-6400**
1401 Lee Highway   **1-800-228-9290**
Arlington, Virginia

Key Bridge News Stand   **338-2626**
3326 M Street, N.W.

Kid's Closet, The
1226 Connecticut Avenue, N.W.   **429-9247**
1919 K Street, N.W.   **466-5589**

Kids R Us
11818 Rockville Pike,
  Rockville, Maryland   **1-301-770-0660**
3524 Jefferson Street,
  Falls Church, Virginia   **1-703-820-0034**

Kilmanjaro   **328-3838**
1724 California Avenue, N.W.

Kimberly Gallery of Art   **223-6246**
One Westin Center, 2445 M Street, N.W.

Kindness Animal Hospital   **949-2511**
2130 University Boulevard, West

King of France Tavern   **1-301-226-2206**
Maryland Inn, 16 Church Circle, Annapolis, Maryland

Kite Store, The   **965-4230**
3101 M Street, N.W.

KLM   **1-800-777-5553**

Korea (Embassy of)   **939-5600**
2320 Massachusetts Avenue, N.W.

Korean Air	**1-800-223-1155**

Kramerbooks & Afterwords Cafe 387-1400
1517 Connecticut Avenue, N.W.

Kron Chocolatier 966-4946
Mazza Gallerie, 5300 Wisconsin Avenue, N.W.

Krupsaw's Antique Shop 1-301-654-5658
7825 Old Georgetown Road, Bethesda, Maryland

Kuwait (Embassy of) 966-0702
2940 Tilden Street, N.W.

L

L'Auberge Chez François 1-703-759-3800
332 Springvale Road (two miles North of Georgetown Pike), Great Falls, Virginia

L'il Sister 231-4213
237 2nd Avenue, N.W.

L.R. Duehring Jewelers, Inc. 652-0252
6935 Wisconsin Avenue, N.W.

La Bergerie 1-703-683-1007
218 N. Lee Street (King/Queen Sts.), Alexandria, Virginia

La Bonbonniere 333-6425
1724 H Street, N.W.

La Brasserie 546-6066
239 Massachusetts Avenue, N.E. (3rd St.)

La Chaumiere 338-1784
2813 M Street, N.W. (28th/29th Sts.) Georgetown

La Colline 737-0400
400 North Capitol Street, N.W. (D/E Sts.)

La Ferme 1-301-986-5255
7101 Brookeville Road (East-West Hwy./Western Ave.) Chevy Chase, Maryland

La Fourchette 332-3077
2429 18th Street, N.W.

La Maree 659-4447
1919 I Street, N.W. (19th/20th Sts.)

La Plaza 667-1900
1847 Columbia Road, N.W. (Biltmore St.)

Lafitte   466-7978
Hampshire Hotel, 1310 New Hampshire Avenue, N.W.
(20th/N Sts.)

Lambda Rising   462-6969
1625 Connecticut Avenue, N.W.

Lan Chile   1-800-225-5526

Landmark Shopping Center
Alexandria, Virginia

Langston Golf Course   397-8638
66th Street & Benning Road, N.E.

Laos (Embassy of)   332-6416
2222 S Street, N.W.

Latvia (Embassy of)   726-8213
4325 17th Street, N.W.

LAUNDRY/DRY CLEANING

Allstate Repair   582-8444
3423 Minnesota Avenue, S.E.
24-hour emergency service available.

Laura Ashley   338-5481
3213 Wisconsin Avenue, N.W.

Laural Racetrack   1-301-725-0400

Lauriol Plaza   387-0035
1801 18th Street, N.W. (S/T Sts.)

Le Caprice   337-3394
2348 Wisconsin Avenue, N.W. (south of Calvert St.)

Le Gaulois   466-3232
2133 Pennsylvania Avenue, N.W. (Washington Circle)

Le Lion D'Or   296-7972
1150 Connecticut Avenue, N.W. (18th St. between
L/M Sts.)

Le Pavillon   833-3846
1050 Connecticut Avenue, N.W. (L St.)

Le Rivage   488-8111
1000 Water Street, S.W. (Maine Avenue/9th St.)

League of Republican Women of DC   296-2877
1100 17th Street, N.W.

Lebanon (Embassy of)   939-6300
2560 28th Street, N.W.

Lee Bord Jewelers   1-301-530-2800
10400 Old Georgetown Road, Bethesda, Maryland

Leland Memorial Hospital   **1-301-699-2000**
4409 East-West Highway, Riverdale, Maryland

Lenore & Daughters   **1-703-836-3356**
130 South Royal Street, Alexandria, Virginia

Les Amis Du Vin   **1-301-588-0980**
2302 Perkins Place, Silver Spring, Maryland

Lesotho (Embassy of)   **797-5533**
2511 Massachusetts Avenue, N.W.

Liberia (Embassy of)   **723-0437**
5201 16th Street, N.W.

Liberty of London   **338-3711**
Georgetown Park Mall, 3222 M Street, N.W.

LIBRARIES

Washington is a city of libraries, perhaps as many as 500. Almost all of the institutions and many of the organizations have specialized collections which are available to the public. The following are only a few of the more interesting.

D.A.R. Library   **628-1776**
1776 D Street, N.W.
    Monday-Friday 9:00 A.M.–4:00 P.M.
    Sunday 1:00 A.M.–5:00 P.M.
    Metro Station: Farragut West on Blue or Orange lines
The Daughters of the American Revolution restricts membership to women who can prove that they are direct lineal descendants of those who participated in the wars of independence. Because of this requirement, the DAR has developed one of the greatest genealogical libraries in the country. It is available to serious researchers.

Folger Shakespeare Library, The   **544-4600**
201 East Capitol Street, S.E.
    Monday-Saturday 10:00 A.M.–4:00 P.M.
    Closed: Sunday
    Metro Station: Capitol South on the Blue or Orange Line
One of the wonders of Washington, this is another of the more specialized attractions that will not be to everyone's taste. The value of this library can hardly be exaggerated. It has the largest collection of Shakespeare's works in the world, and incidentally includes books by his peers, and about his era, that boggle the mind. The library is worthy of a major write-up, but the nature of this book denies us that pleasure. If you are here as a scholar, there is little we can

tell you about the Folger that you don't already know. If you are here as a tourist, you are probably not interested in doing research on Shakespeare and his friends. However, given the fact that Shakespeare is the most important figure in the history of Western literature, this is one of the most important libraries in the world.

Library of Congress, The   287-5458
1st Street, S.E. (Independence Avenue/
East Capitol St.)
  Monday–Saturday 8:30 A.M.–9:00 P.M.
  Sunday 1:00 P.M.–6:00 P.M.
  Metro Station: Capitol South on Blue or Orange lines
Superlatives abound when one starts to describe the Library of Congress, the world's largest. Every book published in the United States must be deposited here in order to be protected by copyright. Containing 84 million items, almost anything one might wish to read can be found here. Officially the reference library for Congress, its resources are available to the public, as are the many special exhibits and programs provided by its many specialized libraries. For visitors, a brief slide show introduces the library. You might wish to take the 45-minute guided tour.

Martin Luther King, Jr., Library   727-1111
901 G Street, N.W. (9th/10th Sts.)
  Monday-Thursday 9:00 A.M.–9:00 P.M.
  Friday-Saturday 9:00 A.M.–5:30 P.M.
  Sunday 1:00 P.M.–5:00 P.M.
  Metro Station: Gallery Place or Metro Center
This steel and glass building, designed by Mies van der Rohe, is not a memorial library for Martin Luther King, Jr. It is the main branch of the Washington public library system which has been named in his honor.

Library of Congress, The   287-5000
1st Street & East Capitol Street, S.E.

Library of Congress, Annex   287-5458
2nd Street, S.E. (Independence Avenue/A St.)

LIMOUSINES

Limousines are an ideal alternative to the usual sightseeing bus, add comfort and speed to your business day, take the hassle out of trips to and from the airport, add that touch of class to an evening on the town, and generally make one's life much more pleasant. The cost is not as high as one might think and, if you don't know the city, it can really be worth the price. Washington is full of limousine companies which offer a wide variety of services and automobiles. Keep in mind that there are major occasions in this city of diplomats when all of the cars are fully booked. Try to plan far in advance for these events. We can only list a few of the companies which we feel will be of interest to you. If they aren't to your taste, shop around. All of them are listed in the yellow pages.

A-1 Quality Limousine   **575-2040**
1234 Massachusettes Avenue, N.W., Suite 119

Admiral Limousine Service   **554-1000**
1243 1st Street, S.E.

Babel Limousine Service   **328-1297**

Classy Chassis   **829-7050**
6505 Chillum Place, N.W.
Classic cars are a real treat. If you can think of any way to justify it on your expense account, try one. An antique Rolls Royce can really pick up your spirits. Classy Chassis has a beautiful selection.

Diplomat Limousine Service   **589-7620**
1511 K Street, N.W.
A very reliable company which sticks to the standard and stretch limos.

Fantasy Limousines   **236-9363**
Call for a Rolls or Bentley if you are tired of the usual stretch limos.

Morrill Limousine Services, Inc.   **420-0165**
5000 Pennsylvania Avenue   **Evenings 575-2344**

Top Center Ticket & Limousine
     Service   **1-301-585-0046**
8653 Georgia Avenue, Silver Spring, Maryland
The name says it all. They provide both the tickets and the transportation. An easy way to handle the whole package, especially if tickets are scarce.

Welty's London Limos   **1-301-656-2429**
Bethesda, Maryland

Lincoln Memorial   **426-6841**
23rd Street off Constitution Avenue, N.W.

LIQUOR STORES

Of the many liquor stores in DC, the following have some of the largest and best supplies of wines and liquor. Unfortunately, none of them have exceptionally long hours.

A & A Fine Wines and Spirits   **337-3161**
2201 Wisconsin Avenue, N.W.

Central Liquor 737-2800
516–518 9th Street, N.W.

Mayflower Wines & Spirits 463-7950
2115 M Street, N.W.

Schneider's of Capitol Hill 543-9300
300 Massachusetts Avenue N.E.

Lithuania (Embassy of) 234-5860
2622 16th Street, N.W.

Little Caledonia Shop 333-4700
1419 Wisconsin Avenue, N.W.

Little German World 1-703-684-5344
1512 King Street, Alexandria, Virginia

Little Sprout, Inc. 342-2273
Georgetown Pike Mall, 3222 M Street, N.W.

Lloyd Books, Ltd. 333-8989
3145 Dumbarton Avenue, N.W.

Lloyd's Row 1-703-549-7517
119 South Henry Street, Alexandria, Virginia

Lord & Taylor 362-9600
5255 Western Avenue, N.W.

LOST AND FOUND

AMTRAK 484-7540

Metro (subway) 637-1195

Taxi Commission 767-8370

Lost & Found 1-301-946-8666
3734 Howard Avenue, Kensington, Maryland

Lost & Found 488-1200
56 L Street, S.E.

Louis Vuitton 296-6838
Washington Square, 1028 Connecticut Avenue, N.W.

Lowen's 1-301-652-1289
7201 Wisconsin Avenue, Bethesda, Maryland

Lucie 265-1600
Embassy Row Hotel, 2015 Massachusetts Avenue, N.W.

Lufthansa 1-800-645-3880

Luxembourg (Embassy of) 265-4171
2200 Massachusetts Avenue, N.W.

M

M.E. Swing Co., Inc.	**628-7601**
1013 E Street, N.W.	
MacArthur Animal Hospital	**337-0120**
4832 MacArthur Boulevard, N.W.	
Madagascar (Embassy of)	**265-5525**
2374 Massachusetts Avenue, N.W.	
Madison Hotel, The	**862-1600**
15th and M Streets, N.W.	**1-800-424-8577**
Maison Blanche	**842-0070**
1725 F Street, N.W. (17th/18th Sts.)	
Maita (Embassy of)	**462-3611**
2017 Connecticut Avenue, N.W.	
Malawi (Embassy of)	**797-1007**
2408 Massachusetts Avenue, N.W.	
Malaysia (Embassy of)	**328-2700**
2401 Massachusetts Avenue, N.W.	
Mali (Embassy of)	**332-2249**
2130 R Street, N.W.	

THE MALL

The Mall is a two and a half mile stretch of open space that functions as the center of all tourist activities, stretching from the Lincoln Memorial to the Capitol between Constitution and Independence Avenues. Most of the attractions that tourists want to see are located around its perimeter. To help plan your itinerary, the following list itemizes the possibilities. All of the major places are described in the section entitled SIGHTSEEING.

    The White House
    The Old Executive Office Building
    Treasury Building
    Constitution Gardens
    Reflecting Pool
    Lincoln Memorial
    Tidal Basin
    Jefferson Memorial
    Washington Monument
    Department of Agriculture Building
    U.S. Holocaust Memorial Museum
    Bureau of Engraving & Printing

Smithsonian Institution Building
Arts & Industries Building
The Quadrangle
- Enid Haupt Garden
- National Museum of African Art
- Arthur M. Sackler Gallery
Freer Gallery of Art
National Museum of American History
National Museum of Natural History/National Museum of Man
- Hall of Gems
- Insect Zoo
- Children's Discovery Room
National Gallery of Art
National Air & Space Museum
Hirshhorn Museum & Sculpture Garden
U.S. Botanic Gardens
Voice of America
L'Enfant Plaza

MALLS
See **SHOPPING MALLS**

Map Store, The	**628-2608**
1636 I Street, N.W.	
Marie Claire	**466-2680**
1330 Connecticut Avenue, N.W.	
Marie Coreen	**537-1667**
Mazza Gallerie, 5300 Wisconsin Avenue, N.W.	
Mark Turner Flowers	**547-2020**
7 8th Street, S.E.	
Marquee Cabaret	**745-1023**
The Omni Shoreham Hotel, 2500 Calvert Street, N.W.	
Marrakesh	**393-9393**
617 New York Avenue, N.W. (6th/7th Sts.)	
Marsha Mateyka Gallery	**328-0088**
2012 R Street, N.W.	
Marston Luce	**775-9460**
1314 21st Street, N.W.	
Martin Luther King, Jr. Library	**727-1111**
901 G Street, N.W. (9th/10th Sts.)	
Maryland Poison Center	**1-800-492-2414**
Maryland State House	**1-301-269-3400**
State Circle, Annapolis, Maryland	

Massage Associates   495-9375
The J.W. Marriott Hotel   393-2000
1331 Pennsylvania Avenue, N.W.

MASSAGE

When those knotted muscles can stand no more, call your hotel concierge for an appointment with the masseur or masseuse. They will come to you, bringing their portable table, and you will soon feel like a million dollars.

It is more difficult to find someone you can trust if you are not staying in one of the hotels. Massage Associates and the Watergate Health Club are the two places we feel comfortable reccommending.

Massage Associates	393-2000
The J.W. Marriott Hotel	495-9375
1331 Pennsylvania Avenue, N.W.	
Watergate Health Club, The	298-4460
265 Virginia Avenue, N.W.	
Massey's Johnston & Murphy	429-9053
1814 M Street, N.W.	
Masters Tuxedo & Bridal Shop	289-7788
1301 Pennsylvania Avenue, N.W.	
Mauritania (Embassy of)	232-5700
2129 Leroy Place, N.W.	
Mauritius (Embassy of)	244-1491
4301 Connecticut Avenue, N.W.	
Mayflower Wines & Spirits	463-7950
2115 M Street, N.W.	
Mayflower, The	347-3000
1127 Connecticut Avenue, N.W.	**1-800-HOTELS-1**
Mazza Gallerie	
5300 Wisconsin Avenue, N.W.	
McIntosh/Drysdale Gallery	783-5190
406 7th Street, N.W.	
Medical Referral Service for Doctors	872-0003
Melrose	955-3899
The Park Hyatt Hotel, 24th and M Streets, N.W.	
Memorial General Hospital	774-8882
Merriweather Post Pavilion	**1-301-982-1800**
Meskerem	462-4100
2434 18th Street, N.W. (Columbia Rd.)	

MESSENGER SERVICES

Messenger and delivery services are important to those of us in the business world. Listed below are some of the many choices available. They have been selected not only because they do good work, but because they have the most important qualification—they are always open.

BIB Couriers, Inc. 817 Delafield Street, N.E.	**529-3966**
Central Delivery Service 1014 K Street, N.W.	**589-8500**
Panic Deliveries 1275 K Street, N.W.	**966-8966**
QMS 1275 K Street, N.W.	**966-8966**

Metro (Lost & Found)	**637-1195**
Metro Center Grille & Bar 12th and H Streets, N.W.	**737-2200**

METROBUS

The bus system in Washington is best left to the local residents who can figure out its complexities. For those of you who are tourists, there is a much better way to travel. The Metro, which is the subway, will take you almost anywhere you want to go. The city has been well designed for visitors (since almost everybody is one), and this modern, clean, and well-maintained system goes to all sightseeing attractions except Georgetown, which didn't want an even greater influx of people. For transportation to the few restaurants not near a Metro station, take a taxi. They're not terribly comfortable, but they are cheap and they do get there.

Metropolitan AME Church 1518 M Street, N.W.	**331-1426**
Metropolitan Cigar & Tobacco 921 19th Street, N.W.	**223-9648**
Metropolitan Club, The 17th and H Streets, N.W.	**835-2500**

METRORAIL

The Metrorail subway system is the most convenient and least expensive means of getting around our nation's capital. Opened in 1976, the system is clean, safe, and fast. It currently consists of four lines: the Orange Line (New Carroll-ton, Maryland, to Vienna, Virginia), the Blue Line (Addison Rd., Maryland, to National Airport), the Red Line (Shady Grove to Silver Spring, Maryland) and the Yellow Line (Alexandria and Fairfax, Virginia, to downtown Gallery Pl.). The Metro operates weeekdays, 5:30 A.M. to Midnight; Saturday, 8:00 A.M. to Midnight; Sunday, 10:00 A.M. to Midnight. Metro stations are marked by bronze pillars topped with the letter M and with bands in one or more colors that designate the Metro lines. Elevators are available at all stations, and so are maps. Inside, you will find a list of travel times and fares for each destination. Because of its two-tiered fare system based on time of day and distance traveled, the Metro uses a Farecard system. After consulting the fare board, step over to a vending machine and purchase your ticket. Farecard vendors accept nickels, dimes, quarters, $1 and $5 bills. No change is available in the stations, so come prepared. If you plan on doing a great deal of traveling by Metro, you will save time by purchasing a $10 ticket (available at the Sales Office at Metro Center), rather than individual ones. The fares are automatically deducted as you travel. On Saturday, Sunday, and holidays except July 4th, Family Tourist Passes may be purchased. For a mere $5, you receive four passes which are valid for the entire day.

Mexico (Embassy of)	**234-6000**
2829 16th Street, N.W.	
Michelines's Antiques	**1-703-836-1873**
1600 King Street	**1-703-256-0950**
Alexandria, Virginia	
Middendorf Gallery	**462-2009**
2009 Columbia Road, N.W.	
Midway Airlines	**1-800-621-5700**
Midwest Express	**1-800-452-2022**
Milton Pitts	**333-3488**
The Sheraton Carlton Hotel, 16th and K Streets, N.W.	
Miniatures From the Attic	**1-703-237-0066**
2442 North Harrison Street, Arlington, Virginia	
Monday's Child	**1-703-548-3505**
218 North Lee Street, Alexandria, Virginia	

MONEY MACHINES

No matter where you go in Washington, you will find a money machine (ATM) near by. They are in almost all of the banks, which are everywhere in our nation's capital. They are also in all tourist areas. We have been pleasantly surprised to find machines in almost every museum, at the zoo, all of the airports, and anyplace else one might need money. We list only the ones most convenient to the tourist areas.

National Air & Space Museum
National Gallery of Art
National Museum of Natural History
Washington National Airport
301 7th Avenue, N.W.
412 1st Street, S.E.
417 6th Street, N.W.
420 4th Street, S.W.
425 11th Street, N.W.
444 North Capitol Street, N.W.
502 23rd Street, N.W.
509 7th Street, N.W.
740 15th Street, N.W.
1000 Connecticut Avenue, N.W.
1001 Pennsylvania Avenue, N.W.
1100 Connecticut Avenue, N.W.
1100 17th Street, N.W.
1111 Constitution Avenue, N.W.
1123 15th Street, N.W.
1129 20th Street, N.W.
1130 Connecticut Avenue, N.W.
1200 Wisconsin Avenue, N.W.
1201 Pennsylvania Avenue, N.W.
1225 Connecticut Avenue, N.W.
1300 Connecticut Avenue, N.W.
1300 L Street, N.W.
1300 New York Avenue, N.W.
1301 Pennsylvania Avenue, N.W.
1325 G Street, N.W.
1337 Connecticut Avenue, N.W.
1350 F Street, N.W.
1400 G Street, N.W.
15th and York Avenue, N.W.
1503 Pennsylvania Avenue, N.W.
1510 K Street, N.W.
1627 K Street, N.W.
17th and H Street, N.W.
1701 Pennsylvania Avenue, N.W.
1750 New York Avenue, N.W.
1750 Pennsylvania Avenue, N.W.
1775 Pennsylvania Avenue, N.W.
1800 K Street, N.W.

1800 M Street, N.W.
1829 Connecticut Avenue, N.W.
1875 Connecticut Avenue, N.W.
1913 Massachusetts Avenue, N.W.
1919 M Street, N.W.
1919 Pennsylvania Avenue, N.W.
1920 L Street, N.W.
1925 K Street, N.W.
2000 K Street, N.W.
2000 M Street, N.W.
2033 K Street, N.W.
2035 K Street, N.W.
2905 M Street, N.W.
2929 M Street, N.W.

Montgomery General Hospital　　　**1-301-774-8882**
18101 Prince Phillip Drive, Olney, Maryland

Monticello　　　**1-804-295-8181**
Routes 20/I-64 (Exit 24-A), (two miles south/east of
Charlottesville), Charlottesville, Virginia

Montpelier　　　**862-1712**
The Madison Hotel, 1177 15th Street, N.W. (M St.)

Moon, Blossoms & Snow　　　**543-8181**
225 Pennsylvania Avenue, S.E.

Moonstone Bookcellars　　　**659-2600**
2145 Pennsylvania Avenue, N.W.

Mora Camera Service　　　**362-9866**
4027 Brandywine Street, N.W.

Morocco (Embassy of)　　　**462-7979**
1601 21st Street, N.W.

Morrill Limousine Services, Inc.　　　**420-0165**
5000 Pennsylvania Avenue　　　**575-2344**

Morrison-Clark Hotel　　　**898-1200**
Massachusetts Avenue and 11th Street, N.W.

Morrison House　　　**1-703-838-8000**
116 South Alfred Street　　　**1-800-367-0800**
Alexandria, Virginia

Morton's of Chicago　　　**342-6258**
3251 Prospect Street, N.W., Georgetown

Morven Park　　　**1-703-777-2414**
Old Waterford Road, (two miles north of Leesburg),
Leesburg, Virginia

MOTELS

One of the "finds" in accommodations can be the motels, some of which are located in prime spots throughout the city. The ones on New York Avenue are located on the main road into the city if you are driving down from the north. While they are not geared toward full service, they compensate by having lower prices than the big hotels. Remember that, like all of the hotels, they are quite often fully booked. As soon as you know your travel plans, call for reservations.

Best Western Regency	**546-9200**
600 New York Avenue, N.E.	
Budget Motor Inn	**529-3900**
1615 New York Avenue, N.E.	
Channel Inn	**554-2400**
650 Water Street	
Days Inn	**832-5800**
2700 New York Avenue, N.E.	
Downtown Motel	**544-2000**
New York Avenue & 4th Street, N.E.	
Econo Lodge	**832-3200**
1600 New York Avenue, N.E.	
Holiday Inn	
550 C Street, S.W.	**479-4000**
Thomas Circle, N.W.	**737-1200**
J & D Inn	**832-1492**
1007 Rhode Island Avenue, N.E.	
Quality Inn Capitol Hill	**638-1616**
415 New Jersey Avenue, N.W.	
Quality Inn Downtown	**232-8000**
1315 16th Street, N.W.	
Quality Hotel Embassy Suites	**659-9000**
2000 N Street, N.W.	

Mother's Aides, Inc.	**1-703-250-0700**
Fairfax, Virginia	
Mount Vernon Plantation	**1-703-780-2000**
George Washington Parkway, Mount Vernon, Virginia	
Mozambique (Embassy of)	**293-7146**
1990 M Street, N.W.	
Mr. Henry's	**546-8412**
601 Pennsylvania Avenue, S.E.	

Mr. Henry's Adams Morgan   **797-8882**
1836 Columbia Road, N.W.

Mr. K's   **331-8868**
2121 K Street, N.W.

Mrs. Simpson's   **332-8300**
2915 Connecticut Avenue, N.W.

Murray's Tickets   **1-703-770-5233**
1750 Rockville Pike, Rockville, Maryland

Museum of Modern Art of Latin America   **789-6016**
201 18th Street, N.W. (Virginia Ave.)

MUSEUMS

Armed Forces Medical Museum   **576-2348**
Walter Reed Army Medical Center, 6825 16th Street,
N.W., (Building 54 on Dahlia St.)

It isn't easy anymore to find exhibits that startle or surprise, but this one will. Designed to trace the development of medical practice in the military, many of the exhibits are built around the human body. Among the most popular are the body parts damaged by bullets. See the bullet that killed Abraham Lincoln and some of the bone fragments from his skull. On a lighter note, there is a wonderful display of microscopes showing how they developed through the ages. The skeleton of Able, the monkey who traveled into space in the nose cone of a rocket in 1959, is also popular.

Arthur M. Sackler Collection of Asian & Near Eastern Art   **357-2700**
Smithsonian Institution, 1050 Independence
Avenue, S.W.

    Daily 10:00 A.M.–5:30 P.M.
    Closed Christmas Day
    Admission: Free
    Metro: Smithsonian on the Blue or Orange Lines

Hidden beneath the Enid A. Haupt Garden is a treasure that could only be assembled by a merchant prince or a doctor. In this case, a doctor, Arthur M. Sackler, M.D. Opened in 1987, it is a unique collection of art focused on the Orient and the Near East. China, Japan, India, and Persia are among the many countries from which the works come. Lacquer, jade, bronze, silver, and gold are but a few of the materials which we find here. Dr. Sackler had a superb eye for acquiring fine art, and we are the benefactors. A relatively new museum, this is a real treat.

B'nai B'rith Klutznick Museum   857-6583
1640 Rhode Island Avenue, N.W.
 Monday–Friday, Sunday 10:00 A.M.–5:00 P.M.
 Closed Saturday and Jewish holidays
 Metro Station: Farragut North

Twenty centuries of Judaica are on permanent exhibit. In addition to material from the World War II era showing the many ways in which Jews were persecuted, it has many items of significance which relate to the daily life of a people whose civilization knew no national borders.

Capital Children's Museum, The   543-8600
800 3rd Street N.E. (H Street)
 Daily 10:00 A.M.–5:00 P.M.
 Closed Major Holidays
 Admission: $5.00
 Metro Station: Union Station

Like similiar institutions which are springing up in other cities, this is not really a museum. It is a learning center where children can be exposed to techniques of learning which they perceive as play. There are things to play on, tactile things to feel, and sophisticated computers that talk and can be used for drawing upon.

Corcoran Gallery of Art   638-3211
17th Street & New York Avenue, N.W.
 Tuesday-Sunday 10:00 A.M.– 4:30 P.M.
 Thursday 10:00 A.M.–9:00 P.M.
 Closed Monday
 Admission: Free
 Metro Station: Farragut West on the Blue or Orange Lines

Washington is blessed with wonderful public museums of art which began as the private collections of the very wealthy. The Corcoran is another example. William Wilson Corcoran, like his peers, was interested in American and European art and had the means to acquire it. His magnificent collection was originally housed in what is now called the Renwick Gallery. When it became too big, it was moved to quarters in the beautiful Beaux-Arts building it now occupies. The collection of Senator William Clark was added, in a separate wing, at a later date. The collections include many works of art we all know well. The most popular may be the portrait of Washington which is reproduced on the one dollar bill. The European selections were not the most important to Mr. Corcoran. He loved the American art that forms the basis for a comprehensive survey of our artists. The work ranges from early portraits through contemporary work. All of the various schools of art in between are represented here; the Hudson River School, with its beautiful paintings of the Hudson River Valley, American Impressionism, Abstract Expressionism, and yes, even Minimalism have found a home here. We must not forget to add that one of the most famous schools in the country is the Corcoran Art School. It has always been an intregal part of the museum and indicates the interest that Mr. Corcoran took in the young artists who produced the work he loved to collect. This was the first Washington museum McDowell visited when he was in charge of the arts programs for the state of Pennsylvania, and he has never forgotten it. We think you, too, will find it a worthwhile stop.

Dumbarton Collections   342-3200
1703 32nd Street, N.W.
  Tuesday–Sunday 2:00–5:00 P.M.
  Closed Monday
  Admission: Free
  Metro Station: There are none close-by. Take a taxi.

Dumbarton Oaks has such a unique place in the history of Washington and the United Nations that it is hard to isolate the portion which is the museum. The entire house contains museum quality furnishings. But in 1963, Robert Woods Bliss and his wife commissioned Philip Johnson to design a museum specifically for their collection of Byzantine and pre-Columbian art—before those art forms became popular. Johnson, whose small commissions are often his best, built a wonderful museum of nine glass cylinders, with domes, which became as famous as the collection it contains.

Freer Gallery of Art, The   357-2104
Smithsonian Institution, Jefferson Drive &
12th Street, S.W.
Closed for renovations until 1991.

Goddard Space Flight Center (NASA)   1-301-286-8981
Soil Conservation Road, (Baltimore–Washington
Pkwy./Greenbelt Rd.), Greenbelt, Maryland
  Wednesday–Sunday 10:00 A.M.–4:00 P.M.

This is one of NASA's largest research centers. In addition to its scientific work and its function as a tracking station, it also houses a fascinating Visitor's Center. Dr. Robert Goddard was one of the pioneers in rocketry, and his early work is reflected in a great collection of rockets which ranges from a replica of his 1926 model to some of the most recent designs. On the first and third Sunday of each month, model rockets are launched here—call for exact times.

**Hirshhorn Museum & Sculpture
    Garden**   **357-1461**
Smithsonian Institution, Independence Avenue and
8th Street, S.W.

> Daily 10:00 A.M.–5:30 P.M.
> Closed Christmas Day
> Admission: Free
> Metro Station: Smithsonian on the Blue or Orange
> Lines

The round building on the Mall houses the art that Joseph Hirshhorn collected during his lifetime. He was a notorious collector who bought in quantity when he found an artist whose work he liked. Today, we reap the benefit of his limitless passion for acquisition. When he died, he left his huge collection to the nation. Over 4,000 paintings and 2,000 sculptures formed the nucleus of the museum. Now under the management of the Smithsonian Institution, work is continually being added, and is beautifully displayed. There is reason to believe that the sculpture collection outshines the paintings. A wonderful collection of Henry Moore's work (the largest in the U.S.) and representative work from most of the important sculptors of the nineteenth and twentieth centuries are gathered here. Don't miss the sculpture garden which shows the outdoor pieces to perfection.

**Museum of Modern Art of Latin
    America**   **789-6016**
201 18th Street, N.W. (Virginia Ave.)

> Tuesday-Friday 10:00 A.M.–5:00 P.M.
> Saturday Noon–5:00 P.M.
> Closed Sun. & Monday
> Admission: Free
> Metro Station: Federal Triangle or Farragut West on
> the Blue or Orange Lines

Latin America has yet to carve a niche for itself in terms of modern or contemporary art. This is not to say that none of the Latin artists is interesting. But it is true that with the exception of a very few artists, this is an area whose time is yet to come. We recommend the headquarters of this OAS for its tropical gardens and lush setting.

National Air & Space Museum   **357-2700**
Smithsonian Institution, 6th Street & Independence
    Avenue, S.W.

> Daily 10:00 A.M.–5:30 P.M.
> Closed Christmas
> Admission: Free

Metro Station: Smithsonian on the Blue or Orange Lines

This is the most popular museum in the world, and there is not much we can say to improve upon that. If the combination of space exploration, rockets, astronomy, Lunar vehicles, space suits, missiles and spacecraft, Skylab, and the mystery of other planets doesn't get to you, we recommend the Work Horse Museum.

National Building Museum   783-0690
440 G Street, N.W.
> Monday–Saturday 10:00 A.M.–4:00 P.M.
> Sunday Noon–4:00 P.M.
> Admission: Free
> Metro Station: Judiciary Square on the Red Line

We've not been able to ascertain the value of this building. Built as the Pension Building in 1882, it seems to have outlived its usefulness and, for no apparent reason, was turned into a museum for the "building trades." The courtyard is the city's largest open indoor space and boasts the largest corinthian columns in the world (for what that's worth). Because of its size, it has been used for many presidential inaugural balls including those of Nixon, Carter, Reagan, and Bush.

National Capital Trolley Museum   1-301-384-6088
1313 Bonifant Road (Layhill/Notley Rds.),
Silver Spring, Maryland
> Saturday & Sunday Noon–5:00 P.M.
> Admission: Free
> Trolley rides:
> Adults $1.50
> Children under 18 $1.00

Trolley cars and related memorabilia occupy a reproduction of an old terminal building. There is also a working trolley that will take you on a one-and-a-half mile ride.

National Firearms Museum   828-6253
1600 Rhode Island Avenue, N.W.
> Daily 10:00 A.M.–4:00 P.M.
> No admission charge
> Metro Station: Farragut North on Red Line

The National Rifle Association has assembled a large collection of guns here. While many of them are used to trace the development of this type of weapon, there are also a number of guns that have belonged to famous people, like the shotgun of President Eisenhower. Well worth a visit if you like guns.

National Gallery of Art—East
  Building   737-4215
4th Street, N.W. (Constitution Ave./Madison Dr.)
  Monday–Saturday 10:00 A.M.–5:00 P.M.
  Sunday Noon–9:00 P.M.
  Closed Christmas & New Year's Day
  Admission: Free
  Metro Station: Judiciary Square on the Red Line. Archives on the Yellow Line. Smithsonian on the Blue or Orange Lines

Paul Mellon and his sister, Alisa Mellon Bruce, children of the original donor, gave the East Building to the nation in order to house the rapidly growing collection of modern art. A work of art in itself, the building was designed by I.M. Pei & Partners, who connected it to the West Building with an underground passageway, making it easy for visitors to move from one collection to the other. Works by the modern masters (and by younger artists who are just beginning to make their mark) are beautifully displayed in this contemporary building. Popular with local residents and tourists, the fine permanent collection and many changing exhibitions have made the East Wing a major focus for the arts in our capital.

National Gallery of Art—West
  Building   842-6188
Constitution Avenue, N.W. (3rd/7th Sts.)
Monday–Saturday 10:00 A.M.–5:00 P.M.
  Sunday Noon–9:00 P.M.
  Closed Christmas & New Year's Day
  Admission: Free
  Metro Station: Judiciary Square on the Red Line. Archives on the Yellow Line. Smithsonian on the Blue or Orange Lines

Opened in 1941, The National Gallery has taken its place as one of our leading fine art museums. The West Building and original collection were a gift of Andrew W. Mellon, and while federal funds are available for daily operations, all artworks continue to be acquired by donation. The collection, reflecting the interests of Mr. Mellon, has been focused primarily upon European and American art and excells in these areas. The section covering Italian painting and sculpture is considered to be the finest in the western hemisphere. Dutch, German, French, Flemish, British, and of course, American work are also displayed. Many of the great masters are represented here, and one shouldn't visit Washington without spending a few hours wandering these marble halls.

National Museum of African Art   **364-1001**
Smithsonian Institution   **357-2700**
The Quadrangle (950 Independence Avenue, S.W.)
Jefferson Drive between 11th and 12th Streets, S.W.
> Daily 10:00 A.M.–5:30 P.M.
> Closed Christmas
> Admission: Free
> Metro Station: Smithsonian on the Blue or Orange Lines

This claims to be the only museum in the country dedicated to the study and exhibition of the art of sub-Saharan Africa. Having looked at exhibitions in major museums for over 30 years, we find that hard to believe. It is impossible to study African art without studying the culture which made it. Most of the objects were made for a purpose—there was no art made just for art's sake. The museum therefore studies the way the various civilizations interact and influence each other. One of the problems affecting the collection of African art is that the materials the artisans used were easily destroyed. Wood, fiber, fur, feathers, textiles, all are susceptible to rot, cracking caused by high humidity, and the breakage caused by everyday use. It is difficult, therefore, to find objects that have survived, and we are lucky to have such treasures as this museum provides.

National Museum of American Art   **357-3156**
Smithsonian Institution   **357-2700**
Gallery Place at 8th and G Streets, N.W.
> Daily 10:00 A.M.–5:30 P.M.
> Closed Christmas
> Admission: Free
> Metro Station: Gallery Place on Red or Yellow Lines

The former U.S. Patent Office now houses two museums: the National Museum of American Art on the North side and the National Portrait Gallery on the South side. If you are pressed for time (and what tourist isn't?) see both galleries on the same day. The National Gallery of Art is a chronologically arranged survey of the whole of American art. It is the oldest art collection in the country and currently contains more than 33,000 items. It presents material from every period and makes it possible to view the way in which art has progressed and developed in the United States.

National Museum of American
      History   **357-2700**
Smithsonian Institution, 14th Street and Constitution Avenue, N.W.
> Daily 10:00 A.M.–5:30 P.M.
> Closed Christmas

Admission: Free
Metro Station: Smithsonian or Federal Triangle on
Blue or Orange Lines

Whether a tourist or a local resident you'll find plenty here to interest and fascinate. With a mandate to deal with both scientific and cultural areas, it seems to have almost everything that relates to our history. To give you an idea: an enormous collection of models from the U.S. Patent Office, such as a Model T Ford from 1913, Alexander Graham Bell's first telephone, and Edison's light bulb. Mementos from the movies and TV, such as Judy Garland's famous ruby slippers, and Archie Bunker's chair. McDowell's favorite is a locomotive, Adele's is the gowns of some of our First Ladies.

National Museum of Health & Medicine 576-2348

Walter Reed Army Medical Center, 6900 Georgia
Avenue, N.W. (Fern/Aspen Sts.)
Monday–Friday 9:30 A.M.–4:30 P.M.
Saturday–Sunday 11:30 A.M.–4:30 P.M.
Admission: Free
Metro Station: Tacoma on the Red Line

Originally founded to research medical problems during the Civil War, this is not a museum for the squeamish. For example, it has a famous exhibition of severed limbs. It may have more appeal if you are a doctor or a researcher of medical questions.

National Museum of Man. *See* National Museum of Natural History

National Museum of Natural History 357-2700

Smithsonian Institution, 10th Street and Constitution
Avenue, N.W.
Daily 10:00 A.M.–5:30 P.M.
Closed Christmas
Admission: Free
Metro Station: Smithsonian or Federal Triangle on the
Blue or Orange Lines

Another wonderful experience and another reason why it takes so long to see the Washington museums. This is a huge collection, and you will probably have to choose between exhibits instead of seeing everything. From the time you are greeted by the giant elephant in the entrance hall to your last lingering look at the Hope Diamond, you will be enthralled by the marvelous collections. Children will enjoy the Insect Zoo, where they can actually fondle the little critters, and the Discovery Room, where there are all kinds of things with which they can interact.

**National Museum of Women in the
    Arts**   783-5000
801 13th Street, N.W.
    Monday-Saturday 10:00 A.M.–5:00 P.M.
    Sunday Noon–5:00 P.M.
    Closed Thanksgiving/Christmas/New Years Day
    Admission:
    Adults: $3.00
    Children: $2.00
A very controversial museum which segregates the art
made by women from the rest of art history (apparently
made by men). The question is whether this helps women
to claim their rightful place or simply isolates them more.
While it is true that many women whose names are unknown to the public are represented here, there are also
many whose place in history is assured and whose work is
coveted by museums large and small. Sonia Delaunay and
Mary Cassatt were in our art history textbooks, as were
Kathe Kollwitz, Georgia O'Keefe, Alice Neel, Louise Nevel-
son, and Sophie Taeuber-Arp. Other renowned artists represented are Anne Truitt, Elizabeth Murray, Nancy Graves,
Helen Frankenthaler, and Audrey Flack. Only time will sort
out the politics, but in the meantime, this is an interesting
place to see a lot of good art.

National Portrait Gallery   357-2920
Smithsonian Institution   357-2137
Gallery Place at F and 8th Streets, N.W.
    Monday–Saturday 10:00 A.M.–5:00 P.M.
    Sunday Noon–9:00 P.M.
    Closed Christmas & New Year's Day
    Admission: Free
    Metro Station: Judiciary Square on the Red Line. Ar-
    chives on the Yellow Line. Smithsonian on the Blue or
    Orange Lines
Located on the South side of the former U.S. Patent Office, this collection shares the building with the National
Museum of American Art. There are literally thousands of
portraits here. Many of them are familiar to us from school-
books, but others will be totally unknown. Almost every
artist who did portraits, whether famous or not, is represented, and the experience is overwhelming. Try to coordi-
nate a visit here with one to the National Museum of
American Art.

Phillips Collection, The   387-0961
1600 21st Street, N.W. (Q St.)
    Tuesday–Saturday 10:00 A.M.–5:00 P.M.
    Sunday 2:00 P.M.–7:00 P.M.

Closed Monday
Admission: Contribution
Metro Station: Red Line to Dupont Circle

Started as the personal collection of Duncan Phillips, this is one of the most beautiful in Washington and should not be missed. During extensive and time-consuming renovations, the collection was sent on tour to numerous museums in the United States and around the world and was seen by almost a million people. Phillips concentrated on French and American artists and acquired works by masters such as Renoir, Cezanne, Bonnard, Klee, and Van Gogh. Although lesser known at the time, Americans like Steiglitz, Hartley, Demuth, Arthur Dove, Georgia O'Keeffe, Marin, and Scheeler were bought and occupy prominent places in the collection.

Renwick Gallery, The   357-1300
The National Museum of American Art
Pennsylvania Avenue and 17th Street, N.W.
    Daily 10:00 A.M.–5:30 P.M.
    Closed Christmas
    Admission: Free
    Metro Station: Farragut West on the Blue or Orange
    Lines

Originally built by William Wilson Corcoran to house his personal collection of art, it was quickly outgrown. When he built the Corcoran Gallery to re-house his collection, the Renwick was used as the Court of Claims for 65 years. It has been restored and is now used by the Smithsonian as an exhibition area for American crafts and decorative arts.

Sackler Collection, The . *See* the
    Arthur M. Sackler Collection

Smithsonian Institution, The. *See*
    SIGHTSEEING

Sumner School Museum & Archives   727-3419
1201 17th Street, N.W. (M St./Rhode Island Ave.)
Monday–Saturday 9:00 A.M.–5:00 P.M.
Admission: Free

The first school for African American children in Washington. It now features exhibitions concerning culture and the local history of the neighborhood. All of the public school records are also housed here. This is a historical site because of the use to which the building was first put, but if you are on a tight schedule there are more important museums commemorating African American history.

Textile Museum, The   667-0441
2320 S Street, N.W.
>   Tuesday–Saturday 10:00 A.M.–5:00 P.M.
>   Sunday 1:00–5:00 P.M.
>   Closed Monday & Holidays
>   Admission: Free
>   Metro Station: Dupont Circle on the Red Line

Primarily for the Mediterranean and North Africa, this collection was started by collector George H. Myers. His former home, which now houses over 14,000 textiles and about 1500 rugs is a must if you want to see textiles. There is also a large and important research library on the premises.

U.S. Navy Memorial Museum   433-2651
The Navy Yard, 9th and M Streets, Building 76
>   Monday–Friday 9:00 A.M.–4:00 P.M.
>   Saturday–Sunday 10:00 A.M.–5:00 P.M.
>   Admission: Free
>   Metro Station: Eastern Market on the Blue or Orange Lines

When we think of the early history of our country we always think first of ships. The ships that brought our ancestors here and the navy that protected them after they arrived. This museum depicts the history of the navy from 1775 to the present. There is everything you might want to see, including the weapons that the children can actually play with. Of course, since we are dealing with the navy, there is a submarine room—one of the most popular with the kids.

U.S. Marine Corps Museum   433-3840
The Navy Yard, 9th and M Streets, Building 58
>   Monday–Saturday 10:00 A.M.–4:00 P.M.
>   Sunday Noon–5:00 P.M.
>   Admission: Free
>   Metro Station: Eastern Market on Blue or Orange Lines

Exhibits trace the history of the Marine Corps and re-create events that are famous in their annals, including the memorabilia that are part of such a glorious military past. Uniforms, weapons, and the flags that went before them.

Victualling Warehouse Maritime
     Museum. *See* **Annapolis,**
     Maryland

Washington Dolls' House & Toy
     Museum   1-301-244-0024
5236 44th Street, N.W. (Jenifer/Harrison Sts.), Chevy Chase, Maryland

Tuesday–Saturday 10:00 A.M.–5:00 P.M.
Sunday Noon–5:00 P.M.
Closed Monday
Admission:
Adults: $3.00
Children: $1.00
Metro Station: Friendship Heights on the Red Line

Flora Gill Jacobs is recognized as the leading authority on the history of doll houses, and this is her museum. As she says, "It is dedicated to the proposition that doll's houses of the past comprise a study of the decorative arts in miniature, and that toys of the past reflect social history." There are so many things to see that we can't begin to list them—several hundred dolls are shown in the many interiors provided by the shops, houses, and rooms. If you are interested in rare dolls, they are here, too. Don't miss the shops! There are two, one for collectors of doll houses, furniture, little stuff for decorating, and of course, dolls. The second shop is for people who like to build doll houses and supplies everything necessary to do just that.

MUSIC

"Where can we go for some live music?" is a question frequently asked of concierges. Washington offers an excellent variety, with the following among the most popular. *See* JAZZ for additional listings.

Bayou, The (Rock & Roll, New Wave, Blues)   333-2897
3135 K Street, N.W.

Comedy and national and local blues and rock groups perform at this club on the Georgetown waterfront. Tickets are available at the Bayou box office after 8:00 P.M. or through TicketCenter.

Birchmere, The (Country, Folk, Bluegrass)   1-703-549-5919
3901 Mt. Vernon Avenue, Alexandria, Virginia

This intimate club features country, folk, and bluegrass performed by both local and national acts. Thursday belong to the Bluegrass band the Seldom Scene. Tickets are usually not available in advance, so it's best to arrive early for popular acts.

Cafe Lautrec (Jazz, Tap Dancing)   265-6436
2431 18th Street, N.W.

You can hear anything from piano and jazz combos to vocalists at this lively Adams Morgan bistro. In addition, tap dancer Johne Forges performs on the long wooden bar Thursday through Saturday nights.

Dubliner, The (Irish Folk Singers)   737-3773
520 North Capitol Street, N.W.

Nightly entertainment at this authentic Irish pub in the Phoenix Park Hotel features old Irish and Celtic tunes and jigs.

**Mr. Henry's Adams Morgan
(Rhythm & Blues)**   797-8882
1836 Columbia Road, N.W.

Julia Nixon, who performed a lead role in "Dreamgirls" on Broadway, leads her rhythm-and-blues group, Julia and Company, in this unassuming locale. When she sings gospel, the decor doesn't matter.

Nightclub 9:30 (New Wave, Reggae)   393-0930
930 F Street, N.W.

Washington's reigning (at this writing, anyway) new wave nightclub hosts alternative and progressive rock bands of both local and national quality.

Music Box Center   783-9399
918 F Street, N.W.

My Other Secretary   429-1997
1133 15th Street, N.W., Suite 1010

N

Nam Viet   1-703-522-7110
1127 North Hudson Street (Wilson Blvd.),
Arlington, Virginia

**National Capital Area Federation of
Garden Clubs**   399-5958
2402 R Street, N.E.

Nathan's   338-2000
3150 M Street, N.W.

National Air & Space Museum   357-2500
The Smithsonian Institution, 6th Street and Independence Avenue, S.W.

National Aquarium, The   377-2825
Department of Commerce Building, 14th Street and Constitution Avenue, N.W.

National Arboretum, The   475-4815
3501 New York Avenue, N.E.

National Archives, The   523-3000
8th Street and Constitution Avenue, N.W.

**National Association of Colored
    Women's Clubs**   726-2044
5808 16th Street, N.W.

**National Association of Executives
    Club**   223-1770
1400 M Street, N.W.

National Building Museum   783-0690
440 G Street, N.W.

National Capital Poison Center   625-3333
Georgetown University Hospital

National Capital Trolley Museum   1-301-384-6088
1313 Bonifant Road (Layhill/Notley Rds.), Silver Spring,
Maryland

National Car Rental   1-800-328-4567

National Cathedral, The   537-6200
Massachusetts & Wisconsin Avenues, N.W.

National Democratic Club, The   543-2035
30 Ivy Street, S.E.

National Economists Club, The   293-2698

National Firearms Museum   828-6258
1600 Rhode Island Avenue, N.W.

**National Gallery of Art—East
    Building**   737-4215
4th Street (Constitution Avenue/Madison Dr., N.W.)

**National Gallery of Art—West
    Building**
6th Street (Constitution Avenue/Madison Dr., N.W.)

**National Geographic Society
    Headquarters**   857-7000
17th & M Streets, N.W.

National Lawyers Club, The   638-3200
1815 H Street, N.W.

National Map Gallery & Travel Center   789-0100
Union Station (West Hall), 50 Massachusetts Avenue, N.E.

National Museum of African Art   364-1001
The Smithsonian Institution, The Quadrangle

**National Museum of American Art,
The**   357-3156
The Smithsonian Institution, Gallery Place
(8th/G Sts., N.W.)

**National Museum of American
History**   357-2700
The Smithsonian Institution, 14th Street and Constitution
Avenue, N.W.

**National Museum of Health &
Medicine**   576-2348
Walter Reed Army Medical Center, 6900 Georgia Avenue,
N.W. (Fern/Aspen Sts.)

National Museum of Natural History   357-2700
The Smithsonian Institution, 10th Street and Constitution
Avenue, N.W.

**National Museum of Women in the
Arts**   783-5000
801 13th Street, N.W.

National Portrait Gallery, The   357-2920
The Smithsonian Institution   357-2137
Gallery Place (F/8th Sts., N.W.)

National Sculpture Garden Ice Rink   347-9042
Across the Mall from the Hirshhorn Museum

**National Shrine of the Immaculate
Conception**   526-8300
4th Street and Michigan Avenue, N.W.

National Theater, The   554-1900
1321 East Street, N.W.   628-6161

National Zoological Park   673-4800
3001 Connecticut Avenue, N.W.

Nautical & Scientific Shop   1-301-942-0636
3760 Howard Avenue, Kensington, Maryland

Neiman Marcus   966-9700
Mazza Gallery, Wisconsin and Western Avenue, N.W.

Nepal (Embassy of)   667-4550
2131 Leroy Place, N.W.

Netherlands (Embassy of)   244-5300
4200 Linnean Avenue, N.W.

Neuchatel Chocolates   347-8570
The Willard Hotel, Suite 115

New Heights   234-4110
2317 Calvert Street, N.W. (Connecticut Ave.)

New Orleans Cafe	**234-5111**
1790 Columbia Road, N.W. (Columbia Rd.)	
New Orleans Emporium	**328-3421**
2477 18th Street, N.W. (Columbia Rd.)	
New Playwright's Theater, The	**232-1122**
1742 Church Street, N.W.	
New York Avenue Presbyterian	
Church	**393-3700**
1313 New York Avenue, N.W.	
New Zealand (Embassy of)	**328-4800**
37 Observatory Circle, N.W.	
News Room, The	**332-1489**
1753 Connecticut Avenue, N.W.	

NEWSSTANDS

B & B News Stand	**234-0494**
2621 Connecticut Avenue, N.W.	**234-0497**
Chronicles	**293-6247**
2000 Pennsylvania Avenue, N.W.	
Hudson Country News	**783-1720**
The Shops at National Place, 1331 Pennsylvania Avenue, N.W.	
Key Bridge News Stand	**338-2626**
3326 M Street, N.W.	
News Room, The	**332-1489**
1753 Connecticut Avenue, N.W.	
Huge selection of out-of-town newspapers.	
Periodicals	**223-2526**
1825 I Street, N.W.	

Nicaragua (Embassy of)	**387-4371**
1627 New Hampshire Avenue, N.W.	
Nicholas	**347-8900**
The Mayflower Hotel, 1127 Connecticut Avenue, N.W. (L/DeSalles Sts.)	
Niger (Embassy of)	**483-4224**
2204 R Street, N.W.	
Nigeria (Embassy of)	**822-1500**
2201 M Street, N.W.	
Nightclub 9:30	**393-0930**
930 F Street, N.W.	

NIGHTCLUBS

The term "Nightclub" means a lot of different things in Washington. There is only one real nightclub in town: Anton's 1201 Club. None of the other nightspots seem to mean the Ginger Rogers/Fred Astaire type of evening on the town.

Anton's 1201 Club   783-1201
1201 Pennsylvania Avenue, N.W.

Featuring big name entertainers like Carmen McRae, Anthony Newley, and the McGuire Sisters, this Art Deco supper club is unique in the city. They are open for lunch and dinner daily. Call for information on current entertainment. If Anton's is not your cup of tea, refer to one of the following subject headings in order to identify other nightlife: Bars, Gay Bars, Piano Bars, Singles Bars, Sports Bars, Comedy, Dancing, Dance Clubs/Discos, Jazz, Music

Nora   462-5143
2109 R Street, N.W.

Northwest Airlines   1-800-225-2525

Northwest Park   1-301-598-6100
15701 Layhill Road, Wheaton, Maryland

Norway (Embassy of)   333-6000
2720 34th Street, N.W.

O

Oatlands   1-703-777-3174
State Road 15, (six miles south of Leesburg), Leesburg, Virginia

Occidental   783-1475
1475 Pennsylvania Avenue, N.W. (14th/15th Sts.)

Occidental Grill   783-1476
1475 Pennsylvania Avenue, N.W. (14th/15th Sts.)

Octagon, The   638-3105
1799 New York Avenue, N.W. (18th St.)

Officers Club of Walter Reed   726-8806
6825 16th Street, N.W.

Okyo   342-2675
1519 Wisconsin Avenue, N.W.

Old Ebbitt Grill   347-4800
675 15th Street, N.W. (F/G Sts.)

Old Post Office Tower   523-5691

Old Stone House, The   426-6851
3051 M Street, N.W., Georgetown

OLD TOWN

Alexandria, Virginia

Once the home of both George Washington and Robert E. Lee, Alexandria is located about five miles south of Georgetown. It's easily reachable by Metro—just take the Yellow Line to the King Street Station and transfer to a DASH bus which will deliver you to the visitors' center at the Ramsay House (221 King Street, 1-703-838-4200). There you can pick up maps, a self-guided walking tour brochure, and tips on where to dine. Founded as a trading port by a group of Scottish tobacco merchants in the mid-eighteenth century, Alexandria is extremely history-conscious. George Washington, the town's most famous native son, shopped, ate, drank, prayed, and joined the Masons here. The George Washington Masonic National Memorial contains a bronze statue of Washington, a replica of the Masonic meeting room where he was the Worshipful Master of Lodge 22, and relics including Washington's Masonic apron and the silver trowel he used to lay the cornerstone of the Capitol. George Washington, Robert E. Lee, and a host of other influential and famous families worshipped at Christ Church (118 North Washington St., 1-703-549-1450). Designed by architect James Wren, the church has been in continuous use since 1773. Gadsby's Tavern (134 North Royal Street, 1-703-838-4242), Washington's headquarters during the French and Indian War, later became the scene of Alexandria's most lavish parties. During August Tavern Days (call for exact dates), Colonial life is recreated here with eighteenth- and nineteenth-century music, food, and entertainment. Other sites of interest are Robert E. Lee's boyhood home (607 Oronoco St., 1-703-548-8485), the Lee-Fendall House (614 Oronoco St., 1-703-548-1789), and the Carlyle House (121 North Fairfax St., 1-703-549-2997)—one of Virginia's most architecturally impressive eighteenth-century houses. Alexandria is a browser's paradise. The red-brick sidewalks are lined with unusual shops selling everything from souvenir T-shirts to priceless antiques. On the waterfront, a former munitions plant, the Torpedo Factory, has been converted to studio space for some 200 professional artists and craftspeople. The works for sale are of mixed quality, but you have unique opportunity to see the artists at work. The lower level houses Alexandria architects at work in the laboratory and museum. Alexandria offers all forms of fare, from fast food to haute cuisine. The Hard Times Cafe (1404 King St., 1-703-685-5340) specializes in chili—both Cincinnati and Texas style served in a raucous atmosphere with loud country and western music. Terrazza (710 King St., 1-703-683-6900) offers the same refined Northern Italian fare as its Downtown brother, Tiberio.

Old Town Coffee, Tea & Spice   **1-703-683-0856**
215 South Union Street, Alexandria, Virginia

Old Town Holiday Inn   **1-703-549-6080**
480 King Street   **1-800-368-5047**
Alexandria, Virginia

Old Town Trolley Tours   **1-703-269-3021**
Arlington, Virginia

Old Town Trolley Tours of Washington   **269-3020**
3150 V Street, N.E.

Old Treasury Building, The   **1-301-267-8149**
State Circle, Annapolis, Maryland

Olsson's Books & Records   **338-9544**
1239 Wisconsin Avenue, N.W.

Olsson's Books & Records   **785-2662**
3249 M Street, N.W.

Olympic Airlines   **1-800-223-1226**

Oman (Embassy of)   **387-1980**
2342 Massachusetts Avenue, N.W.

Omega   **745-9158**
1858 Columbia Road, N.W. (Belmont/18th Sts.)

Omni Georgetown Hotel, The   **293-3100**
2121 P Street, N.W.   **1-800-THE-OMNI**

Omni Shoreham Hotel   **234-0700**
2500 Calvert Street, N.W.   **1-800-THE-OMNI**

One Good Tern   **1-703-820-8376**
170 Fern Street, Alexandria, Virginia

One Step Down   **331-8863**
2517 Pennsylvania Avenue, N.W.

One Washington Circle Hotel   **872-1680**
One Washington Circle

Onslow Square   **1-301-530-9393**
4131 Howard Avenue, Kensington, Maryland

Opera House, The   254-3770
Kennedy Center for the Performing Arts,
New Hampshire Avenue, N.W. and Rock Creek Parkway

Organization of American States, The   789-3751
17th Street, N.W. and Constitution Avenue

Orpheus Records   337-7970
3249 M Street, N.W.

Osuna Gallery   296-1963
406 7th Street, N.W.

P

Paint Brush Golf Course   1-301-935-0330
4690 University Boulevard, College Park, Maryland
Pakistan (Embassy of)   939-6200
2315 Massachusetts Avenue, N.W.
Pall Mall   965-5353
3235 M Street, N.W.
Palm, The   293-9091
1225 19th Street, N.W. (M/N Sts.)
Pampillonia
1213 Connecticut Avenue, N.W.   628-6305
Mazza Gallerie, 5300 Wisconsin Avenue, N.W   363-6305
Pan Am   1-800-421-5330
Panama (Embassy of)   483-1407
2862 McGill Terrace, N.W.
Panic Deliveries   589-9006
Silver Spring, Maryland
Paper Moon   965-6666
1073 31st Street, N.W.
Paraguay (Embassy of)   483-1407
2400 Massachusetts Avenue, N.W.
Park Hyatt, The   789-1234
24th and M Streets   1-800-922-PARK

PARKS

    **Chesapeake & Ohio Canal National
        Historic Park**   1-301-739-4200
  Borders the Potomac River from Georgetown to
  Cumberland, Maryland.

Constitution Gardens
Constitution Avenue between 17th and
23rd Streets, N.W.

Dumbarton Oaks　　　　　　　　　　**342-3212**
31st and R Streets, N.W.

Hillwood Museum Gardens　　　　　**686-0410**
4155 Linnean Avenue, N.W.

Kenilworth Aquatic Gardens　　　　**426-6905**
Kenilworth Avenue and Douglas Street, N.E.

Lady Bird Johnson Park
Across Memorial Bridge and off George Washington
Parkway in Virginia

National Arboretum　　　　　　　　**475-4815**
3501 New York Avenue, N.E.

Rock Creek Nature Center　　　　　**426-6829**
5200 Glover Road, N.W., Rock Creek Park

Rock Creek Park
Cathedral Avenue and Rock Creek Parkway, N.W.

Theodore Roosevelt Island　　**1-703-285-2600**
Off the George Washington Memorial Parkway, north
of the Theodore Roosevelt Bridge.

Tulip Library
Near the Tidal Basin and the Jefferson Memorial

U.S. Botanic Garden　　　　　　　　**225-8333**
Maryland Avenue at 1st Street, S.W.

Patriot Center　　　　　　　　**1-703-323-2675**
4400 University Drive, Fairfax, Virginia

Peking Inn Gourmet　　　　　　**1-703-671-8088**
6029 Leesburg Pike, Falls Church, Virginia

Pen Arts Club　　　　　　　　　　**785-1643**
1300 17th Street, N.W.

Penderbrook Club　　　　　　　**1-703-385-3700**
3700 Golf Trail Lane, Fairfax, Virginia

Penguin Feathers　　　　　　　　**965-7172**
3225 M Street, N.W.

Penn Camera　　　　　　　　　　**347-5777**
915 E Street, N.W.

Pentagon, The　　　　　　　　**1-703-695-1776**
Route 1 & I-395, Arlington, Virginia

Peoples Drug Stores, Inc.
7 Dupont Circle, N.W.   **785-1466**
14th Street and Thomas Circle, N.W.   **628-0720**

Periodicals   **223-2526**
1825 I Street, N.W.

Perry's   **234-6218**
1811 Columbia Road, N.W.

Pershing Park   **737-6938**
15th Street & Pennsylvania Avenue, N.W.

Peru (Embassy of)   **833-9860**
1700 Massachusetts Avenue, N.W.

Peterson House   **426-6830**
516 10th Street, N.W.

PHARMACIES/DRUG STORES (24 HOUR)

There are thousands of pharmacies in Washington. We list below only the ones that are open 24-hours a day.

Peoples Drug Stores, Inc.
7 Dupont Circle, N.W.   **785-1466**
14th Street and Thomas Circle, N.W.   **628-0720**

Phase One   **544-6831**
525 8th Street, S.E.

Philippine Airlines   **1-800-435-9725**

Philippines (Embassy of)   **483-1414**
1617 Massachusetts Avenue, N.W.

Phillips Collection, The   **387-0961**
1600 21st Street, N.W.

Philly's Finest   **635-7790**
1601 Rhode Island Avenue, N.E.

Phineas Frogg & Friends   **543-1686**
210 7th Street, S.E.

Phoenix Park Hotel   **638-6900**
520 North Capitol Street, N.W.

Phyllis Van Auken Antiques   **1-301-933-3772**
10425 Fawcett Street, Kensington, Maryland

PIANO BARS

For the transition between a hard day's business and an entertaining evening, there's nothing more relaxing than a drink in pleasant surroundings with piano music in the background. The following locations are also recommended for after-dinner drinks.

Allegro 638-2626
The Sheraton Carlton Hotel, 923 16th Street, N.W.

Anton's Loyal Opposition 546-4545
400 1st Street, S.E.

Bar, The 393-1000
The Capital Hilton Hotel, 16th & K Streets, N.W.

Federal Bar, The 429-1700
Vista International Hotel, 1400 M Street, N.W.

John Hay Room 638-2260
The Hay-Adams Hotel, 800 16th Street, N.W.

Old Ebbitt Grill 347-4800
675 15th Street, N.W.

Terrace Room, The 293-2100
Ritz-Carlton Hotel, 2100 Massachusetts Avenue, N.W.

Town & Country, The 347-3000
The Mayflower Hotel, 1127 Connecticut Avenue, N.W.

Piedmont Airlines 620-0400

Pierre Deux 244-6226
Mazza Gallerie, 5300 Wisconsin Avenue, N.W.

Pietro Hair Salon 628-3706
The Capitol Hilton Hotel, 1001 16th Street, N.W.

Pimlico Racetrack 1-301-542-9400
Baltimore, Maryland

Pineapple, Inc., The 1-703-836-3639
132 King Street, Alexandria, Virginia

Plain Jane's 1-703-548-2457
222 North Lee Street, Alexandria, Virginia

PLANTATIONS

It's fascinating to tour the plantations near Washington. For some of them, like Mt. Vernon, there are bus or boat tours to transport you. You will need a car to visit others. The plantations are restored and maintained so that they give a view of life as it was in the good old days. There is wide variety among the plantations included on our list; they range from elegant, stately homes to working farms.

Gunston Hall 1-703-550-9220
10709 Gunston Road (Route 1), Lorton, Virginia

Hampton National Historic Site 1-301-962-0688
535 Hampton Lane (Delaney Valley Rd.), Towson, Maryland

Monticello   **1-804-295-8181**
Routes 20 and I-64, (exit 24A), two miles southeast of
Charlottesville, Virginia

Morven Park   **1-703-777-2414**
Old Waterford Road, two miles north of Leesburg,
Virginia

Mount Vernon   **1-703-780-2000**
South end of George Washington Parkway, (16 miles
south of Washington) Mount Vernon, Virginia

Oatlands   **1-703-777-3174**
State Road 15, six miles south of Leesburg, Virginia

Sotterley Mansion   **1-301-373-2280**
Route 235 (south of Waldorf), Hollywood, Maryland

Stratford Hall Plantation   **1-804-493-8038**
State Road 214, east of Fredericksburg, Virginia

Sully Plantation   **1-703-437-1794**
Sully Road (off State Road 28), Chantilly, Virginia

Woodlawn Plantation   **1-703-780-4000**
9000 Richmond Highway (U.S. 1/Route 235), 14 miles
south of Washington, Virginia

Poison Control Center	**625-3333**
Poland (Embassy of)	**234-3800**
2640 16th Street, N.W.	
Police	**911**
Politics & Prose	**364-1919**
5015 Connecticut Avenue, N.W.	
Polo Shop (Ralph Lauren)	**463-7460**
1220 Connecticut Avenue, N.W.	
Portugal (Embassy of)	**332-3007**
2310 Tracy Place, N.W.	

POSTAGE

The following are the standard rates for postage:
    Letters (U.S.) $.25 per half ounce (a normal letter)
    Postcards (U.S.) $.15 each
    Letters (overseas) $.45 per half ounce (a normal letter)
    Postcards (overseas) $.36 each
    Rate increases are anticipated for 1991, however, data is
not available as we go to press

POST OFFICES

Main Post Office   **523-2323**
North Capitol Street & Massachusettes Avenue, N.E.
Open 24 hours a day.

Potomac Appalachian Trail Club, The   638-5306
1718 N Street, N.W.

Potomac Boat Club, The   333-9737
3530 Water Street, N.W.

Potomac Butter & Egg Co., Inc.   554-9200
220 E Street, S.W.

Potomac Party Cruises   683-6076

Potomic Mills
2700 Potomac Mills Circle, Prince William, Virginia

Powerscourt   737-3776
The Phoenix Park Hotel, 520 N. Capitol Street, N.W.
(Massachuetts Ave.)

Presentation Group/Washington   337-5500
2121 Wisconsin Avenue, N.W.

PRESIDENTS

George Washington	1789–1797
John Adams	1797–1801
Thomas Jefferson	1801–1809
James Madison	1809–1817
James Monroe	1817–1825
John Quincy Adams	1825–1829
Andrew Jackson	1829–1837
Martin Van Buren	1837–1841
William H. Harrison	1841
John Tyler	1841–1845
James K. Polk	1845–1849
Zachary Taylor	1849–1850
Millard Fillmore	1850–1853
Franklin Pierce	1853–1857
James Buchanan	1857–1861
Abraham Lincoln	1861–1865
Andrew Johnson	1865–1869
Ulysses S. Grant	1869–1877
Rutherford B. Hayes	1877–1881
James A. Garfield	1881
Chester A. Arthur	1881–1885

Grover Cleveland	1885–1889
Benjamin Harrison	1889–1893
Grover Cleveland	1893–1897
William McKinley	1897–1901
Theodore Roosevelt	1901–1909
William H. Taft	1909–1913
Woodrow Wilson	1913–1921
Warren G. Harding	1921–1923
Calvin Coolidge	1923–1929
Herbert C. Hoover	1929–1933
Franklin D. Roosevelt	1933–1945
Harry S. Truman	1945–1953
Dwight D. Eisenhower	1953–1961
John F. Kennedy	1961–1963
Lyndon B. Johnson	1963–1969
Richard M. Nixon	1969–1974
Gerald R. Ford	1974–1977
James E. Carter, Jr.	1977–1981
Ronald W. Reagan	1981–1989
George Bush	1989–

Prime Plus 783-0166
727 15th Street, N.W. (H St./New York Ave.)

Prime Rib 466-8811
2020 K Street, N.W. (20th/21st Sts.)

Primi Piatti 223-3600
2013 P Street, N.W. (20th/21st Sts.)

Prince George's Hospital Center 1-301-341-3300
3001 Hospital Drive, Cheverly, Maryland

Pro Photo 223-1292
1919 Pennsylvania Avenue, N.W.

Providence Hospital 269-7000
1150 Varnum Street, N.E.

Provisions 543-0694
218 7th Street, S.E.

Pyramid Bookstore 328-0190
2849 Georgia Avenue, N.W.

Q

QMS 966-8966
1275 K Street, N.W.

Quality Hotel Capitol Hill 638-1616
415 New Jersey Avenue, N.W.

Quality Hotel Embassy Suites 659-9000
2000 N Street, N.W.

Quality Inn Capitol Hill Hotel 638-1616
415 New Jersey Avenue, N.W. 1-800-228-5151

Quality Inn Downtown 232-8000
1315 16th Street, N.W.

Quator (Embassy of) 338-0111
600 New Hampshire Avenue, N.W.

R

R. Saunders Jewelers 772-8210
Capital Plaza Mall

R.T.'s 1-703-684-6010
3804 Mount Vernon Avenue (Glebe Rd.), Alexandria,
Virginia

RACE TRACKS

Laurel Racetrack (Thoroughbreds) 1-301-725-0400
Laural, Maryland
Open from October until March and from June until early
July. The Washington DC International is run in October.

Pimlico (Thoroughbreds) 1-301-542-9400
Baltimore, Maryland
Open from March until the end of May and from July
until the end of October. The Preakness, the second race in
the Triple Crown, is run on the third Saturday in May.

Rosecroft Raceway (Trotters) 1-301-567-4000
Oxon Hill/Fort Washington, Maryland
Open from mid-January until the end of May and from
October until the middle of December.

Radisson Park Terrace 232-7000
1515 Rhode Island Avenue, N.W.

RAILROADS

Amtrak	**1-800-872-7245**
Metroliner Service	**1-800-523-8720**
Ticket offices:	
1721 K Street, N.W.	**484-7540**
Union Station	**484-7540**

Raleigh's   **785-7070**
1130 Connecticut Avenue, N.W.

Ramada Renaissance Techworld   **898-9000**
999 9th Street, N.W.   **1-800-228-9898**

Rape Crisis Center   **333-7273**

Racquet & Jog   **861-6939**
915 19th Street, N.W.

Record Mart   **1-703-683-4583**
217 King Street, Alexandria, Virginia

RECORDS/TAPES

Birchmere, The   **1-703-549-5919**
3901 Mt. Vernon Avenue, Alexandria, Virginia

Compact Discovery   **1-301-587-1963**
8223 Georgia Avenue, Silver Spring, Maryland

Olsson's Books & Records   **785-2662**
3249 M Street, N.W.

Orpheus Records   **337-7970**
3249 M Street, N.W.

Penguin Feathers   **965-7172**
3225 M Street, N.W.

Record Mart   **1-703-683-4583**
217 King Street, Alexandria, Virginia

Serenade Record Shop   **638-5580**
1710 Pennsylvania Avenue, N.W.

Tower Records   **333-2400**
2000 Pennsylvania Avenue, N.W.

Red Balloon, The   **965-1200**
1073 Wisconsin Avenue, N.W.

Redgate Golf Course   **1-301-340-2404**
14500 Avery Road, Rockville, Maryland

Reflecting Pool, The
Between the Lincoln Memorial and
Washington Monument

**Reiter's Scientific & Professional
        Books**   223-3327
2021 Pennsylvania Avenue, N.W.

Remington's   543-3113
639 Pennsylvania Avenue., S.E.

Rent–A–Computer, Inc.   1-301-951-0811
4853 Cordell Avenue, Bethesda, Maryland

RENTAL, AUDIO VISUAL

Avcom   638-1513
919 12th Street, N.W.

Presentation Group/Washington   337-5500
2121 Wisconsin Avenue, N.W.

Total Audio-Visual Systems, Inc.   737-3900
303 H Street, N.W.

RENTAL, AUTO

Avis   1-800-331-1212

Budget
Wisconsin Avenue   244-7437
National Airport   920-3360
Dulles Airport   437-9373

Dollar Rent–A–Car   1-800-421-6868
National Airport   739-2255
Dulles Airport   661-8577

Envoy Rentals   1-301-657-2304
2070 Chain Bridge Road, Bethesda, Maryland

Hertz   1-800-654-3131

International Limousine Service, Inc.   388-6800
2300 T Street, N.E.
This limo service has mini-coaches for up to 20 people.

National Car Rental   1-800-328-4567

Thrifty Car Rental   1-800-367-2277
1201 K Street, Arlington, Virginia   1-703-783-0400
This company has 20 metropolitan locations, free local
pick-up, and is open 24-hours a day.

RENTAL, BICYCLE

Bicycle rental companies sometimes have a brief lifespan.
These are a few of the ones which have demonstrated some
staying power. They are also in areas where you will want
to ride.

Big Wheel Bikes

1004 Vermont Avenue, N.W.	638-3301
315 7th Street, S.E.	543-1600
1034 33rd Street, N.W.	337-0254

Fletcher's Boathouse   244-0461
4940 Canal Road, N.W. (C & O Canal Towpath)

Thompson Boat Center   333-4861
Rock Creek Parkway and Virginia Avenue, N.W.

RENTAL, BOAT

To some of us, nothing is as much fun as sailing. The following companies can provide the boats to make your days blissful. Some of them also teach sailing.

Annapolis Boat Rentals, Inc.   1-301-261-1947
601 6th Street, Annapolis, Maryland

Fletcher's Boat House   224-0461
4940 Canal Road, N.W.

Guest Services, Inc.   484-3475
15th Street and Maine Avenue, S.W.

Tidal Boat House   484-3475
1501 Main Avenue, S.W.

Thompson's Boat Center   333-4861
Rock Creek Parkway and Virginia Avenue

Washington Boat Lines, Inc.   554-8011
6th and Water Streets, S.W.

Washington Sailing Marina   1-703-548-9027
George Washington Parkway, (south of National
Airport), Alexandria, Virginia

RENTAL, COMPUTER

The ability to rent computer equipment can be a godsend when you are desperate. We found, however, that one must be very sure of the costs involved. Three weeks of rental fees for the printer we needed was equal to the retail purchase price.

Avcom   638-1513
919 12th Street, N.W.

Computer Rental Corp.   347-1582
666 11th Street, N.W.

Easy Rentals, Inc.   342-9114
2121 Wisconsin Avenue, N.W.

Rent–A–Computer, Inc.   **1-301-951-0811**
4853 Cordell Avenue, Bethesda, Maryland

RENTAL, COSTUME

Washington is a party town. The embassies, lobbies, and many individuals have found that this is one of the easiest and most impressive ways of meeting and doing business. If you want to give or are invited to a costume party, the places below are the source for those wonderful disguises.

A.T. Jones & Sons   1-301-748-7087
708 North Howard Street, Baltimore, Maryland
Claiming to have one of the largest collections of costumes in the country, A.T. Jones & Sons is a goldmine of material. It has been the mainstay of the Gridiron Club for many years. They have a particularly fine selection of costumes relating to musicals.

Backstage Rental & Sales   775-1488
2101 P Street, N.W.
This is the easiest shop to get to, it's only a couple of blocks from the Dupont Circle Metro station. Their collection is not the largest, but it is quite adequate for most needs. Their prices are among the lowest, too.

Stein's Theatrical & Dance Center   1-703-522-2660
1180 North Highland Street, Arlington, Virginia
All kinds of theatrical clothing at reasonable prices.

RENTAL, EXERCISE EQUIPMENT

A-Allied Rentals   1-301-229-5400
6825 Reed Street, Bethesda, Maryland

RENTAL, FORMAL WEAR, MEN'S

Washington demands formal occassions. If you are caught without the proper attire, you may want to call one of the following companies in order to rent what you need. They all provide good service, some with no advance notice, and most of them will pick up and deliver. Remember to order well in advance if it is a major city-wide event because they all sell out.

After Hours (No advance notice
required)
4612 East-West Highway,   **1-301-654-2929**
Bethesda, Maryland
2715 Wilson Boulevard   **1-703-522-6455**
Arlington, Virginia

Bethesda Custom Tailors   **1-301-656-2077**
7836 Wisconsin Avenue, Bethesda, Maryland

Friendly Formals   **842-5132**
1220 L Street, N.W.

Masters Tuxedo & Bridal Shop   **638-3773**
1301 Pennsylvania Avenue, N.W.

Woodward & Lothrop   **289-7788**
11th and F Streets, N.W.

RENTAL, FORMAL WEAR, WOMEN'S

Why wear the same dress twice when you can rent a formal for that gala occasion? It's nice to see that there are now places where women can rent gowns on short notice—men have been renting formal wear for years. Keep in mind that, because women need more alterations than men, it may require more advance notice.

Black & White   **337-6660**
1235 Wisconsin Avenue, N.W.
Designer gowns for ladies.

Friendly Formals   **842-5132**
1220 L Street, N.W.

Renwick Gallery, The   **357-1300**
The National Gallery of American Art, Pennsylvania
Avenue and 17th Street, N.W.

REPAIR, CAMERA

Baker's Photo Supply, Inc.   **362-9100**
4433 Wisconsin Avenue, N.W.

Congressional Photo Shoppe   **543-3206**
209 Pennsylvania Avenue, S.E.

Embassy Camera Center   **483-7448**
1709 Connecticut Avenue, N.W.

Mora Camera Service   **362-9866**
4027 Brandywine Street, N.W.

Pro Photo   **223-1292**
1919 Pennsylvania Avenue, N.W.

REPAIR, GLASSES

Embassy Opticians
1325 Connecticut Avenue, N.W.   **785-5700**
617 Pennsylvania Avenue, S.E.   **544-6900**

Voorthuis Opticians, Inc.   **362-7977**
4250 Connecticut Avenue, N.W.

REPAIR, JEWELRY

Benson's Jewelers   **628-1838**
1319 F Street, N.W. (Second Floor)

Compton Jewelers   **393-2570**
1709 G Street, N.W.

Woodward & Lothrop   **347-5300**
1025 F Street, N.W.

REPAIR, LUGGAGE

Doudaklian Leathers Custom
    Designer   **293-0442**
2150 P Street, N.W.
Voted best luggage repair shop in Washington by *Washingtonian* magazine.

Expert Luggage & Shoe Repair   **362-6681**
3808 Northhampton, N.W.

REPAIR, WATCH

L.R. Duehring Jewelers, Inc.   **652-0252**
6935 Wisconsin Avenue

Lee Bord Jewelers   **1-301-530-2800**
10400 Old Georgetown Road, Bethesda, Maryland

R. Saunders Jewelers   **772-8210**
Capital Plaza Mall

Woodward & Lothrop   **347-5300**
11th and F Streets, N.W.

RESTAURANTS

Every city has plenty of restaurant guides: books abound, along with reviews in weekly and monthly magazines. We love to read them and often do. Our experience with travelers, however, is that they want only a limited amount of information about restaurants and they want it fast. We are giving you, therefore, the same amount and type of information for which our hotel guests ask. The majority of the restaurants included here are the best and most popular in Washington, but we also note some that are only recommended for their atmosphere and others that should be avoided altogether.

♀ Our favorites

L Late (open after midnight)

S Open on Sunday

Adirondacks (American) S
   (Expensive)   **682-1840**
Union Station, 50 Massachusetts Avenue, N.E.
    All major credit cards

Everything is just right in this modern American restaurant located in what was once the magnificent Presidential Suite at Union Station. Few restaurants can boast the atmosphere created by this huge room whose soaring, vaulted ceiling requires no sight-blocking supporting columns. In contrast to the serene, classical appearance of Union Station's main lobby, Adirondacks utilizes an ornate combination of patterns, colors, and renovated bronze lighting fixtures to achieve an overall effect of elegance and richness. Large, well-spaced tables, weighty Georg Jensen silverware, fresh flowers, and classical music playing softly in the background set the stage for delicious, beautifully presented cuisine. The menu, which changes daily, reflects owner Michael McCarty's devotion to California cuisine—a variety of salads and simply prepared meats and fish. Desserts range from sorbets and cookies to our favorite—the chocolate caramel torte. The very efficient service is provided by a casually dressed (by Ralph Lauren) crew of waitpeople whose attentiveness to detail reflects their careful training. Although a newcomer to the Washington scene, all indications are that Adirondacks will make an important contribution to Washington dining.

Allegro (American) S (Expensive)   **638-2626**
The Sheraton Carlton, 923 16th Street, N.W.
    All major credit cards

The moment we were welcomed by Maitre D' Roland Venturini, we knew we had come to the right place. Since McDowell had been concierge at the St. Regis Sheraton in New York, we were expecting their usual standard of luxurious service, and we got it. Sitting at the huge Palladian windows that stretch from the floor almost to the ceiling in this Italian Renaissance room, one can enjoy watching the passing scene as well as observing one's fellow diners. The food was quite good, and the service was excellent. Encouraged by Roland, we returned the following day for brunch, which was a particular treat. Since the hotel is frequented by visitors to the White House as well as Hollywood stars, it can be a great place for people-watching.

Aux Beaux Champs (American) S (Expensive)   342-0810
Four Seasons Hotel, 2800 Pennsylvania Avenue, N.W.
    All major credit cards
Nouvelle cuisine, a spa menu, and sumptuous brunches.

Bacchus (Lebanese) (Moderate)   785-0734
1827 Jefferson Place, N.W. (M/N Sts.)
    All major credit cards
We wish the owners would open a branch in our home town—New York—where it's impossible to find sophisticated Middle Eastern fare on a par with this. Rather than go the standard appetizer, main course, dessert route, we recommend making a meal from a selection of eight to ten appetizers. The stuffed grape leaves, tabbouleh, and spicy Turkish sausages are sure to please.

Bamiyan (Afghan) (Inexpensive)   338-1896
3320 M Street, N.W. (33rd St.), Georgetown
    All major credit cards
Georgetown is noted for the variety of its ethnic restaurants, and Bamiyan stands out as one of the best. The cuisine blends Indian and Middle Eastern influences, and is very reasonably priced.

Bombay Palace (Indian) S (Moderate)   331-0111
1835 K Street, N.W. (19th St.)
    All major credit cards
Although it's on the pricey side of Indian restaurants, the Bombay Palace's authentic tandoori cooking and discrete atmosphere still make it a relative bargain. The house specialty "Butter Chicken" with its delicately spiced sauce is a winner.

Broker, The (Swiss) (Moderate)   546-8300
713 8th Street, S.E. (G & I Sts.)
    Credit cards: AE, MC, V
Swiss specialties such as fondue, raclette, and Bunderfleisch share the menu with lighter American fare at this Capitol Hill favorite. The homemade bread is outstanding, and the brick-walled, skylit setting is serene and relaxing.

Cambodian S (Inexpensive)   1-703522-3832
1727 Wilson Boulevard (Quinn St.), Arlington, Virginia
    All major credit cards
Washingtonians always seem to be searching for a new cuisine, and Cambodian may be the latest in a trend that has brought great popularity to Ethiopian and Thai restaurants. Food, service, and value are all outstanding.

Carnegie Deli (Deli) L/S
    (Inexpensive)   **1-703-790-5001**
Embassy Suites Hotel, 8517 Leesburg Pike, Tysons
Corner, Virginia
    Credit cards: AE, MC, V
Ex-New Yorkers complain that the pickles and bread
aren't quite right, and the waiters lack the original
Carnegie's gruffness. Washingtonians don't seem to un-
derstand what all the fuss is about. Still, when you need a
pastrami or corned beef "fix," the Carnegie comes closest.

Chardonnay (American) S (Moderate)   **232-7000**
Radisson Park Terrace Hotel, 1515 Rhode Island
Avenue, N.W.
    All major credit cards
At the moment, Chardonnay's reasonably-priced wine
list is more dependable than the food, but this is definitely
a kitchen to watch. The setting, complete with fireplace at
one end, is formal and warm. The menu is new American
with some Southwestern touches. Homemade ice creams
are a highlight of the desserts.

Chaucer's (American) S (Moderate)   **296-0665**
Canterbury Hotel, 1733 N Street, N.W. (17th/18th Sts.)
    All major credit cards
Located on a quiet, residential street near bustling Dupont Circle, the Canterbury is a little gem of a hotel, and its
restaurant, Chaucer's, offers dependable fare.

China Inn (Cantonese) L/S
    (Inexpensive)   **842-0909**
631 H Street, N.W. (6th/7th Sts.)
    Credit cards: AE, MC, V
Chinatown's oldest (and at 450 seats, also largest) restaurant continues to please both those seeking authentic Cantonese cuisine and those for whom chop-suey represents
the outer limits of daring.

China Pearl (Cantonese/Seafood)
    S (Moderate)   **223-9888**
2020 K Street (20th/21st Sts.)
    Credit Cards: AE, MC, V
This lovely, spacious Cantonese offers delicious seafood
at a fraction of the prices you'd pay at nearby Mr. K's.

Cities (American) L/S (Moderate)   **328-7194**
2424 18th Street, N.W.
    All major credit cards
Not just a restaurant—a happening! Every four months,
Cities is redecorated to honor one of the world's great cities,

with the menu adjusted accordingly. The decor and concept may sound frivolous, but the cooking is perfectly serious. The upstairs disco attracts Eurotrash and young professionals who party until the wee hours.

Collonade (Seafood) S (Moderate)   457-5000
Westin Hotel, 24th & M Streets, N.W.
     All major credit cards
Washington hotel dining is of particularly high quality, and Collonade stands out among its competition. Sunday brunch ($29 *prix fixe* with unlimited champagne) in the beautiful courtyard setting is highly recommended.

Crisfield (Seafood) S (Moderate)   1-301-589-1306
8012 Georgia Avenue, Silver Spring, Maryland
     No credit cards
     Closed Monday
Honest, old-fashioned Eastern Shore cooking is presented in a totally unpretentious (painted cinder-block walls, no-frills decor) atmosphere. Their no-reservations policy means you may have to wait for a table, but it's well worth it to sample their definitive imperial crab, clam chowder, fried oysters, and made-from-scratch French fries.

Dakota (American) L/S (Moderate)   265-6600
1777 Columbia Road, N.W.
     All major credit cards
Dakota follows the trend of combining a restaurant, bar, and dance club. They start with the very freshest ingredients, cook them with imagination, and serve them with panache.

Dar es Salam (Moroccan) L/S
          (Moderate)   342-1925
3056 M Street, N.W. (31st St.), Georgetown
     All major credit cards
Excellent Moroccan cuisine in an impressively authentic decor. The "diffas," a feast of representative dishes, offers an easy introduction to this exotic cuisine. Although diners are encouraged to eat with their hands in authentic Moroccan style, spoons will be provided on request.

Dominique's (French) L (Moderate)   452-1126
1900 Pennsylvania Avenue, N.W.
     All major credit cards
Although the food can be uneven, Dominique's legendary hostess, Diana, creates an exuberant atmosphere that makes diners forgive the chef's shortcomings. The extensive menu includes everything from alligator and rattle-

snake to filet mignon and duck a l'orange, but we recommend sticking to the simpler dishes.

Donatello (Italian) L/S (Moderate)   333-1485
2514 L Street, N.W. (Pennsylvania Ave.)
    All major credit cards
Convenient to the Kennedy Center, this charming old townhouse with contemporary decor is a favorite with lawyers and businessmen who work nearby. The outdoor terrace attracts throngs during Washington's long and sticky summer.

Duangrat's (Thai) S (Moderate)   1-703-820-5775
5878 Leesburg Pike, Falls Church, Virginia
    All major credit cards
Attentive service, a strikingly attractive setting, and a menu where variety and reliability go hand in hand have made Duangrat the best Thai restaurant in the metropolitan area. Newcomers to this cuisine are urged to try their beef with green curry, "Panang Beef," and deep-fried whole flounder. Connoisseurs will enjoy the exotic daily specials.

East Wind (Vietnamese) S (Moderate)   836-1515
809 King Street (Washington St./Route 1), Alexandria, Virginia
    All major credit cards
Beautifully prepared and presented Vietnamese cuisine served in a tranquil surrounding. Open only Monday through Friday.

**El Tamarindo
    (Mexican/Salvadorian) L/S
    (Inexpensive)   1-703-328-3660**
1785 Florida Avenue, N.W. (18th/U Sts.)
    All major credit cards
El Tamarindo's cheap but tasty fare keeps crowds flocking here.

English Grill (Grill) S (Moderate)   638-6600
Hay Adams Hotel, 1 Lafayette Square, N.W.
(16th/H Sts.)
    All major credit cards
Simple dishes are your best choice at this clubby locale. Situated just across the street from the White House, it's the site for many "power dinners."

Enriqueta's (Mexican) S (Inexpensive)   338-7772
2811 M Street, N.W. (28th/29th Sts.)
    All major credit cards
Owner Pepe Montesinos and Chef Arnulfo Luengas

Rosales prove that there's more to Mexican food than tacos and enchiladas. Chicken with a chile-and-chocolate "mole" (pronounced mo-lay) sauce is particularly delicious. Whitewashed walls, brightly colored tablecloths, and tin fiesta decorations help to create a festive atmosphere. The chairs are the only cause for complaint. They look "rustic"; they feel downright uncomfortable.

Filomena's (Italian) S/L (Moderate)   338-1800
1063 Wisconsin Avenue, N.W. (M/K Sts.), Georgetown
     All major credit cards

The food is just so-so, but the people-watching is marvelous here. They must be doing something right—overbooking is a constant problem despite lackadaisical service and multi-decibel noise levels.

Fish Wings & Tings (Caribbean)
(Inexpensive)   234-0322
2418 18th Street, N.W. (Columbia Rd.)
     Credit cards: AE

One of the best bargains in town, serving spicy Jamaican fare at unbelievably low prices. This tiny (eleven tables), lively restaurant attracts eager customers with its curried dishes and grilled fishes.

Foong Lin (Chinese) S
(Inexpensive)   1-301-656-3427
7710 Norfolk Avenue (Fairmont Ave.), Bethesda, Maryland
     All major credit cards

For a change of pace from the normal eggs Benedict brunch routine, try Foong Lin's delicious dim sum.

Fuji (Korean/Japanese) S
(Moderate)   1-703-524-3666
77 North Glebe Road (Route 50), Arlington, Virginia
     All major credit cards

Both sushi and sashimi fans and those (like us) who prefer their food cooked will enjoy the mixture offered here.

Galileo (Italian) S (Moderate)   293-7191
2014 P Street, N.W. (20th/21st Sts.)
     All major credit cards

Chef–proprietor Roberto Donna offers both traditional Northern Italian dishes and an Italian version of nouvelle cuisine. Mr. Donna oversees this operation carefully, periodically touring the dining room to make sure that everybody's happy.

Genji (Sushi) S (Moderate)   1-703-573-0112
2816 Graham Road (Lee Hwy.), Falls Church, Virginia

Impeccably fresh sushi and the comfort of warmed sake are an unbeatable combination.

Georgetown Bar & Grill
(American) S (Moderate)   **337-7777**
1310 Wisconsin Avenue, N.W. (N St.)
    All major credit cards

There are many adjectives to describe Georgetown, but "roomy" and "airy" seldom come to mind. The Georgetown Bar & Grill is a delightful exception with its spaciousness and beautiful woodwork. Unfortunately, you can't eat the paneling. The chef and staff turnover eliminates any consistency in food quality or service. However, the drinks and piano music are always reliable.

Germaine's (Vietnamese) S
(Moderate)   **965-1185**
2400 Wisconsin Avenue, N.W. (Calvert St.), Georgetown
    All major credit cards

Vietnamese cooking combines the zest of the Orient with the subtleties of French cuisine, and it doesn't get any better than here at Germaine's. Grilled fish, meat, and shellfish are uniformly excellent. Pay attention to the daily specials—they live up to their name.

Ginza's (Japanese) (Moderate)   **833-1244**
1009 21st Street, N.W. (K/L Sts.)
    Credit cards: AE, CB, MC, V

The full range of Japanese dishes is offerred, from sushi to sukiyaki and shabu shabu. However, the service is *very* slow.

Hisago (Japanese) S (Expensive)   **944-4181**
3020 K Street, N.W. (Washington Harbour)
    All major credit cards

Visiting Japanese businessmen form the core clientele at Hisago, where they can reserve a tatami room, enjoy a formal meal, and end the evening in song. Hisago's special "kaiseki" menus are exquisitely subtle multi-course preparations, meant to be studied and reflected upon before being consumed. The sushi and tempura bars satisfy those with more moderate tastes and incomes.

Houston's (American) L/S
(Inexpensive)   **338-7760**
1065 Wisconsin Avenue, N.W. (M St.), Georgetown
    All major credit cards

Simple fare (burgers, salads, ribs), good drinks and low prices result in a mob scene. Don't arrive too hungry; you may have to wait an hour for a table.

Hunan Chinatown (Chinese) S
    (Inexpensive)   **783-5858**
624 H Street (6th/7th Sts.)
    All major credit cards
Classic hot and spicy Hunan cuisine in a subdued setting.

Hunt Club (American) (Moderate)   **347-2200**
Jefferson Hotel, 1200 16th Street, N.W. (M St.)
    All major credit cards
This room is so lovely, we'd enjoy being here even if the food were terrible. Fortunately, it isn't—although it doesn't quite live up to the promise of the private club decor. Simple dishes fare best.

Inn at Little Washington
    (American) S (Expensive)   **1-703-675-3800**
Middle & Main Streets, Washington, Virginia
    Credit cards: MC, V
    Closed Monday and Tuesday
Everyone's idea of the "perfect country inn": exquisite, romantic setting, beautifully prepared and presented food, and the possibility (if you've planned ahead) to linger over dinner and stay overnight. The Inn is 80 miles West of Washington, DC, and well worth the detour

I Ricchi (Italian) (Expensive)   **835-0459**
1220 19th Street, N.W.
    All major credit cards
I Ricchi leapt to stardom when George Bush dined here shortly after it opened, and it quickly became a favorite of diplomats, journalists, and business leaders. But what goes up may come down, and, in our opinion, this place has. The noise level is so high as to be almost unbelievable, and it is certainly not in keeping with a first-class restaurant's image. We found the service slow, inattentive, and graceless. The food continued in the same negative vein. Not a place we could, in good conscience, recommend.

Jean-Louis (French) (Very Expensive)   **298-4488**
Watergate Hotel, 2650 Virginia Avenue, N.W.
(New Hampshire Ave.)
    All major credit cards
Everyone we've talked to agrees that while Jean-Louis Palladin can be one of the city's (and country's) best and most innovative chefs, his skills are very unreliable. To dine here on one of his off nights is extremely annoying. Our recent experience was a major disappointment. We have had far better food and service in several of Washington's less touted restaurants. As concierges, we cannot recommend

restaurants where the quality is so unreliable that the guests must take their chances.

Jean-Pierre (French) S (Expensive)   466-2022
1835 K Street, N.W. (18th/19th Sts.)
     All major credit cards
Both classic French and creative contemporary dishes served by a smoothly efficient staff in an elegant room. Washington's French restaurants compete fiercely in a small market, and Jean Pierre is one of the finest. Don't miss it.

Jockey Club (French) (Expensive)   293-2100
Ritz Carlton Hotel, 2100 Massachusetts Avenue, N.W. (21st St.)
     All major credit cards
Grand, solid, conservative and, above all, reliable, the Jockey Club continues to pamper its customers with stunning tableside service and sophisticated Continental food. Still one of *the* places to see and be seen.

Kabul Caravan (Afghan) S
     (Inexpensive)   1-703-522-8394
Colonial Shopping Center, 1725 Wilson Boulevard, Arlington, Virginia
     All major credit cards
Washington is a city of contrasts, so it really shouldn't come as a great surprise to discover this friendly, family-run restaurant nestled in a modern shopping center in Arlington. Moderate prices and a wine list add to its appeal.

La Bergerie (French) (Moderate)   1-703-683-1007
218 N. Lee Street (King/Queen Sts.), Alexandria, Virginia
A delightful townhouse restaurant whose Basque-inspired menu has attracted a loyal following.

La Brasserie (French) L/S (Moderate)   546-6066
239 Massachusetts Avenue N.E. (3rd St.)
     All major credit cards
Within easy walking distance of both Union Station and the Capitol, La Brasserie serves sophisticated bistro fare and knockout créme brulee—either cold or hot. Old standbys such as onion soup and quiche are balanced by modern creations such as belon oysters with raspberry vinagrette and monkfish with sauce Americaine. The staff is friendly, personable, and extremely attentive. Co-owner Raymond Campet boasts that many of his staff have been there ten years or more, and it's easy to see why. La Brasserie hums with the pleasant air of people doing their jobs both gladly and well.

L'Auberge Chez Francois (French)
    S (Moderate)   1-703-759-3800
332 Springvale Road (2 Miles North of Georgetown
Pike), Great Falls, Virginia
    Credit cards: AE, MC, V

This charming Alsatian inn fulfills everyone's dream of the idealized French country restaurant. The rustic setting provides the perfect background for hearty dishes such as chicken stewed in Alsatian Riesling, stuffed rabbit, or choucroute garnie. Reserve well in advance for a Friday or Saturday night.

La Chaumiere (French Bistro)
    (Moderate)   338-1784
2813 M Street, N.W. (28th/29th Sts.), Georgetown
    All major credit cards

In a setting reminiscent of a country inn, simple bistro-style cuisine served with warm hospitality have earned La Chaumiere a loyal clientele. Daily specials such as Wednesday's couscous or Thursday's cassoulet are too delicious to ignore.

La Colline (French) (Moderate)   737-0400
400 North Capitol Street, N.W. (D/E Sts.)
    All major credit cards

Open for breakfast, lunch, and dinner, La Colline serves over 400 meals daily. Fortunately, this quantity does not seem to diminish the quality of chef Robert Greault's inventions. The menu offers great variety—you can choose anything from a simple omelette to duck breast with cassis or tripe stew. Be sure to save room for dessert—the cart selection is heavenly. "Nondescript" is the kindest word for the decor. "Efficient" describes the service. "Picky eaters" describes us, and we loved this place.

La Ferme (French) S (Moderate)   1-301-986-5255
7101 Brookeville Road (East-West Hwy./Western Ave.)
Chevy Chase, Maryland
    All major credit cards

Traditional French dishes served in a warm, countrylike setting. The dessert souffles are worth every delicious calorie.

Lafitte (Cajun) S (Moderate)   466-7978
Hampshire Hotel, 1310 New Hampshire Avenue, N.W.
(20th/N Sts.)

A Dupont Circle Cajun particularly noted for its Creole-style breakfasts and Sunday brunch.

La Fourchette (French) S (Moderate)   332-3077
2429 18th Street, N.W.

All major credit cards

The fare runs to simple rather than fussy at this hospitable family-run bistro. Traditional items such braised veal or lamb shanks, onion soup, patés, and aioli are expertly prepared and cheerfully served. Moderate prices add to La Fourchette's appeal.

La Marée (French Seafood)
   (Moderate)   659-4447
1919 I Street, N.W. (19th./20th Sts.)
   All major credit cards

Seafood prepared in the classical French style is the specialty at this elegant, romantic townhouse restaurant. Don't look for trendiness here, just the charm of reliability.

La Plaza (Spanish/Mexican) S
   (Moderate)   667-1900
1847 Columbia Road, N.W. (Biltmore St.)
   All major credit cards

A lovely combination of Spanish and Mexican dishes are served in a bright, congenial atmosphere that invites lingering. Huge portions of such classics as paella, zarzuela, and seafood enchiladas plus moderate prices make this a standout in the lively Adams Morgan neighborhood.

Lauriol Plaza (Mexican) S
   (Inexpensive)   387-0035
1801 18th Street, N.W. (S/T Sts)
   All major credit cards

A good choice for either a snack or a full meal, Lauriol Plaza shares both ownership and some dishes with La Plaza. But here, the emphasis is on the Mexican side of the menu. Passersby provide a constant show for diners on the sidewalk terrace.

Le Caprice (French) S (Moderate)   337-3394
2348 Wisconsin Avenue, N.W. (South of Calvert St.)
   All major credit cards

The jury is still out on this Georgetown French. Elaborate presentations cannot disguise the erratic nature of the cooking. If you don't mind playing Russian roulette with your evening meal, you might risk venturing out here.

Le Gaulois (French) (Moderate)   466-3232
2133 Pennsylvania Avenue, N.W. (Washington Circle)
   All major credit cards

Fans, willing to overlook noise and overcrowding, pack into this small, very popular bistro for its modest prices, extensive choice of daily specials, and excellent, traditional dishes.

Le Lion D'Or (French) (Moderate)   296-7972
1150 Connecticut Avenue, N.W. (18th St. between
L/M Sts.)
      All major credit cards

Since chef Jean-Pierre Goyenvalle's classical French cuisine had been so highly recommended, we expected a superb dining experience. Alas, this was not the case. Although the foie gras ravioli and poached char fish were luscious, our enjoyment was marred by the condescending attitude of our waiter, who fairly threw the plates down, never inquired how things were, and left before we had finished lunch—leaving the bus boy to present our check.

Le Pavillon (French Nouvelle)
      (Very Expensive)   833-3846
1050 Connecticut Avenue, N.W. (L St.)
      All major credit cards

Just as we were beginning to despair of finding the quality service and hauntingly memorable food for which several Washington restaurants are (in our opinion, unjustifiably) renowned, we dined at Le Pavillon. Janet Lai Cam's warm welcome, the absolutely perfect service by Michael, our waiter, and Chef Yannick Cam's wonderfully imaginative and creative cuisine restored our faith. Havilland china and Sevres crystal vases enhance the tables in the spacious, modern dining room. The wine list is among the best in the nation, with a daunting list of Burgundies.

Le Rivage (French) S (Moderate)   488-8111
1000 Water Street, S.W. (Maine Avenue/9th St.)
      All major credit cards

If you're determined to dine on the waterfront, this is one of your best options. Just remember that you can't eat the view.

Lucie (American) S (Very Expensive)   265-1600
Embassy Row Hotel, 2015 Massachusetts Avenue, N.W.
(off Dupont Circle)
      All major credit cards

Quite simply, our favorite. Chef James Papovich, who established his reputation at Le Chardon d'Or in Alexandria, has brought many of his staff (including Maître d'Hôtel Pierre Robert) to this extensively renovated location. Pierre Robert espouses the philosophy that there are no excuses and trains his staff accordingly. The food and service here rival Michelin-rated two-star restaurants in France. As we were being seated on our first visit, other diners purred their contentment. This is the sort of place where you can relax and know that everything will be done perfectly. The *prix fixe* daily offering ($60 at this writing) is a relative bargain, and includes just enough of five courses. Some folks stop by just for a dessert souffle. Lucie sets a standard by which all District restaurants must be measured.

Maison Blanche (French) (Expensive)   842-0070
1725 F Street, N.W. (17th/18th Sts.)
    All major credit cards
This top spot for power lunches and dinners has retained its popularity for over 30 years. Classical French cuisine served with great formality.

Marrakesh (Moroccan) S (Moderate)   393-939
617 New York Ave, N.W. (6th/7th Sts.)
    No credit cards
You sit on low cushions, eat with your hands, and are treated to a floor show including belly dancers. Once is enough.

Melrose (Modern American) S
    (Expensive)   955-3899
Park Hyatt Hotel, 24th & M Sts., N.W.
    All major credit cards
A good choce for Sunday buffet brunch, breakfast, or afternoon tea. Every seat overlooks a sunken outdoor patio with a cascading fountain.

Meskerem (Ethiopian) L/S
    (Inexpensive)   462-4100
2434 18th Street, N.W. (Columbia Rd.)
    All major credit cards
Washington has many Ethiopian restaurants, but its bright, skylit rooms, relaxed atmosphere and carefully seasoned preparations set Meskerem apart from the competition.

Metro Center Grille & Bar
    (American) S (Moderate)   737-2200
Holiday Inn Crowne Plaza at Metro Center,
775 12th Street, N.W.
    All major credit cards
Holiday Inns aren't what they used to be—they're after a share of the upscale market. Executive chef Melissa Ballinger, given free rein by General Manager David Woodward, has created a varied menu in the New American style, ranging from hamburgers to saffron linguini with lobster sauce. Side dishes, such as sauteed spinach with garlic and olive oil or potato pancakes are a lovely indulgence. Ballinger welcomes and gladly accommodates special requests. The pastries here rank with the best we've tasted around town.

Mr. K's (Chinese) S (Expensive)   **331-8868**
2121 K Street, N.W.
    All major credit cards
Not your average Chinese restaurant. Elaborate presentations with prices to match, impeccably served are the story here. It's a wonderful place for entertaining if you're on an expense account.

Mrs. Simpson's (American) S
    (Moderate)   **332-8300**
2915 Connecticut Avenue, N.W.
    All major credit cards
We all know that Edward VIII renounced his throne for Mrs. Wallis Simpson. If her cooks hadn't served something more imaginative than the fare served here, the history books would be rewritten.

Montpelier (Continental) S
    (Expensive)   **862-1712**
Madison Hotel, 1177 15th Street, N.W. (M St.)
    All major credit cards
First class service, excellent French and Continental cuisine, and opulent surroundings make this a consistent favorite.

Morton's of Chicago (Steak) S
    (Expensive)   **342-6258**
3251 Prospect Street, N.W. , Georgetown
    All major credit cards
Reservations are accepted only before 7:00 P.M., and the din can be excruciating. Still, enthusiasts endure these discomforts to dine on superbly aged steaks, filets, and prime ribs. The latter are so popular that they are frequently sold out by 8:00 P.M. However, it is possible to reserve a portion by calling beforehand and giving a credit card number to guarantee your arrival.

Nam Viet (Vietnamese) S
    (Inexpensive)   **1-703-522-7110**
1127 N. Hudson Street (Wilson Blvd.), Arlington, Virginia
    All major credit cards
An extensive menu of Vietnamese delicacies.

New Heights (American) S
    (Moderate)   **234-4110**
2317 Calvert Street, N.W. (Connecticut Ave.)
    All major credit cards
When you're in the mood to experiment, try this elegant modern dining room overlooking Rock Creek Park. The somewhat bizarre food combinations don't always suc-

ceed, but when they do, they are not only delicious, they're works of art.

New Orleans Café   (Creole/Cajun)
S   (Inexpensive)   234-5111
1790 Columbia Road, N.W.

   All major credit cards

It looks like Cajun food is here to stay, if the popularity of this casual, friendly, and inexpensive café is any indication. From beignets to bread pudding with whiskey sauce, the food is authentic and very good.

New Orleans Emporium
(Creole/Cajun) S (Moderate)   328-3421
2477 18th Street, N.W.(Columbia Rd.), Georgetown

   All major credit cards

The full range of Cajun seafood specialties, including hot oysters, wonderful soups, blackened redfish, fabulous barbecued shrimp, and beggars' purses can compete with the best in New Orleans itself.

Nicholas (American) S (Expensive)   347-8900
Mayflower Hotel, 1127 Connecticut Avenue, N.W.
(L/DeSalles Sts.)

   All major credit cards

The Mayflower Hotel's elegant, spacious dining room with its Modern American food is a popular choice for power lunches.

Nora (American) (Moderate)   462-5143
2109 R Street, N.W.

   No credit cards

Nora proves that eating healthy can be delicious: meats grown without hormones and vegetables raised without pesticides are the chosen ingredients. Simple preparations, beautiful presentations, and a romantic townhouse atmosphere attract an enthusiastic clientele.

Occidental (American) S
(Expensive)   783-1475
1475 Pennsylvania Avenue, N.W. (14th/15th Sts.)

   All major credit cards

Once a Washington institution, the Occidental has reopened as part of the Pennsylvania Avenue redevelopment. The formal dining room upstairs serves contemporary interpretations of classic American dishes.

Occidental Grill (Grill) L/S
(Moderate)   783-1476
1475 Pennsylvania Avenue, N.W. (14th/15th Sts.)

   All major credit cards

Lined with photos of the famous, the Occidental Grill serves excellent hamburgers and its trademark swordfish club sandwich to a power clientele.

Old Ebbitt Grill (American) L/S
          (Moderate)   347-4801
675 15th St., N.W. (F /G Sts.)
          All major credit cards

We can't think of a nicer start to a day than breakfast at the Old Ebbitt Grill. From the crowds we've encountered there, many Washingtonians agree. The plush, green velvet banquettes, plethora of potted palms, and gaslights welcome you into a bygone era. The staff actually seems interested in serving you. While the menu makes some concessions to the health-conscious (granola, oatmeal), we found the lure of homemade biscuits and gravy or eggs Benedict irresistible. In the evening, the restaurant expands into an indoor courtyard, where pianist Peter Robinson performs with a rare combination of skill and charm.

Omega (Cuban) S (Inexpensive)   745-9158
1858 Columbia Road, N.W. (Belmont/18th Sts.)

One of the mainstays of the Adams Morgan neighborhood, Omega offers huge portions of authentic Cuban food at minimal prices. This is a storefront restaurant, so don't expect much in the way of decor.

Palm, The (Steak) (Moderate)   293-9091
1225 19th Street, N.W. (M/N Sts.)
          All major credit cards

The Palm's philosophy is simple: they serve juicy steaks with mountains of thick homemade potato chips, gargantuan (4 1/2 pound) lobsters, and the occasional fish. Their loyal customers approve.

Peking Gourmet Inn (Chinese) S
          (Inexpensive)   1-703-671-8088
6029 Leesburg Pike, Falls Church, Virginia
          All major credit cards

Washington's concierges are unanimous in their praise for this Arlington Chinese. The Peking Duck is the best in the area.

Perry's (Japanese) L/S (Moderate)   234-6218
1811 Columbia Road, N.W.
          All major credit cards

This New-Wave sushi grazing bar, complete with Japanese videos, offers a long list of sushi and spectacular views of the city.

Powerscourt (Irish) (Moderate)   737-3776
Phoenix Park Hotel, 520 N. Capitol Street, N.W.
(Massachusetts Ave.)
    All major credit cards

Who says "Irish cuisine" is an oxymoron? At the recommendation of Kevin McMooney, a concierge at the luxurious Sheraton Carlton, we stopped by here for a delicious meal of oysters Rockefeller, potato soup, and veal, and finished off with a Bailey's mousse. "Powerscourt" is the name of a famous Irish estate, but it also provides a good indication of the clientele. We seemed to be the only non-politicians.

Prime Plus (American) (Moderate)   783-0166
727 15th Street, N.W. (H St./New York Ave.)
    All major credit cards

Proximity to the National Theater makes this an excellent choice for a pre-theater dinner. Simple dishes with innovative accompaniments followed by sensational desserts keep the most discerning diners happy.

Prime Rib (Steak) (Moderate)   466-8811
2020 K Street, N.W. (20th/21st Sts.)
    All major credit cards

Many consider Prime Rib Washington's most civilized steakhouse. Concierges love it because they actually take reservations! A pianist playing unobtrusively in the glamorous black-and-gold dining room creates a soothing atmosphere for your enjoyment of superb steaks and prime rib. The extensive wine list includes a number of half-bottles, and excellent wines are also served by the glass. Like most steakhouses, the Prime Rib bows to the cholesterol-conscious by including broiled fish on the menu. However, we recommend throwing caution to the winds and opting for crab imperial.

Primi Piatti (Italian) (Moderate)   223-3600
2013 P Street, N.W. (20th/21st Sts.)
    All major credit cards

We have mixed feelings about this Galileo spin-off. We don't like standing in line, nor receiving food of undependable quality.

**Rio Grande Café (Tex-Mex) S
(Moderate)**   1-301-656-2981
4919 Fairmont Avenue (off Old Georgetown Rd.),
Bethesda, Maryland
    Credit cards: AE, MC, V

The real thing. The Rio Grande Café's menu was imported directly from Dallas.

R. T.'s (Seafood) S (Moderate)   **1-703-684-6010**
3804 Mount Vernon Avenue (Glebe Rd.), Alexandria, Virginia
  All major credit cards
Wonderful New Orleans style seafood served in a friendly atmosphere draws throngs to this unassuming Arlington bar.

Sakura Palace (Japanese) S (Moderate)   **1-301-587-7070**
7926 Georgia Avenue (Eastern Ave.), Silver Spring, Maryland
  All major credit cards
While this is one of the top-rated Japanese restaurants in the area, many tourists may find that Silver Spring is a long ride for Japanese food.

Sarinah Satay House (Indonesian) S (Moderate)   **337-2955**
1338 Wisconsin Avenue, N.W. (N/O Sts.), Georgetown
  All major credit cards
Moderate prices, a soothing atmosphere, and an opportunity to sample a new cuisine make this very appealing.

1789 (French/American) S (Moderate)   **965-1789**
1226 36th Street, N.W. (Prospect St.), Georgetown
  All major credit cards
This beautiful, Colonial-style townhouse recalls the charming inns of days gone by. Chef George Odachowski combines a native appreciation of American foods with training in some of Washington's best French kitchens, giving classic dishes an interesting twist.

Sushi-Ko (Japanese) S (Moderate)   **333-4187**
2309 Wisconsin Avenue, N.W. (Observatory Lane), Georgetown
  Credit cards: AE, MC, V
The city's first sushi bar is still going strong.

Sushi Taro (Japanese) (Moderate)   **462-8999**
1503 17th Street, N.W. (P St.)
  Credit cards: AE, MC, V
This attractive Dupont Circle restaurant features those yummy skewers called yakitori, 14 kinds of tempura, and noodle dishes in addition to sushi and sashimi.

Szechuan (Chinese) S (Inexpensive)   **393-0130**
615 I Street, N.W. (6th/7th Sts.)
  All major credit cards
The expansion of this chain has led to some inconsisten-

cies in the kitchen. Nevertheless, the Szechuan-style whole fish and crispy beef are usually excellent.

Taberna del Alabardero (Spanish)
(Very Expensive)   429-2200
1776 I Street, N.W. (18th St.)
    All major credit cards

When we asked the Four Seasons' Chef Concierge, Jack Nargil, for one of his favorite spots, he named Taberna del Alabardero. Luis de Lezama has recreated his critically acclaimed Madrid restaurant, serving Spanish haute cuisine. It's a pleasure to taste traditional dishes such as paella prepared by a serious chef. In keeping with the current trend toward "grazing," the tapas bar serves pre- and post-theater snacks.

Tachibana (Japanese) (Moderate)   1-703-558-1122
4050 Lee Highway (Military Road/Quincy St.),
Arlington, Virginia
    All major credit cards

The Washington area's best Japanese is just across the Potomac in Arlington. Tachibana offers generous portions of impeccably fresh sushi at reasonable prices. Sukiyaki, tempura, and yosenabe complete the selection.

Takesushi (Japanese) (Moderate)   466-3798
1010 20th Street, N.W. (K/L Sts.)
    All major credit cards

When the clientele is largely Japanese, as it is here, you can be sure of two things: the sushi will be sophisticated, and the prices will be high.

Taverna Cretekou (Greek) S
(Moderate)   1-703-548-8688
818 King Street (South Henry St.), Alexandria, Virginia
    All major credit cards

While this is one of the better Greek restaurants in the area, their ratings for cuisine are not overwhelming. We suggest you go mainly for the friendly atmosphere and the Greek dances.

Terrazza (Italian) S (Moderate)   1-703-683-6900
710 King Street (Washington/Columbus Sts.),
Alexandria, Virginia
    All major credit cards

Terrazza serves the same superb Northern Italian food as its downtown brother, Tiberio, at slightly lower prices.

Thai Flavor (Thai) S (Moderate)   966-0200
3709 Macomb Street, N.W. (Wisconsin Ave.)
One of several very good Thai restaurants, it is

particularily popular with the local residents. Tends to be overpriced by comparison to the other Thai places.

Thai Kingdom (Thai) S
     (Inexpensive)   835-1700
2021 K Street, N.W. (20th/21st Sts.)
     All major credit cards

Beautiful surroundings enhanced by fresh orchids and Thai art set the background for the exquisitely prepared and beautifully presented delicacies. This is the city's best Thai restaurant.

Thai Taste (Thai) S (Inexpensive)   387-8876
2606 Connecticut Avenue, N.W. (Calvert St.)
     All major credit cards

Reasonable prices and friendly service have made this one of Washington's most popular Thai restaurants.

Tiberio (Italian) (Expensive)   452-1915
1915 K Street, N.W. (19th/20th Sts.)
     All major credit cards

Contrary to rumors of cold and haughty service, we have nothing but the best to report about Tiberio. Service may have improved since Adele speaks flawless Italian, but we doubt if that explains why the chef is so good. We accidentally broke the ice by asking the chef to prepare something that wasn't on the menu, which seemed to increase the waiter's interest and to call forth even more virtuosity from the kitchen.

Tony Cheng's Mongolian Barbecue
     (Chinese) S (Inexpensive)   842-8669
619 H Street, N.W. (6th/7th Sts.)
     Credit cards: AE, MC, V

Food as theater, with chefs wielding long chopsticks over cast-iron grills at center stage. Diners choose from the bins of neatly arranged raw meats and vegetables, season them at the sauce station, then hand their selections to the grill cooks for a quick turn. This is then consumed by stuffing portions into split, sesame-seed rolls. Or they might elect to have a coal-fired hot pot placed on the table to cook their own meats, seafoods, and vegetables in the boiling broth. Either way, it's a bargain—$11.95 for the barbecue (all you can eat). The Mongolian hot pot starts at $5.00 per person, with additional charges for the raw meat, chicken, seafood, and vegetables ordered.

Trader Vic's (Polynesian) S Moderate   347-7100
The Capitol Hilton, 16th and K Streets, N.W.
     All major credit cards

Everyone should go to Trader Vic's at least once—if not for the food, for the shamelessly funky South Seas atmosphere and lethal rum drinks.

Tragara (Italian) S (Expensive)   1-301-951-4935
4935 Cordell Avenue (Old Georgetown Rd./Norfolk Ave.), Bethesda, Maryland

This is one of the best of the area Italians and has become an "in" place for the limo set. The food is usually first class and is supported by both the decor and service. Like some of the other Italian restaurants, Tragara receives complaints about an "attitude" problem from the staff. We have always found that an aggressively friendly attitude on our part breaks through this almost immediately.

21 Federal (American) (Expensive)   331-9771
1736 L Street, N.W. (18th St./Connecticut Ave.)
     All major credit cards

Chef Robert Kinkead's intensely flavored and creative cooking encompasses a wide variety and is inspired by regional American and international cuisines. Blond oak walls, gray banquettes, bright floral arrangements, and generously spaced tables create a refined atmosphere which, unfortunately, can get very noisy.

Vincenzo (Italian) (Expensive)   667-0047
1606 20th Street, N.W. (Q St./Connecticut Ave.)
     All major credit cards

Uncomplicated preparations and uncompromisingly excellent raw materials make Vincenzo the District's best seafood restaurant. Homemade breads and pastas are the prelude to precisely grilled fish with just the barest of seasonings, wonderful fish stews, and perfectly deep fried fritto misto di mare. This elegant simplicity does not come cheap, however. Dinner checks can easily reach $75.00 per person.

Willard Room (American) S
     (Expensive)   637-7440
Willard Hotel, 1401 Pennsylvania Avenue, N.W. (14th/15th Sts.)
     All major credit cards

We have a particular weakness for hotel dining rooms where the tables are large and well-distanced from one another, the staff is well-trained, and the food is consistently excellent, if not innovative. The Willard Room never disappoints us.

Windows of the East (Vietnamese)
     S (Moderate)   1-301-654-6444
4747 Elm Street (off Wisconsin Ave.), Bethesda, Maryland

If you like Vietnamese food, you will want to know about this one. The cuisine is excellent and our only complaint is that tourists may not want to travel to Bethesda for dinner. For those of you who live in the area and know your way around, this is ideal for both food and decor.

RESTAURANTS, BRUNCH

🗝 Adirondacks

Allegro

Aux Beaux Champs

Chardonnay

Chaucer's

Collonade

Foong Lin

Georgetown Bar & Grill

Lafitte

🗝 Lucie

Melrose

Meskerem

Metro Center Grill & Bar American

Mr. K's

Mrs. Simpson's

New Heights

New Orleans Café

🗝 Old Ebbitt Grill

🗝 Powerscourt

Rio Grande Café

🗝 Willard Room

RESTAURANTS BY CUISINE

AFGHAN

Bamiyan

Kabul Caravan

AMERICAN

🗝 Adirondacks

213

♟ Allegro

    Aux Beaux Champs

    Bridge Street Cafe

    Chardonnay

    Chaucer's

    Cities

    Dakota

    Georgetown Bar & Grill

    Houston's

    Hunt Club

♟ Inn at Little Washington

♟ Lucie

    Melrose

    Metro Center Grille & Bar American

    Mrs. Simpson's

    New Heights

    Nicholas

    Nora

    Occidental

♟ Old Ebbitt Grill

    Prime Plus

    1789

♟ 21 Federal

♟ Willard Room

CREOLE/CAJUN

    Lafitte

    New Orleans Café

    New Orleans Emporium

CAMBODIAN

    Cambodian

CARIBBEAN

    Fish Wings & Tings

CHINESE

China Inn (Cantonese)

China Pearl (Cantonese seafood)

Foong Lin

Hunan Chinatown

🔑 Mr. K's

🔑 Peking Gourmet Inn

🔑 Szechuan

Tony Cheng's Mongolian Barbecue

CONTINENTAL

Montpelier

CUBAN

Omega

DELI

Carnegie Deli

ETHIOPIAN

Meskerem

FRENCH

Dominique's

🔑 Jean-Louis

Jean-Pierre

Jockey Club

La Bergerie

🔑 La Brasserie

🔑 L'Auberge Chez François

🔑 La Colline

La Ferme

La Fourchette

La Maree

Le Caprice

Le Gaulois

Le Lion D'Or

🔑 Le Pavillon

Le Rivage

🗝 Maison Blanche

FRENCH BISTRO

La Chaumiere

GREEK

Taverna Cretekou

GRILL

Occidental Grill

English Grill

INDIAN

Bombay Palace

Sarinah Satay House

IRISH

🗝 Powerscourt

ITALIAN

Donatello

Filomena's

🗝 Galileo

I Ricchi

Primi Piatti

🗝 Terrazza

🗝 Tiberio

Tragara

🗝 Vincenzo

JAPANESE

Genji (Sushi)

Ginza's

🗝 Hisago

Perry's

Sakura Palace

Sushi-Ko

Sushi Taro

🍴 Taachibana

Takesushi

KOREAN/JAPANESE

Fuji

LEBANESE

Bacchus

MEXICAN

El Tamarindo

Enriqueta's

Lauriol Plaza

Mixtec

Rio Grande Café (Tex-Mex)

MOROCCAN

Dar es Salam

Marrakesh

POLYNESIAN

Trader Vic's

SEAFOOD

Collonade

🍴 Crisfield

R.T.'s

SPANISH

La Plaza

🍴 Taberna del Alabardero

STEAK

Palm, The

🍴 Prime Rib

🍴 Morton's of Chicago

SWISS

Broker, The

217

THAI

Duangrat's

Thai Flavor

🍴 Thai Kingdom

Thai Taste

VIETNAMESE

🍴 East Wind

🍴 Germaine's

Nam Viet

Windows of the East

GRILL

English Grill

ITALIAN

Donatello

Filomena's

RESTAURANTS BY LOCATION

ADAMS MORGAN

Cities

Dakota

El Tamarindo

Enriqueta's

Fish Wings & Tings

La Fourchette

La Plaza

Meskerem

Mixtec

New Orleans Café

Omega

Perry's

ALEXANDRIA, VIRGINIA

🍴 East Wind

La Bergerie

R.T.'s

Taverna Cretekou

♈ Terrazza

ARLINGTON, VIRGINIA

Cambodian

Fuji

Kabul Caravan

Nam Viet

Tachibana

BETHESDA, MARYLAND

Foong Lin

Rio Grande Café

Tragara

Windows of the East

CAPITOL HILL

♈ Adirondacks

Broker, The

♈ La Brasserie

La Chaumiere

♈ La Colline

♈ Powerscourt

CHINATOWN/CONVENTION CENTER AREA

China Inn

Hunan Chinatown

Marrakesh

Metro Center Grill & Bar American

♈ Szechuan

Tony Cheng's Mongolian Barbecue

DOWNTOWN

Chardonnay

Dominique's

English Grill

Hunt Club

Maison Blanche

Montpelier

Nicholas

Occidental

Occidental Grill

🍸 Old Ebbitt Grill

Prime Plus

🍸 Willard Room, The

DUPONT CIRCLE

Bacchus

Chaucer's

🍸 Galileo

I Ricchi

Jockey Club

Lafitte

Lauriol Plaza

🍸 Lucie

Nora

Palm, The

Sushi Taro

🍸 Vincenzo

FALLS CHURCH, VIRGINIA

Duangrat's

Genji

🍸 Peking Gourmet Inn

FOGGY BOTTOM

Jean-Louis

Le Gaulois

GEORGETOWN

Aux Beaux Champs

Bamiyan

Bridge Street Cafe

Dar es Salam

Filomena's

Georgetown Bar & Grill

🔑 Germaine's

Houston's

Le Caprice

🔑 Morton's of Chicago

New Orleans Emporium

Sarinah Satay House

1789

Sushi-Ko

Thai Taste

GREAT FALLS, VIRGINIA

🔑 L'Auberge Chez François

"K" STREET AREA

Allegro

Bombay Palace

China Pearl

Ginza's

🔑 Jean-Pierre

La Maree

Le Lion D'Or

🔑 Le Pavillon

🔑 Mr. K's

Prime Rib

Primi Piatti

🔑 Taberna del Alabardero

Takesushi

Thai Kingdom

🔑 Tiberio

Trader Vic's

🔑 21 Federal

SILVER SPRING, MARYLAND

🔑 Crisfield

Sakura Palace

TYSONS CORNER, VIRGINIA

   Carnegie Deli

UPPER, N.W.

   Mrs. Simpson's

   New Heights

   Thai Flavor

WASHINGTON HARBOUR

   🔑 Hisago

WASHINGTON, VIRGINIA

   🔑 Inn at Little Washington

THE WATERFRONT

   Le Rivage

WEST END

   Collonade

   Donatello

   Melrose

RESTROOMS/BATHROOMS

For tourists and residents alike, there is nothing as important as a public bathroom. Fortunately, Washington is a city
geared to sightseers and most of the public buildings have
the necessary facilities. Keep in mind that most department
stores and all hotels have bathrooms.

Revolution Books   265-1969
2438 18th Street, N.W.

RFK Stadium   546-3337
East Capitol Street and the Anacostia River

Rio Grande Café   1-301-656-2981
4919 Fairmont Avenue (off Old Georgetown Rd.),
Bethesda, Maryland

Ritz-Carlton, The   835-2100
2100 Massachusetts Avenue, N.W.   1-800-424-8008

River Inn, The   337-7600
924 25th Street, N.W.   1-800-424-2741

Rivermist Kennels   1-301-774-3100
19515 New Hampshire Avenue, Brinklow, Maryland

Rizik Brothers, Inc.   223-4050
1260 Connecticut Avenue, N.W.

Robert F. Kennedy Memorial Stadium   547-9077

Robin Weir & Co.   861-0444
2134 P Street, N.W.

Rock Creek Nature Center   426-6829
5200 Glover Road

Rock Creek Park
Cathedral Avenue and Rock Creek Parkway, N.W.

Rock Creek Park Horse Center   362-0117
Military and Glover Roads, N.W.

Rogue, The   371-2223
476 K Street, N.W.

Rogue's Gallery Mystery Bookstore   1-301-986-5511
4904 Elm Street, Bethesda, Maryland

Romania (Embassy of)   232-4747
1607 23rd Street, N.W.

Rosecroft Raceway   1-301-567-4000
Oxon Hill/Fort Washington, Maryland

Rotary Club of Washington, The   638-3555
Washington Hotel, 15th Street and Pennsylvania
Avenue, N.W.

Royal Jordanian Airlines   1-800-223-0470

Rubesch's, Inc.   1-703-548-0659
119 South Royal Street, Alexandria, Virginia

Ruesch International   887-0990
1140 19th Street, N.W.

Rumors   466-7378
1900 M Street, N.W.

Rwanda (Embassy of)   232-2882
1714 New Hampshire Avenue, N.W.

S

Saint Laurent Rive Gauche   965-3555
600 New Hampshire Avenue, N.W.

Saks-Jandel   1-301-652-2250
5514 Wisconsin Avenue, Chevy Chase, Maryland

Saks-Watergate   337-4200
2522 Virginia Avenue, N.W.

Sakura Palace   1-301-587-7070
7926 Georgia Avenue (Eastern Ave.)
Silver Spring, Maryland

Salon Roi   234-2668
2602 Connecticut Avenue, N.W.

San Marino (Embassy of)   223-3517
1155 21st Street, N.W.

Sarinah Satay House   337-2955
1338 Wisconsin Avenue, N.W. (N/O Sts.), Georgetown

Satin & Lace   659-5223
2000 Pennsylvania Avenue, N.W.

Saudi Arabia (Embassy of)   342-3800
601 New Hampshire Avenue, N.W.

Save the Children   822-8426
International Craft Center, 1341 Connecticut
Avenue, N.W.

Scandinavian Airways   1-800-221-2350

Schneider's of Capitol Hill   543-9300
300 Massachusetts Avenue, N.E.

Secondhand Rose   337-3378
1516 Wisconsin Avenue, N.W.

SECRETARIAL SERVICES

AA Secretarial Services   466-3702
1522 K Street, N.W.

Only three blocks from the White House, they are ideally located in the center of town and are equipped to handle almost any job ranging from regular secretarial work to telephone answering and accounting work. Their computer equipment includes both Wang and IBM.

My Other Secretary   429-1997
1133 15th Street, N.W., Suite 1010

In addition to all of the usual secretarial skills available, they have another major asset: 24-hour emergency service. When you suddenly need help, they are there. They will also pick up and deliver material.

SECURITY GUARDS

In a city that is constantly host to policy makers, there is sometimes a need for special security arrangements. We have selected two companies that offer the most experienced personnel and the most comprehensive service.

Commando K-9 Detectives, Inc.   **1-301-868-7014**
7703 Woodyard Road, Clinton, Maryland

Executive Security, Inc.   **546-5800**
3230 Pennsylvania Avenue, S.E.

Seidner Antiques   **775-8212**
1333 New Hampshire Avenue, N.W.

Senate Barber Shop (U.S. Senate)   **224-4560**
B-68 Russell Senate Office Building, U.S. Capitol

Senegal (Embassy of)   **234-0540**
2112 Wyoming Avenue, N.W.

Serenade Record Shop   **638-5580**
1710 Pennsylvania Avenue, N.W.

Seven Corners Custom Tailors   **1-703-532-7900**
6201 Arlington Boulevard, Falls Church, Virginia

Sheraton Carlton, The   **638-2626**
923 16th Street, N.W.   **1-800-325-3535**

Sheraton Crystal City Hotel   **1-703-486-1111**
1800 Jefferson Davis Highway   **1-800-325-3535**
Alexandria, Virginia

Sheraton Washington Hotel   **228-2000**
2660 Woodley Road, N.W.   **1-800-325-3535**

SHOES, MEN'S

Bally of Switzerland   **429-0604**
1022 Connecticut Avenue, N.W.

Florsheim   **223-0975**
1218 Connecticut Avenue, N.W.

Hahn's   **783-1080**
14th and G Streets, N.W.

Massey's Johnston & Murphy   **429-9053**
1814 M Street, N.W.

SHOES, WOMEN'S

Andre Bellini   **1-301-231-9144**
White Flint Mall, Rockville, Maryland

Bally of Switzerland   **429-0604**
1022 Connecticut Avenue

Shoe Scene   **659-2194**
1330 Connecticut Avenue, N.W.

Charles Jourdan Boutique   **1-301-986-1460**
5506 Wisconsin Avenue, Chevy Chase, Maryland

Chorus Line	**965-7277**

Georgetown Park Mall, 3222 M Street, N.W.

Shoe Scene	**659-2194**

1330 Connecticut Avenue, N.W.

Shooters	**234-0975**

3 Riggs Court, N.W.

SHOPPING

See **STORES or SHOPPING MALLS**

SHOPPING MALLS

Almost all of the shopping in Washington is done in the giant shopping malls. They certainly make it easy to part with your money. There is a wide range in the quality of the shops to be found in the malls, and you can usually judge by the name of the main store. The Neiman Marcus name, for instance, is a sign of a quality mall.

Georgetown Park Mall
3222 M Street, N.W.
> Monday–Friday 10:00 A.M.–9:00 P.M.
> Saturday 10:00 A.M.–7:00 P.M.
> Sunday Noon–6:00 P.M.

Everything for the high-style lifestyle is available in the midst of bustling Georgetown. Abercrombie & Fitch, Ann Taylor, Mark Cross, Polo/Ralph Lauren, and Williams-Sonoma are included.

Landmark Shopping Center
5839 Duke Street, Alexandria, Virginia
> Monday–Saturday 9:30 A.M.–10:00 P.M.
> Sunday Noon–6:00 P.M.

You'll find Sears, branches of Woodward & Lothrop, and Hecht's among the 43 stores at this open-air center with lots of parking.

Mazza Gallerie   966-6114
5300 Wisconsin Avenue, N.W.
> Monday–Friday 10:00 A.M.–9:00 P.M.
> Saturday 10:00 A.M.–6:00 P.M.
> Sunday Noon–5:00 P.M. (Some stores)
> Metro: Friendship Heights

Neiman Marcus anchors this luxurious collection of shops on the District/Chevy Chase line.

Potomac Mills
2700 Potomac Mills Circle, Prince William, Virginia
    Monday–Saturday 10:00 A.M.–9:30 P.M.
    Sunday 1:00 A.M.–6:00 P.M.

You'll need a car to reach this shoppers' paradise—200 stores specializing in discounted merchandise. Take exit 52 off of I-95 South to reach such stores as IKEA and Waccamaw Pottery.

Shops at National Place, The
F Street (13th/14th Sts., N.W.)
    Monday–Saturday 10:00 A.M.–7:00 P.M.
    Sunday Noon–5:00 P.M.
    Metro: Metro Center

Adjoining the J.W. Marriott, 80 shops and six restaurants provide wonderful browsing and snacking.

Springfield Mall
Franconia Road & Loisdale Road, Springfield, Virginia
    Monday–Saturday 10:00 A.M.–9:30 P.M.
    Sunday Noon–5:00 P.M.

J.C. Penney, Montgomery Ward, and Garfinkels are the major attractions here. Plans are underway to convert this from a family-oriented mall to an upscale one.

Tyson's Corner Center   1-703-893-9400
1961 Chain Bridge Road, McLean, Virginia
    Monday–Saturday 10:00 A.M.–9:30 P.M.
    Sunday Noon–5:00 P.M.

One hundred forty of the area's finest shops, including Bloomingdale's, Nordstrom, Woodward & Lothrop, and Hechts.

White Flint
11301 Rockville Pike, North Bethesda, Maryland
    Monday–Saturday 10:00 A.M.–9:30 P.M.
    Sunday Noon–6:00 P.M.

Women's fashions and accessories are the drawing card here, with I. Magnin, Bloomingdale's, Lord & Taylor, and Raleigh's leading the selection. To preserve its upper-crust appeal, White Flint, refuses to label itself as a mall.

Shops at National Place, The
F Street (13th/14th Sts., N.W.)

Sidney Kramer Books, Inc.   293-2685
1825 I Street, N.W.

Sierra Leone (Embassy of)   939-9261
1701 19th Street, N.W.

SIGHTSEEING

See also **TOURS AND MUSEUMS**

Anderson House   785-0540

2118 Massachusetts Avenue, N.W. (21st/22nd Sts.)

  Tuesday–Saturday 1:00 P.M.–4:00 P.M.

  No admission charge

  Metro: Dupont Circle

Now the headquarters of the Society of the Cincinnati, this must have been one of the most overwhelming homes in Washington when it belonged to Larz Anderson, the Ambassador to Japan and Minister to Belgium, who was a member of the Society for 43 years. Named for Lucius Quinctius Cincinnatus, a Roman leader whose military, political, and private life paralleled George Washington's, the Society was founded in 1783 by officers of the Continental Army. Membership is limited to first-born male descendents of those original officers or the French forces who fought alongside them. The furnishings include carved Italian Renaissance choir stalls, seventeenth-century Flemish tapestries which were a gift from King Louis XIII to the Papal emissary to his court, and a 2000-year-old Chinese urn. A glance at the 80 foot long grand ballroom hints at the splendor and elegance that were the everyday life of the Andersons.

Arlington National Cemetery   1-703-692-0931

Across the Potomac River via Memorial Bridge into Arlington, Virginia

  Open daily:

  October–March 8:00 A.M.–5:00 P.M.

  April–September 8:00 A.M.–7:00 P.M.

  Metro Station: Arlington Cemetery

These peaceful acres in Virginia were once the estate of the Custis family. General Robert E. Lee, our most famous confederate leader, married Mary Ann Randolph Custis (daughter of George Washington's adopted son, George Washington Parke Custis) in 1831, and they lived here until Union troops overran the mansion during the Civil War and forced the family out. Later, the federal government seized the land for unpaid taxes, but a Supreme Court decision returned the house to Lee's son, George Washington Custis Lee, in 1883. The Custis–Lee mansion, as it is now known, is open to the public. Right in front of it is the tomb of Pierre Charles L'Enfant, the original designer and city planner of Washington. Thousands of simple markers honor the dead of numerous wars, a solemn sight that causes one to reflect on the rights most dear to all of us. Among the many prominent people buried here are, of course, the Kennedys—JFK and his brother Robert share a hillside with a wonderful view of Washington. Generals Omar Bradley, George Marshall, and John Pershing are here, as is boxing great Joe Louis. But the most moving memorial is the perpetual honor guard at the Tomb of the Unknown Soldier. The changing of the guard is a simple yet stirring ceremony that has taken place every half hour for many years. The best and most comfortable way to tour the cemetery is by Tourmobile. It is the only conveyance allowed on the grounds and will shuttle you back and forth from the Mall area in the city as well as taking you to all of the most interesting places in the cemetery.

Armed Forces Medical Museum   **576-2348**
Walter Reed Army Medical Center, 6825 16th Street, N.W., Building 54 on Dahlia Street

Arts & Industries Building   **357-2700**
Jefferson Drive at 9th Street, N.W.   **Tours 357-3030**
    Daily except Christmas: 10:00 A.M.–5:30 P.M.
    Metro: Smithsonian
It doesn't have the appeal of the National Air & Space Museum; it doesn't contain the Hope Diamond or other baubles, but to us this red-brick Victorian structure embodies the very spirit of "The Smithsonian." Originally built as the National Museum, it was finished in 1881 and was the site of the inaugural ball for James Garfield. Its real purpose, however, was to house all of the stuff left over from Philadelphia's Centennial Exhibition. Looking around, you'll understand why the Smithsonian has been labeled "the nation's attic." You can view a polyglot collection ranging from locomotives to totem poles. All of the Smithsonian's gift shops offer everything from books and bookmarks to expensive reproduction jewelry, but since this museum does not attract hordes of people, shopping here is a particular pleasure.

B'nai B'rith International
Center/Klutznick Museum   **857-6583**
1640 Rhode Island Avenue, N.W. (16th/17th Sts.)
    Monday–Friday, Sun 10:00 A.M.–5:00 P.M.
    Closed Saturday and Jewish Holidays
    Metro: Farragut North

Bureau of Engraving & Printing   **447-9709**
14th and C Streets, S.W.
    Weekdays: 8:30 A.M.–2:30 P.M.
    Metro: Smithsonian
Everyone loves touring this building where all the paper currency in the United States is made. After a short intro-

ductory film, you'll see the complicated intaglio process by which those lovely greenbacks are produced. Postage stamps, treasury notes, military certificates, and invitations to the White House are also printed here.

Capitol, The

Pennsylvania Avenue and	**Senate 224-3121**
1st Street, S.E.	**House 225-3121**

    Daily 9:00 A.M.–3:45 A.M.

    Metro: Capitol South

Built on a hill which Pierre L'Enfant described as "a pedestal waiting for a monument," the Capitol is the first landmark that visitors to Washington search for on the horizon. This building once contained not only both houses of Congress, but the Supreme Court and Library of Congress as well. Write to your congressperson well in advance of your visit to request tickets to the morning congressional tour. Otherwise, take one of the free 35-minute guided tours that leave from the Rotunda every 15 minutes between 9:00 A.M. and 3:45 P.M.

Every President from Andrew Jackson through George Bush (except Reagan who changed tradition and was inaugurated on the West Front) has taken his oath of office on the East Front steps. It was here that Abraham Lincoln asked a divided nation to forge ahead "with malice toward none, with charity for all...," Franklin Delano Roosevelt reminded us that "the only thing we have to fear is fear itself," and John F. Kennedy challenged us to "Ask not what your country can do for you—ask what you can do for your country."

The huge Rotunda (180 feet high and 97 feet across) is the hub of the Capitol. Nine presidents have lain in state here. The House of Representatives met from 1807 to 1857 in what is now the National Statuary Hall. A curious acoustical effect enables one to hear what is whispered 45 feet away.

Cedar Hill. *See* Frederick Douglass
National Historic Site

Cherry Blossom Festival, The

Washington's cherry trees have become the symbol of spring for the entire country. When they bloom, in late March or early April, hundreds of thousands of people are drawn to the capital to see the 3,000 trees of twelve varieties that glorify the Tidal Basin. A gift from Japan in 1912, the trees remind us each year of our many and varied ties to that country. Although the "Greenhouse Effect" has made it increasingly difficult for meteorologists to predict when the blossoms will appear, Festival planners have settled on the first week of April for the celebratory pageants, parades, concerts, and marathon. Be prepared for massive traffic jams, crowds, and the heart-breaking beauty of fragile, delicate blossoms that a strong wind might scatter.

Chesapeake & Ohio Canal (C&O)   229-3614

One of the best preserved of the old American canals, this stretches 184½ miles from Georgetown to Cumberland, Maryland. Walking or biking along the old towpath provides a pleasant afternoon's excursion. From mid-April to mid-October, canal boats the Georgetown (653-5844) and the Canal Clipper (299-2026) operate.

Chinatown

Located roughly between H and K Streets, N.W. from 6th to 9th Streets, Washington's Chinatown is graced by the spectacular Friendship Archway, decorated in classical Chinese art of the Qing and Ming Dynasties. Compared to its New York and San Francisco counterparts, this is a small area. As one would expect, restaurants offering outstanding cuisine and value abound.

Christ Church, Capitol Hill   547-9300

620 G Street, S.E.

Built in 1767–1773, it was the church George Washington attended. Many of the interior appointments are the originals.

Christian Heurich Mansion
Columbia Historical Society   785-2068

1307 New Hampshire Avenue, N.W. (19th/20th Sts.)
   Wednesday–Saturday Noon–4:00 P.M.
   Metro: Dupont Circle

A monument to the time-honored path to success. Heurich started life, in Germany, as a butcher's apprentice, emigrated, managed a brewery, married the boss's widow and inherited everything upon her death. Now the home of the Columbia Historical Society, the house is one of the most opulent in Washington and is well worth a visit.

Columbia Historical Site. *See*
Christian Heurich Mansion

Daughters of the American
Revolution Headquarters &
Museum   628-1776

1776 D Street, N.W.
   Monday–Friday 9:00 A.M.–4:00 P.M.
   Sunday 1:00 P.M.–5:00 P.M.
   Metro: Farragut West

One of our most famous historical organizations, the DAR headquarters building houses their offices, a magnificent genealogical library, and museum. Founded in 1890, membership is limited to direct descendants of those who fought in the war for independence. The rooms furnished with period furniture are well worth a visit.

Decatur House   673-4030
748 Jackson Place, N.W. (H Street/Lafayette Square)
    Tuesday–Friday 10:00 A.M.–2:00 P.M.
    Saturday & Sunday Noon–4:00 P.M.
    Metro: Farragut West, Farragut North
It was said that Commodore Stephen Decatur, hero of the War of 1812, built this splendid Late Federal style house with proceeds from government-sanctioned privateering against Barbary pirates. Admiring the splendid second-floor ballroom may convince you there's some truth to these rumors.

Dumbarton Oaks   338-8278
1703 32nd St., N.W. (R/S Sts.)
    Collections: Tuesday–Sunday 2:00 P.M.–5:00 P.M.
    Gardens: Daily, except holidays 2:00 P.M.–5:00 P.M.
This gorgeous estate on the upper reaches of Georgetown is rich in historical significance. Named after the Rock of Dumbarton in Scotland, the original home was built in 1801. After taking possession of the house in 1920, Robert Bliss, former U.S. Ambassador to Sweden and Argentina, and his heiress wife, Mildred, created a small, but important, museum of pre-Columbian, Byzantine, and Hellenistic art and jewelry. Mrs. Bliss and Beatrix Farrand designed the 16 acres of gardens, manicured walkways and fountains—one of the most dramatically beautiful in the United States.

In 1944, talks held here laid the foundations for the creation of the United Nations. Igor Stravinsky wrote his Concerto in E Flat, the Dumbarton Oaks Concerto to commemorate the Bliss's 30th wedding anniversary.

Embassy Row
    Metro: Dupont Circle
Diplomats from over 130 countries are concentrated in the Northwest quadrant in opulent houses built earlier this century for the fabulously rich. When you are feeling "museum-ed out" and desire a change of pace, take the Metro to Dupont Circle and stroll along Massachusetts Avenue past 2020 (the McLean Mansion, now the Indonesian Embassy) up as far as 3100—the British Embassy's stately country house. In mid-May, various embassies open their doors to the public to benefit Davis Memorial Goodwill industries. Call 636-4225 for details.

Explorers' Hall. *See* **National Geographic Society**

FBI Building, The   324-3447
10th Street & Pennsylvania Avenue, N.W.
   Monday–Friday 9:00 A.M.–4:15 P.M.
   Admission: Free
   Metro: Federal Triangle, Gallery Place
Tourists don't flock here to admire the architectural wonders of this building—one of the ugliest in Washington. It's the firearms demonstration that packs 'em in. The well-informed and enthusiastic guides also explain the FBI's current work fighting organized crime, terrorism, espionage, and extortion. During the summer, about 5,000 people visit here daily, so you may have a long wait. If possible, write to your Senator or Congressperson well in advance of your trip and request passes for a VIP tour.

Folger Shakespeare Library, The   544-4600
201 East Capitol Street, S.E.
   Monday–Saturday 10:00 A.M.–4:00 P.M.
   Closed Sunday
   Admission: Free
   Metro Station: Capitol South on the Blue or Orange Line
One of the wonders of Washington, this is another of the more specialized attractions that will not be to everyone's taste. The value of this library can hardly be exaggerated. It has the largest collection of Shakespeare's works in the world, and incidentally includes books by his peers, and about his era, that boggle the mind.

   The library is worthy of a major write-up, but the nature of this book denies us that pleasure. If you are here as a scholar, there is little we can tell you about the Folger that you don't already know. If you are here as a tourist, you are probably not interested in doing research on Shakespeare and his friends. We therefore will simply say that, given the fact that Shakespeare is the most important figure in the history of Western literature, this is one of the most important libraries in the world.

Ford's Theatre & Lincoln Museum   Museum 426-6927
511 10th Street, N.W. (E/F Sts.)   **Box Office 347-6927**
   Daily 9:00AM–5:00 P.M.
   Metro:Metro Center
Best known as the theater where Abraham Lincoln was assassinated as he watched a performance of *Our American Cousin*, Ford's Theater has been beautifully restored and presents small-stage touring productions. The basement

contains a small museum of mementos of both Lincoln and John Wilkes Booth.

Frederick Douglass National Historic Site (Cedar Hill) 426-5960
1411 W Street, S.E. (14th/15th Sts.)
> January–March, October-December 9:00 A.M.–4:00 P.M.
> April–September 9:00 A.M.–5:00 P.M.

Period-costumed guides conduct tours through this simple white Victorian home where Frederick Douglass lived from 1877 until his death in 1895. Born into slavery in Maryland, Douglass escaped from the plantation at the age of 21. An eloquent spokesman for abolition, he ultimately became adviser to four presidents.

George Washington Masonic National Memorial. *See* additional information under Alexandria, Virginia 1-703-683-2007
King Street and Callahan Drive, Alexandria, Virginia

A 333 foot tower which supposedly duplicates the famous lighthouse at Alexandria. While this memorial contains some Washingtoniana, it is also a monument to one of his major interests: free masonry. Tours every half hour.

Goddard Space Flight Center (NASA) 1-301-286-8981
Soil Conservation Road, (Baltimore-Washington Pkwy./Greenbelt Rd.), Greenbelt, Maryland
> Wednesday–Sunday 10:00 A.M.–4:00 P.M.

This is one of the largest of NASA's research centers. In addition to its scientific work and its function as a tracking station, it is also home to a fascinating Visitor's Center. Dr. Robert Goddard was one of the pioneers in rocketry, and his early work is reflected in their great collection of rockets which ranges from a replica of his 1926 model to some of the most recent designs. On the first and third Sunday of each month, model rockets are launched here—call for exact times.

Islamic Mosque & Center 332-8343
2551 Massachusetts Avenue, N.W. (Belmont Rd.)

It is always a delight to see the beautiful architecture of a mosque, with its graceful minaret thrusting into the sky. This one is located in the midst of Embassy Row and is certainly at odds with its more staid neighbors.

Iwo Jima Memorial (Marine Corps Memorial) 1-703-285-2598
Arlington Boulevard and Meade Street, Arlington, Virginia

All of us who remember World War II are familiar with

the famous photograph that inspired this bronze memorial to the marines who have given their lives for their country. Almost 6,000 marines were killed in the battle of Iwo Jima, with thousands of others wounded. Three of the six men who are shown raising the flag were latter killed in battle. It is fittingly located at Arlington National Cemetery.

Jefferson Memorial   426-6822
14th Street and East Basin Drive, S.W.
> Daily 8:00 A.M.–Midnight
> The rotunda is open and lighted all night.

One of Washington's most popular and most beautiful attractions, the Jefferson Memorial is located slightly off the beaten path. The interior of this simple classical structure is dominated by a 19-foot high statue of Thomas Jefferson, an architect of words as well as buildings. In late March or early April when the cherry blossoms are blooming around the Tidal Basin, the whole effect is breathtaking.

Kennedy Center for the Performing Arts, The   254-3600
2700 F Street, N.W.

While Washington has many museums vying for popularity, there is only one major center for the performing arts. Filling a void which had always existed, the Kennedy Center houses a 2750 seat concert hall, a 2300 seat opera house, and the 1200 seat Eisenhower Theater.

Library of Congress   287-5000
10 1st Street, S.E. (East Capitol St./Independence Avenue)

Superlatives abound when one starts to describe the Library of Congress, the world's largest. Every book published in the United States must be deposited here in order to be protected by copyright. Almost anything one might wish to read can be found here. Officially the reference library for Congress, its resources are available to the public, as are the many special exhibits and programs provided by its many specialized libraries. For visitors, there is a brief slide show which introduces the library as well as a guided tour which lasts 45 minutes.

Lincoln Memorial, The   426-6895
23rd Street off Constitution Ave, N.W.

Who can deny that this is one of the nation's outstanding memorials—and certainly a fitting one. Standing at the end of the reflecting pool, its classical Grecian design has been the background for some of the notable events that Lincoln would have championed. When denied the right to perform in the DAR auditorium, Marion Anderson sang to a huge crowd from the steps. Years later, it was the site of the famous "I have a dream" speech made by the Reverend Martin Luther King, Jr.

After climbing the steep flight of steps, one is face to face with the huge statue of Abraham Lincoln by Daniel Chester French. Into the walls surrounding the brooding figure are carved his Gettysburg and Second Inaugural addresses.

Marine Corps War Memorial. *See* **Iwo Jima Memorial**

Marine Corps Museum. *See* **U.S. Marine Corps Museum**

Maryland State House   1-301-269-3400
State Circle, Annapolis, Maryland

Built in 1772, it is the oldest state capitol in continous use. It claims the largest wooden dome in the United States.

Mount Vernon   1-703-780-2000
Southern end of George Washington Parkway, 16 miles south of downtown Washington

Daily 9:00 A.M.–5:00 P.M. (4:00 P.M. November–
February)
Admission:
Adults $5.00
Children $2.00

Five hundred acres remain of George Washington's estate, which once stretched most of the way to present-day Alexandria. Washington loved this house, renovating and expanding it throughout his life. Standing on the splendid verandah overlooking the Potomac, you'll understand why. Since 1860, the house and grounds have been owned and maintained by the Mount Vernon Ladies' Association. It was meticulously restored in the early 1980s and provides a glimpse into the life of Washington the private citizen. Of particular interest is the key to Paris's dreaded Bastille prison, presented to Washington by the Marquis de Lafayette, which hangs on the wall in the central hall. The gardens are splendidly maintained.

A unique way to visit the home of our first president is to take the *Spirit of Mt. Vernon* (see separate listing), a cruise ship. In addition to being a most exciting way to get to the plantation, it is a chance to see Washington and the sights along the Potomac River from a new perspective. A narrator describes the various points of interest en route and the two hours spent at Mt. Vernon are adequate to see everything before the trip back to Washington. Children will love it.

National Aquarium, The   377-2825
Department of Commerce Building, 14th Street and Constitution Avenue, N.W.

Everyone loves an aquarium, and, while this is not one of the "great ones," it is a favorite with adults and children alike. Tucked away in the basement of the Department of Commerce, it is the oldest public aquarium in the country and features a wide variety of salt and fresh water specimens. The children seem to enjoy the "Touch Tank," which allows them to handle some of the hardier varieties of aquatic life. Adults don't mind watching them do it. Feeding time is prime time. Try to visit at 2:00 P.M. any day but Friday. Piranhas eat on Tuesday, Thursday, and Sunday. Sharks dine with equal gusto on Monday, Wednesday, and Saturday.

National Archives   523-3184
Constitution Avenue (7th/9th Sts., N.W.)

A must for everyone. See the documents that are the cornerstones of our democracy. The Declaration of Independence, the Constitution, and the Bill of Rights are preserved here and are on view for all to see. But that's not all. The National Archives is the 21-floor vault that stores millions of documents that are vital to the preservation of the history of our country. Treaties of all kinds, including some made with American Indian tribes, data relating to genealogical history, the famous Civil War photographs of Matthew Brady, share space with more recent items such as Franklin Roosevelt's recorded "Fireside Chats," and the propaganda messages broadcast by Tokyo Rose during World War II.

National Building Museum   272-2448
F Street, N.W. (4th/5th Sts.)
  Metro: Judiciary Square

National Capital Trolley Museum   1-301-384-6088
1313 Bonifant Road (Layhill/Notley Rds.), Northwest Branch Regional Park, Silver Spring, Maryland

National Cathedral, The   537-6200
(Cathedral Church of St. Peter & St. Paul), Wisconsin/ Massachusetts Aves., N.W. (34th/Garfield)

Theodore Roosevelt laid the cornerstone in 1907 of this, the sixth largest cathedral in the world. Although it is the seat of the Episcopal Diocese of Washington, it has no local congregation and serves the entire nation as a house of prayer. The cathedral is built in fourteenth-century Gothic style, complete with flying butresses. The 57-acre grounds contain three gardens, four schools, the London Brass Rubbing Center, and a stone carvers shed where one can watch the carvers at work. In the crypt are the tombs of President Woodrow Wilson and his wife. Helen Keller is buried here as well.

National Firearms Museum   828-6253
1600 Rhode Island Avenue, N.W.

National Geographic
    Society/Explorers' Hall   857-7588
M and 17th Streets, N.W.

National Museum of African Art   357-1300
Smithsonian Institution, The Quadrangle (950 Independence Avenue, S.W.), Jefferson Drive between 11th and 12th Streets, S.W.
> Daily 10:00 A.M.–5:30 P.M.
> Closed Christmas
> Admission: Free
> Metro Station: Smithsonian on the Blue or Orange Lines

National Museum of American Art   357-3156
Smithsonian Institution   357-2700
Gallery Place at 8th and G Streets, N.W.
> Daily 10:00 A.M.–5:30 P.M.
> Closed Christmas
> Admission: Free
> Metro Station: Gallery Place on Red or Yellow Lines

National Museum of American
    History   357-2700
Smithsonian Institution, 14th Street and Constitution Avenue, N.W.
> Daily 10:00 A.M.–5:30 P.M.
> Closed Christmas
> Admission: Free
> Metro Station: Smithsonian or Federal Triangle on Blue or Orange Lines

National Shrine of the Immaculate
    Conception   526-8300
4th Street and Michigan Avemue, N.E.
Pope Pius IX decreed that Mary should be the patron saint of the United States, and this huge church was built as a national shrine in her honor. Seating 6000 people, it is the largest Catholic church in the western hemisphere and the seventh largest in the world. Pope John Paul II, the second pontiff to visit this country, led morning prayers here. Those of you who share our love of church bells will be delighted to find that there is a 56 bell carillon in the Knights Tower. As any student of art history can tell you, the Catholic church has a long and important love of art. Art that depicts and honors the beliefs of the Church. In this church, it takes the form of mosaics, one of the most extensive collections in the world. Take one of the tours so that you can see

them. The architecture is a combination of Byzantine and Romanesque, one of the most romantic forms of the building arts.

National Zoological Park   **673-4800**
3000 Block of Connecticut Avenue
   Metro: Woodley Park
   Open daily except Christmas
   May–September 15th
   Grounds open: 8A.M.–8 P.M.
   Buildings open: 9A.M.–6 P.M.
   September 16th–April 30th
   Grounds open: 8A.M.–6 P.M.
   Buildings open: 9A.M.–4:30 P.M.

A brief trip on Washington's Metro brings you to one of the most popular places in town—the home of the pandas. Adele took a whole roll of photos, the only ones she took in Washington. McDowell wouldn't let her buy the $32 panda sweatshirts so she made him go through the monkey house with her. Yuk! Washington has made a major effort to develop a parklike setting where the animals can live and play in comfort. Children and parents alike enjoy watching the elephants, camels, monkeys, and others. We suggest that you call to verify the exact time of the elephant show and sea lion feeding—two extra special events.

Naval Observatory. *See* **U.S. Naval Observatory**

Navy Memorial Museum. *See* **U.S. Navy Memorial Museum**

Octagon House, The   **638-3105**
1799 New York Avenue, N.W. (18th St.)
   Tuesday–Friday 10:00A.M.–4:00 P.M.
   Saurday–Sunday Noon–4:00 P.M.
   Suggested donations:
   Adults $2.00
   Students $1.00
   Metro: Farragut West

This elegant brick building (Washington's oldest private mansion) was home to President Madison for seven months after the British burned the White House. Now owned by the American Institute of Architects Foundation, the building contains fine examples of period furniture and offers exhibitions of architectural drawings. One of the few attractions in Washington that is not totally free.

Old Post Office Tower, The (Nancy Hanks Center)   **523-5691**
At the turn of the century it was the largest government

building in DC. Among its "firsts"—the first clock tower, the first steel framework, and the first electric power plant for lighting. It still has one of the largest uninterrupted open spaces in the city. Now redesigned for use by lots of fast food and souvenir shops, it is a haven for teenagers and young people. In 1983, The ten Congress Bells were installed in the 315-foot tower. A gift of the Ditchley Foundation of Great Britain, the bells are replicas of the ones in Westminster Abbey in London and weigh between 581 and 2953 pounds each. A complete peal, taking 3½ hours, is rung in honor of the opening and closing of Congress and on State occasions.

Old Stone House, The   426-6851
3051 M Street, N.W., Georgetown
Supposedly the only prerevolutionary house in the Washington area, it may be worth a visit if you have lots of time.

Old Town Trolley Tours. *See*
ALEXANDRIA, VIRGINIA

Old Town Trolley Tours of
Washington   269-3020
3150 V Street, N.E.
Somewhat like the Tourmobile, but more limited, this system offers 17 convenient locations where one can board or re-board.

Old Treasury Building   1-301-267-8149
State Circle, Annapolis, Maryland
Originally the storage depot for Bills of Credit, this building was erected in 1735. It is now the office of a tour company serving the Annapolis area. Of no major importance as a tourist attraction.

Organization of American States, The   789-3751
17th Street, N.W. and Constitution Avenue
While this is an exceptionally important organization, the building and museum are not priority items if you have limited time. The Aztec Gardens are filled with tropical plants from the member countries and are a peaceful and quiet place. The museum exhibits the works of Latin artists.

Pentagon, The   1-301-695-1776
Route 1, I-395, Arlington, Virginia
This is not one of the most interesting tours you can take, particularily if you have the children with you. It sounds much better than it is. The Pentagon, built at the

beginning of World War II, is an unusual building; its shape could easily be a symbol for a contemporary *Star Wars* movie. The statistics about the building itself are staggering (23,000 people work here) and will only be remembered by the kids. What is important is that this is the center of all of the defense systems and the offices of the elite of our defense operations. Regardless of whether you are a hawk or a dove, it's interesting to experience, at first hand, the investment made by our government in just the head office for our defense system.

It is the largest office building in the world, and yet has only five floors above ground. The fact that it is a functioning office building is the reason that it is not interesting. People actually work in this building, and touring it is much like walking through any office building. You see lots of doors but not much else. McDowell has known many of the top officers of the Air Force who served during World War II and is therefore always interested in the exhibit of aircraft models (every aircraft the military has ever flown). One of his friends, a 1924 graduate of West Point, held International Pilots license #1 and test pilots license #50. Without these memories, however, interest fades.

The Navy's scale models of their vessels, submarines, battleships, aircraft carriers, and so forth, make a brave and exciting display outside of the offices of the admirals who control our sea defenses.

There are lots of flags and, for those of you who are afraid this is a male chauvinist operation, there is homage paid to the women who, throughout the history of our country, have dedicated their lives to strengthening and protecting our country. We always leave here feeling more understanding for the stiff-necked attitude of the career military people and sometimes an appreciation for their dedication.

As we say, this is not for everyone. If you are old enough to have memories that support the things you will see, it can be quite interesting, otherwise you should consider allocating your time to more popular tours.

Peterson House   **426-6830**
516 10th Street, N.W.

Except for the fact that Lincoln died here, there is little to recommend this as a tourist attraction. But he was taken here after being shot and thus established this building's place in history. Like most places where many people have experienced strong emotion, there is an aura of spirituality that seems to permeate the atmosphere. Combine it with a visit to Ford's Theater and Museum.

St. John's Episcopal Church   343-8766
Lafayette Square, 16th and H Streets N.W.
Designed by Benjamin Latrobe, this is called "the
Church of the Presidents." It is close to the White House
and has been host to many of them. Pew 54 is "the
President's Pew."

Smithsonian Institution   357-2020
Jefferson Drive, S.W. (10th St.)
    Metro: Smithsonian
After the Capitol and the White House, this is a con-
tender for the most mentioned name in the city. The
Smithsonian is a collection of buildings and collections
that seems to be able to expand indefinitely. "The Castle,"
a familiar red-brick building, is the administration building for the complex of museums and research centers that
comprise the whole. James Smithson, an Englishman, died
in 1829 and left $500,000 to the United States for the
founding of "an establishment for the increase and diffu-
sion of knowledge among men." Little could he have
known of the importance of his bequest. Following is a list
of the various important divisions:

Anacostia Museum
Archives of American Art (New York, Boston, Detroit,
Los Angeles, San Francisco, and Washington, DC)
Arthur M. Sackler Gallery
Arts & Industries Building
Conservation & Research Center (National Zoo)
Cooper–Hewitt Museum (in New York City)
Enid A. Haupt Garden
Freer Gallery of Art
Hirshhorn Museum & Sculpture Garden
International Gallery
Marine Station at Link Port (Ft. Pierce, FL)
National Air & Space Museum
National Gallery of Art
National Museum of African Art
National Museum of American Art
National Museum of American History
National Museum of Natural History
National Portrait Gallery
National Zoological Park
Renwick Gallery
Smithsonian Astrophysical Observatory (Harvard
University, Cambridge, Massachusetts)
Smithsonian Environmental Research Center
(Edgewater, Maryland)
Smithsonian Tropical Research Institute, Panama

Spirit of Mt. Vernon   554-8000
Pier 4 (6th/Water Sts., S.W.)

A wonderful way to visit Mt. Vernon. Sail the Potomac on a comfortable cruise ship and listen to the Captain as he describes the points of interest lining the riverbank. Many colonial homes were built along the river, and this is the way early visitors first saw them in the days when the Potomac was the major highway. You will also pass Old Town Alexandria, and Ft. Washington. At Mt. Vernon, you will have a two-hour visit to the house and grounds before a leisurely trip home.

Spirit of Washington   554-1542
Pier 4, 6th and Water Streets, S.W.

Like the "Spirit" ships in New York and other cities, The *Spirit of Washington* features a live Broadway show review during its dinner cruises. There are also lunch and brunch cruises. It's a wonderful way to enjoy the sights.

State Department Diplomatic
Reception Rooms   647-3241
C and 22nd Streets, N.W.

On the eighth floor of the State Department Building, these rooms are furnished with the cream of eighteenth- and nineteenth-century furniture and art. The John Quincy Adams State Drawing Room is not to be missed.

Supreme Court   479-3211
1st and East Capitol Streets, N.E.

The Supreme Court makes decisions regarding the constitutionality of the decisions of other, lesser courts. Its sole authority for doing this is the Constitution itself. If you have a sincere interest in the most intimate workings of the judicial system, you must attend a session of this court. It is a highly intellectual process and not for the average tourist. There are a limited number of seats so if you want to attend, call for exact information about the case to be discussed and be sure to arrive early.

Courtroom lectures are given, when the court is in session, from 3:30 P.M. to 4:00 P.M. When the court is not in session, the lectures are given from 9:30 A.M. to 3:30 P.M., every hour on the half hour. There is also a short film describing the workings and the history of the court.

The building is a relative newcomer to the Mall, being built in 1935, but with its classical facade it is one of the most impressive. It also has one of the best cafeterias.

Textile Museum   667-0441
2320 S Street, N.W.
Tuesday–Saturday 10:00 A.M.–5:00 P.M.

Sunday 1:00 P.M.–5:00 P.M.
Closed Monday and Holidays
Admission: Free
Metro: Dupont Circle on the Red Line

Primarily for the Mediterranean and North Africa, this collection was started by collector George H. Myers. His former home, which now houses over 14,000 textiles and about 1500 rugs is a must if you want to see textiles. There is also a large and important research library on the premises.

Tomb of the Unknowns (Tomb of the Unknown Soldier)

Arlington National Cemetery, Arlington, Virginia

Dedicated to the memories of all of the dead who remain forever buried in unknown soil. For those who have lost friends, relatives, and loved ones in the various wars, there is no more poignant place. For all of those who remember someone whose body was never identified after the conflicts, this tomb is a symbol of the wastefulness and futility of war—of lives snuffed out before their time. The Third Infantry stands guard over this tomb and is famous for its silent and precise changing of the guard ceremony which takes place every half hour. When you visit Arlington National Cemetery, this is one of the monuments you must visit.

Tourmobile, The   554-7950

1000 Ohio Drive, S.W.

The Tourmobile is one of the most efficient ways of touring we have encountered. As a concessioner authorized by the U.S. Department of the Interior, it obviously has to maintain standards of service that are above reproach. We have found it to be one of the very best ways to reach all of the various sites and to learn about the monuments and buildings that it serves. After paying the fee, you may get off at any of the sites, spend as long there as you want, and get on the next Tourmobile to continue your tour.

There is a narrator on each Tourmobile to tell you in detail about all of the points of interest you pass. Our only complaint was that the speaker system is too loud. Try to not sit under one of the ceiling speakers. This is a wonderful way to see the city and it could only work in a city like Washington—in New York it would be stuck in traffic for hours. There are various tours available. Either call for information or ask at the Tourmobile booths.

Union Station   479-3211

1st and East Capitol Streets, N.W.

One of the busiest places in Washington. It is the main railroad terminal and houses many shops and restaurants including Adirondacks, one of the finest in the city. Re-opened in 1988 after extensive renovation, it is definitely a "must see." The main hall boasts a beautiful vaulted ceiling of white trimmed in gold leaf. Adirondacks occupies the former Presidential Suite where he would wait if taking a trip by train or greeting incoming dignitaries. It was here that Franklin Roosevelt awaited the arrival of the King and Queen of Great Britain.

U.S. Botanic Garden   225-7099
1st Street/Maryland Avenue/Independence
Avenue, S.W.

As orchid fanciers, it's impossible for us to pass this up. A greenhouse on the Mall by the Capitol for the purpose of "collecting, cultivating, and growing the various vegetable production of this and other countries for exhibition and display." In addition to our orchid favorites, there are palms, ferns, cacti, and other plants from tropical, subtropical, and desert habitats.

U. S. National Arboretum   475-4815
New York Avenue/Bladensburg Road and
M Streets, N.E.

Primary concerns at the Arboretum are research on trees and shrubs and educating the public about them. Administered by the U.S. Department of Agriculture, this is a serious research center which shares with the public the beauty of the plants in its care. Occupying 444 acres, its major attractions are the National Bonsai Collection, a bicentennial gift of the Japanese government, the Morrison Azalea Garden, the oriental plantings in the Cryptomeria Valley of the Garden Club of America, the Gotelli Dwarf Conifer Collection, Fern Valley, the National Herb Garden, and the dogwood trees of the Women's National Farm and Garden Association. Parking space is available, and there are picnic grounds.

U.S. Naval Academy   1-301-267-2291
Visitor's Gate, King George Street,
Annapolis, Maryland

The training ground for future naval officers. In Preble Hall are exhibited thousands of items related to the sea and the navy. Ranging from nautical uniforms to scrimshaw, this is a major attraction for those of you with the sea in your blood.

U.S. Naval Observatory   653-1543
34th Street and Massachusetts Avenue, N.W.

Most of us are familiar with this as the location of the home of the Vice President. It actually has had a long and important history of its own. Originally the Depot of Charts and Instruments, it was the storehouse for all of the navigational charts. It was a natural step from this to involvement in the experimentation with chronometers. Observatory Circle was built to keep traffic at a distance so that it wouldn't affect the research on delicate instruments. The Atomic Clock is the key to accurate standard time in the United States. If you're planning a visit, be sure to take valid ID or they won't let you in.

U.S. Navy Memorial   524-0830
Pennsylvania Avenue, N.W. (7th/9th Sts.)
A circular plaza featuring the world's largest grid map of the world. In the summer there are free military band performances here.

Vietnam Veterans Memorial   426-6841
23rd Street at Constitution Ave. N.W.
    Open 24 hours
Washington's most visited monument, Maya Ying Lin's V-shaped black granite walls, inscribed with the names of the almost 60,000 people who gave their lives or remain MIA's, draws a round-the-clock procession of visitors. Many leave flowers or tiny flags. Groups of veterans unite in prayer. No guidebook can prepare you for the emotional impact of this enormously dignified memorial.

Voice of America, The   485-6231
Department of Health and Human Services (North
Bldg.) , 330 Independence Avenue, S.W. (entrance on C
Street between 3rd & 4th Sts.)
Part of the U.S. Information Agency, the VOA broadcasts information and news through more than 100 overseas outlets. Announcers use dozens of languages to reach people who otherwise would be isolated from the rest of the world.

Washington Cathedral. *See* **National
    Cathedral**

**Washington Dolls' House & Toy
    Museum**   1-301-244-0024
5236 44th Street, N.W. (Jenifer/Harrison Sts.), Chevy
Chase, Maryland
    Tuesday–Saturday 10:00A.M.–5:00 P.M.
    Sunday Noon–5:00 P.M.
    Closed Monday
    Admission:
    Adults: $3.00
    Children: $1.00
    Metro Station: Friendship Heights on the Red LIne.
Flora Gill Jacobs is recognized as the leading authority on the history of doll houses, and this is her museum. As

she says, "It is dedicated to the proposition that doll's houses of the past comprise a study of the decorative arts in miniature, and that toys of the past reflect social history." There are so many things to see that we can't begin to list them—several hundred dolls are shown in the many interiors provided by the shops, houses, and rooms. If you are interested in rare dolls, they are here, too. Don't miss the shops! There are two: one for collectors of dolls houses, furniture, little stuff for decorating, and of course, dolls. The second shop is for people who like to build doll houses and supplies everything necessary to do just that.

Washington Harbour   342-7366
3000 K Street, N.W. (31st St.)

Developed to replace a derelict cement factory, this mixed-use project has little to recommend it as an architectural endeavor. It has a wonderful riverside location, however, and the condominums are expensive and popular. Like many similar developments, it has shops and restaurants built around a stone courtyard and makes use of art exhibits, fountains, and landscaping to maintain its aura of luxury.

Washington Monument   426-6841
14th Street and Constitution Avenue, N.W.

Located on the western part of the Mall, this is one of the easiest attractions to find. The needle-like shaft of the marble obelisk towers 555 feet, 5½ inches into the sky and seems to be visible from almost anyplace near the Mall. Built between 1848 and 1885, it opened to the public in 1886. At that time, it was the tallest structure in the world and is still the tallest structure of masonry. Everyone who looks at the monument is immediately aware that there is a slight but definite change in the color of the exterior stone part of the way up. This is where construction was stopped in 1854 by the American Party (the Know-Nothings). They objected to the donation of a block of marble by Pope Pius IX and not only stole the block but managed to sabotage contributions. Construction was unable to continue until 1876 when it was turned over to the Corps of Engineers for completion. They redesigned the proportions by altering the height and set the capstone of aluminum in place on December 6, 1884. Today, you can take a quick elevator ride to the top rather than walking up the 188 steps. The view from the top is all they say it is.

**Washington Visitor Information
    Center**   789-7000
1455 Pennsylvania Avenue (14th/15th Sts.) (inside the Willard Collection Shops)

Go up the steps to the left of the Willard's main entrance (or ask the doorman) and you will find a small office on your left. This is where the Washington Visitor Information Center dispenses information to the general public. The staff is friendly, courteous, and best of all, helpful. They have a fairly complete collection of sightseeing brochures and one of the most useful maps of the city.

White House, The   456-1414
1600 Pennsylvania Ave., N.W.
          Tuesday–Saturday 10A.M.–Noon
More than one and a half million visitors each year take advantage of the opportunity to tour the world's only residence of a head of state that is open to the public free of charge. This can lead to long lines, so we advise that you contact your Senator or Congressperson far in advance of your visit and request tickets for a VIP tour. These are conducted in the mornings before the regular tour hours and include a few more rooms. Visitors on the regular tour will see the East Room, familiar through televised press conferences and concerts, dominated by Gilbert Stuart's famous painting of George Washington. This was daringly saved by Dolley Madison just before the British set fire to the White House in 1814. (Legend has it that she also saved an extremely flattering portrait of herself that now hangs in the Red Room.) In less formal days, Abigail Adams hung her laundry and Theodore Roosevelt's children practiced their roller skating in this room. The tour continues to the Green Room and the oval-shaped Blue Room, used as a wedding chapel by Grover Cleveland in 1886 when he married Frances Folsom. This is where the President brings Heads of State and VIPs after welcoming them on the South Lawn. The final stop in the State Dining Room, which seats up to 140. John Adams's White House Prayer, "I pray heaven to bestow the best of blessings on this house and all that shall hereafter inhabit it. May none but honest and wise men ever rule under this roof," written in a letter to his wife, is inscribed on the marble mantlepiece. Although picture-taking is forbidden within the White House, when you emerge on the north side under the great portico, you'll want to stop to take a snapshot for posterity.

Wolf Trap Farm Park   1-703-255-1860
1551 Trap Road, Vienna Virginia   **Box Office: 255-1900**
          Wolf Trap is an in-door/out-door center for the performing and visual arts. Located on 117 acres of beautiful woodland in Virginia, it annually plays host to some of the biggest names in the entertainment world. The Filine Cen-

ter seats almost 7000 people with about half of the seats open to the skies. A wonderful place to visit.

Woodrow Wilson House, The   387-4062
2340 S Street, N.W.
> Tuesday–Sunday 10:00A.M.–4:00 P.M.
> Admission:
> Adults: $3.50
> Children: $2.00
> Metro: Dupont Circle

The only President to remain in the capital after his term expired, Wilson lived in this red-brick Georgian Revival house from the day he left the White House until his death three years later. The house, bequeathed to the nation by Mrs. Wilson, is preserved much as it was when the Wilsons lived here. The typewriter on which he drafted the League of Nations proposal, the graphoscope (projector) given to Wilson by Douglas Fairbanks, Sr. so he could watch silent movies, and a mosaic of St. Peter given to him by Pope Benedict XV are on view.

Sign of the Whale   223-0608
1825 M Street, N.W.

Silverman Galleries, Inc.   1-703-836-5363
110 North Asaph Street, Alexandria, Virginia

Singapore Airlines   1-800-742-3333

Singapore (Embassy of)   667-7555
1824 R Street, N.W.

SINGLES BARS

Champions   965-4005
1206 Wisconsin Avenue, N.W., Georgetown

Both a singles hang-out and a sports bar, this is a popular place. *Playboy* magazine voted it "the best" for two years in a row.

Clyde's   333-0294
3236 M Street, N.W., Georgetown

Clyde's is one of the oldest of the saloons in Georgetown and also owns Old Ebbitt Grill near the White House. Lots of celebrities are to be found here, and on weekends it's packed.

Duddington's Underground Sports
Bar   544-3500
319 Pennsylvania Avenue, S.E.

If you're in the Capitol Hill area, this is a must. Jukebox, pinball, large screen TV, video games, and a large and noisy crowd make this an ideal watering hole for some. Upstairs is a sports bar.

Jenkins Hill   544-6600
223 Pennsylvania Avenue, S.E.
For weekends only. During the week it hosts locals and employees from the hill.

Rumors   466-7378
1900 M Street, N.W.
Playboy seems to have handed out a lot of awards in Washington. This one received "hottest singles bar." The usual crowd of young professionals, government employees, and students mingle with whatever stars are in town.

Sign of the Whale   223-0608
1825 M Street, N.W.
Playboy has been at it again. "Best Burger, Best Cheap Eats, Best Bar, and most important, Best Male to Female Ratio." What can we possibly add to that?

Sitters Unlimited   250-5250

Sky Terrace, The   347-4499
Hotel Washington, 15th Street and Pennsylvania Avenue, N.W.

Somalia (Embassy of)   342-1575
600 New Hampshire Avenue, NW

Sotterley Mansion   1-301-373-2280
Route 235 (south of Waldorf), Hollywood, Maryland

South Africa (Embassy of)   232-4400
3051 Massachusetts Avenue, N.W.

Spain (Embassy of)   265-0190
2700 15th Street, N.W.

Sparrows   1-301-530-0175
4115 Howard Avenue, Kensington, Maryland

Spinnaker 'N Spoke   1-703-548-9027
George Washington Parkway, Alexandria, Virginia

Spirit of Mt. Vernon   554-8000
Pier 4 (6th/Water Streets, S.W.)

Spirit of Washington   554-8000
Pier 4 (6th/Water Streets, S.W.)

SPORTING GOODS

Barry Ephraim   628-6465
816 15th Street, N.W.

Bicycle Pro Shop   337-0311
3413 M Street, N.W.

Dive Shop   **1-703-998-6140**
1543 North Quaker Lane, Alexandria, Virginia

Eddie Bauer, Inc.   **331-8009**
1800 M Street, N.W.

Herman's World of Sporting Goods   **638-6434**
800 E Street, N.W.

Hudson Trail Outfitters, Ltd.   **393-1244**
The Shops at National Place, 1331 Pennsylvania
Avenue, N.W.

Irving's Sport Shops   **393-2626**
10th and E Streets, N.W.

J. Lynn & Co.   **223-0310**
1900 I Street, N.W.

Racquet & Jog   **861-6939**
915 19th Street, N.W.

Spinnaker 'N Spoke   **1-703-548-9027**
George Washington Parkway, Alexandria, Virginia

Tennis & Fitness Sports Discounters   **1-703-920-6962**
3621 Columbia Pike, Arlington, Virginia

Washington Golf Centers   **1-301-587-4653**
9309 Georgia Avenue, Silver Spring, Maryland

Sports Update (Washington Post)   **223-8060**

SPORTS BARS

Sports bars tend to be very similiar. They all have large TV
screens (usually with satellite dish) and a loyal following of
sports addicts. Try these:

Bottom Line, The   **298-8488**
1716 I Street, N.W.

Champions   **965-4005**
1206 Wisconsin Avenue, N.W.

Chicago Bar & Grill   **463-8888**
19th Street and Dupont Circle

Duddington's Underground Sports
    Bar   **544-3500**
319 Pennsylvania Avenue, S.E.

Springfield Mall
Franconia and Loisdale Roads, Springfield, Virginia

Sri Lanka (Embassy of)   **483-4025**
2148 Wyoming Avenue, N.W.

St. John's Church & Parish House	347-8766

16th & H Street, N.W.

St. John's Episcopal Church	343-8766

Lafayette Square, 16th and H Streets, N.W.

St. Lucia (Embassy of)	463-7378

2100 M Street, N.W.

St. Matthew's Cathedral	347-3215

1725 Rhode Island Avenue, N.W.

St. Sophia Cathedral	333-4730

36th Street & Massachusetts Avenue, N.W.

STADIUMS

Capital Centre   1-301-350-3400
1 Harry Truman Drive, Capital Beltway
(exits 15 & 17 east), Landover, Maryland

D.C. Armory Starplex   547-9077
2001 East Capitol Street, N.W. (22nd St.)
Redskins Ticket Office   546-2222
Starplex Ticket Office   546-3337

Patriot Center, The   1-703-323-2672
George Mason University   **Tickets 432-0200**
4400 University Drive, Fairfax, Virginia
Take the Wilson Bridge to Braddock Road West
(Route 623) and continue for approximately eight miles
to University Drive.

Robert F. Kennedy Memorial Statium   547-9077
East Capitol Street (19th/   **Tickets 432-0200**
20th Sts., S.E.)

**State Department Diplomatic
    Reception Rooms**   647-3241
C and 22nd Streets, N.W.

Stein's Theatrical & Dance Center   1-703-522-2660
1180 North Highland Street , Arlington, Virginia

Stetson's   667-6295
1610 U Street, N.W.

Steven-Windsor   293-2770
1730 K Street, N.W.

STORES

Downtown Washington has some very nice shops and
stores, but it is not a shopper's paradise. Most of the local
residents go to the shopping malls where many of the best

stores are to be found. We list those that merit special mention. Be sure to also check the listing under SHOPPING MALLS. Metro service is available to the best of them, and it's a treat to have everything under one roof.

American Hand, The   965-3273
2906 M Street, N.W.
Wonderful American handmade pottery. Well worth a visit.

Antoinette's Heirloom Jewelry   347-8110
The Willard Hotel, 1400 F Street, N.W.
Adele was impossible! She loves antique jewelry and wanted everything. McDowell let her look through the plate glass window, and the next thing he knew she was inside trying on Victorian earrings. The staff was far too kind and helpful; so was American Express. Be warned, you'll buy something.

Appalachian Spring   337-5780
1415 Wisconsin Avenue NW
As the name would suggest, this shop carries a fine stock of handcrafted objects ranging from pottery to jewelry.

Britches of Georgetown   338-3330
1247 Wisconsin Ave., N.W., Georgetown
Tweedy menswear with pretensions.

Brooks Brothers   659-4650
1840 L Street, N.W.
The most famous men's clothing chain in the country. Unbelievably conservative.

Camalier & Buckley   347-7700
1141 Connecticut Avenue, N.W.
Some of the very best luggage and leather goods passes through these doors. The staff is friendly and the prices are, as usual for this type of store, high.

Full Circle   1-703-683-4500
317 Cameron Street, Alexandria, Virginia
More handcrafted work by both American and international artists. A huge variety is available.

Ginza   331-7991
1721 Connecticut Avenue, N.W.
Buy a beautiful gift, preferably for yourself. They have the fine Japanese items we have all come to cherish. Pottery and porcelain, of course, but also kites and unusual jewelry.

Gucci   965-1700
600 New Hampshire Avenue, N.W.
The best known of the leather specialty stores, Gucci continues to offer fine luggage, handbags, briefcases, and gift items.

Hoffritz   466-4382
1008 Connecticut Avenue, N.W.
Famous for knives and weird gadgets of all kinds.

J.E. Caldwell Co.   466-6780
1140 Connecticut Avenue, N.W.
One of the finest jewelers, they stock a wide variety of expensive watches, crystal, china, gift items, and, of course, jewelry.

Jos. A. Bank Clothiers   466-2282
1118 19th Street, N.W.
Brooks Brothers styling for a lot less money. Experience tells us that "you get what you pay for."

Laura Ashley   338-5481
3213 Wisconsin Avenue, N.W.
Laura Ashley's floral patterns, dainty dresses, and distinctive housewares have won her a large following.

Liberty of London   338-3711
Georgetown Park Mall, 3222 M Street, N.W.
The best buys here are still the old fashioned scarves and fabrics that made this English shop so famous.

Little Caledonia Shop   333-4700
1419 Wisconsin Avenue NW, Georgetown
Small scale furniture and gift items make this an interesting place to browse on your next trip to Georgetown.

Little German World   1-703-684-5344
1512 King Street, Alexandria, Virginia
All kinds of wares made in Germany, including cuckoo clocks.

Louis Vuitton   296-6838
Washington Square, 1028 Connecticut Avenue, N.W.
It's hard to beat Vuitton for beauty and elegance. To know their name is to know what they carry.

Moon, Blossoms & Snow   543-8181
225 Pennsylvania Avenue, S.E.
More American crafts, these taken from the American Crafts Council. Highly recommended.

Music Box Center   783-9399
918 F Street, N.W.
Music boxes, of course. A great selection.

Pampillonia
1213 Connecticut Avenue, N.W.   628-6305
Mazza Gallerie, 5300 Wisconsin   363-6305
Avenue, N.W.
Devoted to both estate and contemporary jewelry, there

is little reason to go anywhere else. Only the very best will do here. Note that they have two locations.

Pierre Deux   244-6226
Mazza Gallerie, 5300 Wisconsin Avenue, N.W.
One of the busiest stores in the Mazza Gallerie and one with which we are all familiar. They feature the usual antiques and reproductions but also carry a lot of clothing and children's things.

Pineapple, Inc., The   1-703-836-3639
132 King Street, Alexandria, Virginia
A large selection of Williamsburg style gifts and things for the home. If you can't make the trip to Williamsburg, this is next best thing.

Raleigh's   785-7070
1133 Connecticut Avenue, N.W.
Conservative men's clothing.

Rubesch's, Inc.   1-703-548-0659
119 South Royal Street, Alexandria, Virginia
One of the few shops we have found that maintains a family tradition. Three generations have made this jewelery store into a must for many families. Be sure to see the antique jewelry.

Saks-Jandel   1-301-652-2250
5514 Wisconsin Ave., N.W., Chevy Chase, Maryland
Women's designer fashions by almost everyone who counts. Needless to say, it's very expensive.

Saks-Watergate   337-4200
2522 Virginia Avenue, N.W.
A boutique featuring women's wear from the workrooms of American designers.

Satin & Lace   659-5223
2000 Pennsylvania Avenue, N.W.
Sexy lingerie of silk and lace. Lots of big name designers' work.

**Save the Children International
     Craft Center**   822-8426
1341 Connecticut Avenue, N.W.
Little goodies from all over the world. You'll find gift items to make your day, and the profits benefit Save the Children.

Secondhand Rose   337-3378
1516 Wisconsin Avenue, N.W.
You can buy designer clothing, including furs, at greatly

reduced prices. Everything is about a third of the original purchase price and is in excellent condition.

Tiny Jewel Box, The   393-2747
1143 Connecticut Avenue, N.W.
Antique jewelry of all kinds, even a nice collection of pocket watches.

Williams-Sonoma   244-4800
Mazza Gallerie, 5300 Wisconsin Avenue NW
A fascinating store that has almost everything for the kitchen. Their catalog lists over 4000 items.

Stratford Hall Plantation   1-804-493-8038
State Road 214, east of Fredericksburg, Virginia

STREET GUIDE

Finding an address in Washington is relatively easy, once you get the hang of it. The city is divided into four sections, Northwest, Northeast, Southwest, and Southeast. Every street address is therefore followed by the all-important N.W., N.E., S.W., or S.E. The Capitol serves as the center of the grid, with North Capitol Street, South Capitol Street, East Capitol Street, and the Mall serving as dividing lines. North–south streets are numbers. East-west streets are letters (except J, X, Y or Z) in alphabetical order. Streets with State names, such as Connecticut, New York, and Pennsylvania, are diagonals. Two-syllable names in alphabetical order (Adams, Bryant, Channing) begin where the letters end. Next come three-syllable names. In a four-digit address, the first two digits indicate the lower-numbered cross street. In a three-digit address, the first digit indicates the lower-numbered cross street. For example, Washington's most famous address, 1600 Pennsylvania Avenue (The White House) is located in the northwest quadrant at 16th Street and Pennsylvania Avenue. 1915 K Street, N.W. (Tiberio, one of our favorite Italian restaurants) is between 19th and 20th Streets. Finding an address on a numbered street is more complicated—figure roughly one block per letter of the alphabet. Going north or south, the blocks between A and B Streets are the 100 blocks, between B and C the 200 blocks, and so forth. If all this seems too confusing, ask someone.

Stuart Aviation Service   1-703-892-2650
National Airport   1-800-225-0990

Studio Antiques, Inc.   1-703-548-5188
628 North Washington Street , Alexandria, Virginia

Studio Theater, The   **265-7412**
1401 Church Street, N.W.

SUBWAYS
See **METRORAIL**

Sudan (Embassy of)   **466-6280**
2210 Massachusetts Avenue, N.W.

Sully Plantation   **1-703-437-1794**
Sully Road (off State Road 28), Chantilly, Virginia

Sumner School Museum & Archives   **727-3419**
1201 17th Street, N.W. (M St./Rhode Island Ave.)

Supreme Court   **252-3000**
1st and East Capitol Streets, N.E.

Surinam (Embassy of)   **244-7488**
4301 Connecticut Avenue, N.W.

Sushi Taro   **462-8999**
1503 17th Street, N.W. (P St.)

Sushi-Ko   **333-4187**
2309 Wisconsin Avenue, N.W. (Observatory Lane),
Georgetown

Sutton Place Gourmet   **363-5800**
3201 New Mexico Avenue, N.W.

Swaziland (Embassy of)   **362-6683**
4301 Connecticut Avenue, N.W.

Sweden (Embassy of)   **944-5600**
600 New Hampshire Avenue, N.W.

Swissair   **1-800-221-4750**

Switzerland (Embassy of)   **745-7900**
2900 Cathedral Avenue, N.W.

Syms   **1-703-241-8500**
1000 East Broad Street, Falls Church, Virginia

SYNAGOGUES
See **CHURCHES, SYNAGOGUES, AND MOSQUES**

Syria (Embassy of)   **232-6313**
2215 Wyoming Avenue, N.W.

Szechuan   **393-0130**
615 I Street, N.W. (6th/7th Sts.)

T

Tabard Inn, The   **785-1277**
1739 N Street, N.W.

Taberna del Alabardero   **429-2200**
1776 I Street, N.W. (18th St.)

TACA   **234-7006**

Tachibana   **1-703-558-1122**
4050 Lee Highway (Military Rd./Quincy St.),
Arlington, Virginia

TAILORS, MEN'S

    Gaetano Gervasi   **544-6772**
    621 Pennsylvania Avenue, S.E. (second floor)

    Ignacy Kunin   **265-5900**
    1725 Wisconsin Avenue, N.W.

    Jos. A. Wilner & Co.   **223-0448**
    1714 L Street, N.W.

Takesushi   **466-3798**
1010 20th Street, N.W. (K/L Sts.)

Tanzania (Embassy of)   **939-6125**
2139 R Street, N.W.

Tartt Gallery   **332-5652**
2017 Q Street, N.W.

Taverna Cretekou   **1-703-548-8688**
818 King Street (South Henry St.), Alexandria, Virginia

Taxi Commission (Lost & Found)   **767-8370**

TAXIS

In our experience, taxis in Washington, almost without exception, have been disreputable and unappealing, tending to be old and in disrepair. Some of the ones we used were station wagons with the back full of junk. We assume this is because the rates are so cheap that there is no incentive to upgrade and maintain equipment. The Taxi Commission should be ashamed of itself. We'd rather pay more and have better service. The good news is that taxis are cheap, and will get you to your destination. Not only can you hail them on the street, you can also telephone and order one. There are three taxi companies providing this service.

Diamond Cab Co.	387-6200
Yellow Cab Co.	544-1212
Capitol Cab	546-2400

TEA ROOMS/SERVICE

High tea is an exclusive gift from the best hotels. They are accustomed to serving the best to the most discriminating. For a quiet and comfortable respite in a busy day, stop in at one of the following between 3:00 P.M. and 5:00 P.M. We've described some of our favorites, but you will be well served at any of these.

Jefferson Restaurant, The   785-0500
The Jefferson, 16th and M Streets, N.W.
Caviar chiffon cake, smoked salmon mousse, smoked chicken and ligonberry sandwiches, walnut shortbread, dipped strawberries, and of course, scones with Devon cream, are among the goodies that distinguish the tea provided by Executive Chef Will Greenwood. As befits one of the most important of the established hotels, this is a power scene. The hotel caters primarily to CEOs of major companies, and you will find them having tea with their counterparts in government between 3:00 P.M. and 5:00 P.M. You can have Informal Tea near the fireplace, from which you can serve yourself, or Formal Tea in the lounge area, featuring full tea service in the English tradition.

Morrison Clark Inn   898-1200
1015 L Street, NW (11th St./Massachusetts Ave.)

Morrison House Hotel   1-703-838-8000
116 S. Alfred Street, Alexandria, Virginia
Tea is served every day in the charming, early American parlor.

Park Hyatt Hotel   789-1234
24th and M Streets, N.W.

Ritz-Carlton Hotel   835-2100
2100 Massachusetts Avenue, N.E.
This fashionable hotel will be under renovation for some time. They intend to stay open during the process and it is a wonderful place for people watching while you have tea.

Sheraton Carlton, The   638-2626
923 16th Street, N.W.
The Great Hall is the perfect place for a quiet stop at the end of a busy day. You may choose from a light tea (scones with double Devon cream and fruit preserves, fruit tartlet, and tea bread), or the complete tea, which includes all of the

above plus finger sandwiches. In addition to a variety of teas, ports, sherries, champagnes and aperitifs are available. The harpist whose music fills the huge room is perfectly in keeping with the Italian Renaissance decor and relaxed atmosphere. Tea is served Monday through Saturday from 3:00 P.M. to 5:30 P.M.

Watergate Hotel, The	**965-2300**
2650 Virginia Avenue, N.W.	
Willard Hotel, The	**628-9100**
1401 Pennsylvania Avenue, N.W.	

One of the most elegant dining rooms we know. The atmosphere is perfect for a little snack and afternoon breather. The food is always a treat.

TELEGRAMS

Western Union (for Information)	**1-800-325-6000**
To send a telegram, cablegram, or	
mailgram	**737-4260**
To send money using a credit card	**1-800-988-2273**
Se habla Espanol	**1-800-988-7726**
Telex service	**1-800-988-1100**

All Western Union offices and their affiliates are listed in the C&P White Pages. They can provide complete service including sending and receiving money. The White Pages will tell you which office is nearest to where you are staying.

TELEPHONE NUMBERS

See **EMERGENCY TELEPHONE NUMBERS**

TENNIS

Washington provides many public courts. We are not tennis players, but we are told that there are so many people who are that it is very difficult to get court time. Call the following numbers for information:

East Potomac Park	**554-5962**
Rock Creek Park	**723-2669**
U.S. Department of Recreation	**673-7646**

There are also the tennis matches for watching, not playing. Now one of the most popular of spectator sports, tennis has a huge following.

Souvran Bank Classic, The	**429-0690**
The Washington Tennis Center, 16th and	
Kennedy Streets, N.W.	

One of the two major tournaments played annually, this is the one for men. Played at the worst possible time of the year, late July to early August, the weather couldn't be hotter or more muggy.

Virginia Slims Tournament, The 1-703-432-0200
The Patriot Center, 4400 University Drive,
Fairfax, Virginia
This is for ladies only and takes place each February.

Tennis & Fitness Sports Discounters 1-703-920-6962
3621 Columbia Pike, Arlington, Virginia

Terrace Room, The 293-2100
The Ritz-Carlton Hotel, 2100 Massachusetts Avenue, N.W.

Terrace Theater, The 254-9895
The Kennedy Center for the Performing Arts,
New Hampshire Avenue and Rock Creek Parkway

Terrazza 1-703-683-6900
710 King Street (Washington/Columbus Sts.),
Alexandria, Virginia

Texas State Society, The 488-5869
600 Maryland Avenue, S.W.

Textile Museum, The 667-0441
2320 S Street, N.W.

Thai Flavor 966-0200
3709 Macomb Street, N.W. (Wisconsin Ave.)

Thai Kingdom 835-1700
2021 K Street, N.W. (20th/21st Sts.)

Thai Taste 387-8876
2606 Connecticut Avenue, N.W. (Calvert St.)

Thailand (Embassy of) 483-7200
2300 Kalorama Road, N.W.

THEATERS

With more than 21 professional stage theaters, Washington has been described by *Variety* as the second-best theater city in the United States outside of New York. Most Broadway productions either preview or play on tour in Washington. We list the major theaters:

Arena Stage 488-3300
6th and M Streets, S.W.

Concert Hall, The 254-3776
John F. Kennedy Center **(Instant Charge)** 857-0900
New Hampshire Avenue, N.W. and Rock Creek
Parkway

Eisenhower Theater, The   254-3670
John F. Kennedy Center   **(Instant Charge)** 857-0900
New Hampshire Avenue, N.W. and Rock Creek
Parkway

Folger Theater, The   546-4000
201 East Capitol Street, S.E.

Ford's Theater (Information)   347-4833
511 10th Street, N.W.   **(Tickets)** 432-0200

John F. Kennedy Center for the
    Performing Arts   254-3600
New Hampshire Avenue, N.W. and Rock Creek
Parkway

National Theater, The   **(Information)** 628-6161
1321 E Street, N.W.   **(Tickets)** 554-1900

New Playwright's Theatre, The   232-1122
1742 Church Street, N.W.

Opera House, The   254-3770
John F. Kennedy Center   **(Instant-Charge)** 857-0900
New Hampshire Avenue, N.W. and Rock Creek
Parkway

Studio Theater, The   265-7412
1401 Church Street, N.W.

Terrace Theater, The   254-9895
John F. Kennedy Center   **(Instant-Charge)** 857-0900
New Hampshire Avenue, N.W. and Rock Creek
Parkway

Third Edition   333-3700
1218 Wisconsin Avenue, N.W.

Thompson Boat Center   333-4861
Rock Creek Parkway and Virginia Avenue, N.W.

Thrifty Car Rental   1-800-367-2277
2900 Jefferson Davis Highway   1-703-548-1600
Arlington, Virginia

Tiberio   452-1915
1915 K Street, N.W. (19th/20th Sts.)

Ticket Connection, The   1-301-587-6850
Silver Spring, Maryland

Ticket Finders   1-301-277-4779
5502 Kenilworth Avenue, Riverdale, Maryland

Ticket Outlet, Inc., The   1-301-740-4236
6041 Majors Lane, Columbia, Maryland

Ticketplace   842-5357
F Street Plaza (12th/13th Sts., N.W.)

Ticketron   **659-2601**
1101 17th Street, N.W.

TICKETS

The following establishments carry tickets to sporting events, the theater, and concerts. They will accept credit card reservations over the telephone, and your tickets will be held at the place of performance. They are all reputable companies from which you can buy with confidence. They normally do not allow cancellations.

Murray's Tickets   **1-301-770-5233**
1750 Rockville Pike, Rockville, Maryland

Ticket Connection   **1-301-587-6850**
Silver Spring, Maryland

Ticket Finders   **1-301-277-4779**
5502 Kenilworth Avenue, Riverdale, Maryland

Ticket Outlet, Inc.   **1-301-740-4236**
6041 Majors Lane, Columbia, Maryland

Ticketplace   **842-5357**
F Street Plaza (12th & 13th Sts., N.W.)
Cut price tickets to most theaters and concerts. Available only on the day of the performance.

Ticketron   Concert & Outlet Info **659-2601**
1101 17th Street, NW

Top Centre Ticket & Limo Service   **585-0046**
This company can provide not only tickets but the car to take you to the performance.

Washington Bullets   **773-2255**
Capitol Beltway (Exits 15 & 17 East)
Tickets for the Washington Bullets only.

Washington Capitals   **432-0200**
Capitol Beltway (Exits 15 & 17 East)
Tickets for the Washington Capitals only.

Tidal Boat House   **484-3475**
1501 Main Avenue, S.W.

Time   **844-2525**

Tiny Dwelling, The   **1-703-548-1223**
1510 King Street, Alexandria, Virginia

Tiny Jewel Box, The   **393-2747**
1143 Connecticut Avenue, N.W.

TIPPING

Nothing smooths your way quite as much as the judiciously placed tip. Remember that people in the service industries in Washington are not well-paid. Since tips make the difference between living well and just surviving, they will work hard to get them. It is important to understand how to use tips to get the best service. While there are some areas in which guidelines may be given, the old adage that it is gauche to overtip is a myth. You will always find people who do their jobs well regardless, but if you like excellent service you must pay for it—particularly in the restaurant and hotel business.

There are no rules for tipping a concierge. In general, these are the people who will consistantly give you the most and best regardless. A favorite guest of McDowell's was a judge from Texas who gave $1.00. On the other hand there are guests who think nothing of giving $500 tips. It's up to you. We list people whose tips have become reasonably well established by custom. The amounts mentioned are the minimums, and you should feel free to increase the tip based on the amount of satisfaction you have received.

- Taxi drivers: 15% to 20% of the fare
- Bellmen: $1.00 per bag
- Restaurant Captain: 5% to 10% of the check
- Waiters: 15% to 20% of the check
- Airport porters: $1.00 per bag

In Washington you will frequently meet the owners of restaurants; it is not correct to tip them. Many people bring gifts to owners (and to others they frequently encounter) as a way to express their gratitude for fine service. Another of McDowell's guests (a permanent resident) used to bring him little desserts every day. He looked forward to these expressions of her appreciation. So you can see that tipping is not as cut and dried as most advisors would have you believe. Just remember, if you are happy with the service, tip what you think the extra effort was worth.

TOBACCO

Draper W. Curtis Tobacconist, Inc.   638-2555
640 14th Street, N.W.

Conveniently located near Metro Center, Draper W. Curtis carries a full line of pipes, cigars, and tobacco users' accessories. They carry McDowell's favorite Dunhill cigars—his Montecruz supply is always our first quest in any city we visit.

Earthworks Tobacco & Snuff	**332-4323**
1724 20th Street, N.W.	

A. Garfinkel, Inc.   **638-1175**
1585 I Street, N.W.
Another well located spot. A small shop with low key, friendly service whose motto is "For the exclusive smoker."

Georgetown Tobacco	**338-5100**
3144 Wisconsin Avenue, N.W.	

John Crouch Tobacconist	**548-2900**
128 King Street, Alexandria, Virginia	

Metropolitan Cigar & Tobacco	**223-9648**
921 19th Street, N.W.	

Togo (Embassy of)   **234-4212**
2208 Massachusetts Avenue, N.W.

Tomb of the Unknowns (Tomb of the Unknown Soldier)

Arlington National Cemetery, Arlington, Virginia

Tony Cheng's Mongolian Barbecue   **842-8669**
619 H Street, N.W. (6th/7th Sts.)

Top Center Ticket & Limousine Service   **1-301-585-0046**
8653 Georgia Avenue, Silver Spring, Maryland

Total Audio-Visual Systems, Inc.   **737-3900**
303 H Street, N.W.

Touchdown Club, The   **223-1542**
2000 L Street, N.W.

Tourist Information—Dial an Event Line   **737-8866**

TOURIST INFORMATION

Washington Visitor Information Center   **789-7000**
1455 Pennsylvania Avenue (14th/15th Sts.) (inside the Willard Collection Shops)
Go up the steps to the left of the Willard's main entrance (or ask the doorman) and you will find a small office on your left. This is where the Washington Visitor Information Center dispenses information to the general public. The staff is friendly, courteous, and best of all, helpful. They have a fairly complete collection of sightseeing brochures and one of the most useful maps of the city.

Tourmobile, The   554-7950
1000 Ohio Drive, S.W.

TOURS

Tours can be one of the fastest and easiest ways to get an overview of the Washington sights. There is so much to see that if you only have a limited amount of time, there is no way to see it all. You must be selective. The following list includes both general tours and some that are more specialized.

American Coach Lines   393-1616
American has all kinds of tours. They can supply one tour that will show you almost everything, to more specific sightseeing. You will have to talk to them to narrow it down to fit your personal needs.

C & O Canal Tours   1-703-472-4376
A narrow and picturesque strip of water that was designed to carry cargo on mule-pulled barges, the Chesapeake & Ohio Canal was replaced almost immediately by the railroad. Today, you can walk along the banks or take a barge trip. It's great fun to see how the locks work and to glide quietly along on the boat. Children love it.

Gray Line   479-5900
One of the major tourist bus companies that can take you everywhere quickly. Their staff is professional and efficient.

Old Town Trolley Tours   269-3021
A brief, two-hour tour of about 13 different sites. They go to the major places that you will want to see and, since you have unlimited boarding rights, you may get off and visit any place that strikes your fancy. They stop at several of the major hotels which makes it easy for you to start and end your trip.

Potomac Party Cruises   683-6076
The Dandy is the boat you will be traveling on, and although it's not gourmet dining, it is a wonderful cruise. After dinner, there is dancing. A very nice way to see the sights from the river.

Spirit of Washington Cruises   554-8000
Tours to Mt. Vernon, plus luncheon, brunch, and dinner cruises on the Potomac. The cruise to Mt. Vernon includes a two hour stop at George Washington's home after the trip down river. Be sure to call for complete information.

Tourmobile   554-7020
Nothing beats the Tourmobile. It has the National Parks

Service concession and, with its running commentary, is our favorite way to see the major federal sights. It takes you everywhere and you have unlimited boarding privileges. Get off whenever you want and reboard when you are ready. You may board at any of the major monuments or at stops along the Mall.

Adults $7.00

Children (3–11 years) $3.50

TOWED CARS

Storage Lot   **For a recorded message call: 727-5000**
Brentwood and W Streets, N E.

(If you are told the line is out of sevice, call the Police Department at 727-1000. They will connect you.) It isn't easy to find out where your car was taken if it has been towed. Cars that are towed, for any reason, are taken to the Brentwood Storage Lot. In order to retrieve your car you must pay all outstanding traffic tickets. The fine for being towed is $50.00. In addition, there is a storage charge of $3.00 per day, starting 24 hours after your car is towed. They will only accept cash, credit cards, or certified checks. A credit card is always the easiest. You must be able to prove that the car is registered to you or that you are authorized by the owner to pick it up.

Tower Records   **333-2400**
2000 Pennsylvania Avenue, N.W.

Town & Country, The   **347-3000**
The Mayflower Hotel, 1127 Connecticut Avenue, N.W.

TOYS

Child's Play   **393-2382**
The Shops at National Place,
1331 Pennsylvania Avenue, N.W.

Easy games and stuffed toys for younger children. They also have a great selection of stuff that winds up or works by battery.

Energy Sciences   **783-1099**
The Shops at National Place,
1331 Pennsylvania Avenue, N.W.

If your children are of a scientific bent, they will find a lot here to interest them. All kinds of microscopes, telescopes, and kits to put together.

FAO Schwartz
Mazza Gallerie,
5300 Wisconsin Avenue, N.W.   **363-8455**
Georgetown Park Mall, 3222 M Street, N.W.   **342-2285**
New York's finest toy store has brought its magic to DC. Not on the same opulent scale as their flagship New York store, it still delights young shoppers.

Flights of Fancy   **783-2800**
The Shops at National Place,
1331 Pennsylvania Avenue, N.W.
Lots of strange stuffed animals with lots of high prices.

John Davy Toys   **1-703-683-0079**
301 Cameron Street, Alexandria, Virginia
Features toys from around the world.

Kite Site, The   **965-4230**
3101 M Street, N.W.
The name says it. All kinds of kites and toys that fly. There are also balloons, windsocks, boomerangs, and model rockets to delight children and adults.

Lowen's   **1-301-652-1289**
7201 Wisconsin Avenue, Bethesda, Maryland
One of the most interesting and complete selections of toys, many of them unusual. When you are tired, try the ice-cream parlor; a little sugar always helps.

Phineas Frogg & Friends   **543-1686**
210 7th Street, S.E.
We're bear collectors and rate Phineas Frogg very high on our list of suppliers. While they have all kinds of strange and wonderful things for children, all else pales beside the "Very Important Bears" from North American Bears of Chicago.

Red Balloon, The   **965-1200**
1073 Wisconsin Avenue, N.W.
Inexpensive! Lots of the little things we all grew up with are available here and the prices will astonish you. Mexican jumping beans, squirt guns, and old-fashioned tops are among the many items that we remember from years gone by.

Tiny Dwelling   **1-703-548-1223**
1510 King Street, Alexandria, Virginia
Everything one needs in order to design, build, and furnish the average dollhouse.

Toys-R-Us   **1-301-770-3376**
11800 Rockville Pike, Rockville, Maryland
One of the most comprehensive collections of toys to be

found in Washington. As usual, this popular chain can supply almost anything one might want. Its popularity make shopping a real headache for those of us who hate crowds. Shop early in the morning.

Washington Doll's House & Toy
  Museum   363-6400
5236 44th Street, N.W.

As we point out in our write up under Museums, this is a fascinating place to visit. Go through the museum first in order to get a feeling for the history and achievements of doll making. In the shops are to be found all of the very best materials and furnishings for your own dollhouse. If dolls are your interest, a visit to this museum and shop is essential.

Why Not   1-703-548-4420
200 King Street, Alexandria, Virginia

Combines toys with an interesting selection of children's clothing.

Toys-R-Us   1-301-770-3376
11800 Rockville Pike, Rockville, Maryland

Tracks   488-3320
1111 First Street, S.E.

Trader Vic's   347-7100
The Capitol Hilton, 16th and K Streets, N.W.

Tragara   951-4935
4935 Cordell Avenue, Bethesda, Maryland

Transworld Airlines (TWA)   1-800-221-2000

Travel Books Unlimited & Language
  Center   1-301-951-8533
4931 Cordell Avenue (Old Georgetown Rd./Norfolk Ave.), Bethesda, Maryland

Travel Merchandise Mart   371-6656
1425 K Street, N.W.

Travelers Aid   347-0101

Trinidad/Tobago (Embassy of)   467-6490
1708 Massachusetts Avenue, N.W.

Trocadero Asian Art   234-5656
1501 Connecticut Avenue, N.W.

Trover Shops
227 Pennsylvania Avenue, S.E.   543-8006
1031 Connecticut Avenue, N.W. (K St.)   659-8138
800 15th Street, N.W. (H St.)   347-2177

Trump Shuttle, The	**1-800-247-8786**
National Airport	
Tune Inn	**543-2725**
3311½ Pennsylvania Avenue, S.E.	
Tunisia (Embassy of)	**862-1850**
1515 Massachusetts Avenue, N.W.	
Turkey (Embassy of)	**387-3200**
1606 23rd Street, N.W.	

TUXEDOS
See **RENTAL, FORMAL WEAR, MEN'S**

TWENTY-FOUR HOUR SERVICES

Aircraft Charter Specialists	**486-0086**
	1-800-327-1966
Allstate Repair	**582-8444**
3423 Minnesota Avenue, S.E.	
Capitol Hill Chevron Service	**543-9456**
2nd Street and Massachusetts Avenue, N.E.	
Embassy Chevron Service Center	**659-8560**
22nd and P Streets, N.W.	
Georgetown Amoco	**337-9759**
2715 Pennsylvania Avenue, N.W. (27th St.)	
Georgetown Texaco	**338-3779**
1576 Wisconsin Avenue, N.W.	
Gibson Aviation, Inc.	**1-301-948-5300**
7901 Queen Air Drive, Gaithersburg, Maryland	
Main Post Office	**523-2323**
North Capitol Street and Massachusettes Avenue, N.E.	
My Other Secretary	**429-1997**
1133 15th Street, N.W., Suite 1010	
Peoples Drug Stores, Inc.	
7 Dupont Circle, N.W.	**785-1466**
14th Street and Thomas Circle, N.W.	**628-0720**
Thrifty Car Rental	**1-800-367-2277**
1201 K Street	**1-703-783-0400**
Arlington, Virginia	
U.S. Jet Aviation	**892-6200**
Washington National Airport	
Vietnam Veterans Memorial	**426-6841**
23rd Street at Constitution Ave. N.W.	

Tyson's Corner Center
1961 Chain Bridge Road, McLean, Virginia

U

U.S. Air	**783-4500**
U.S. Botanic Garden	
Conservatory, The	**225-8333**
1st Street and Maryland Avenue, S.W.	
U.S. Capitol	**224-3121**
U.S. Coast Guard (Search & Rescue)	**576-2520**
U.S. Customs	
U.S. Marine Corps Museum	**433-3840**
9th & M Streets, Building 58	
U.S. National Arboretum	**475-4815**
3501 New York Avenue, N.E.	
U.S. Naval Academy	**1-301-267-2291**
Visitor's Gate, King George Street, Annapolis, Maryland	
U.S. Naval Observatory	**653-1541**
34th Street and Massachusetts Avenue, N.W.	
U.S. Navy Memorial	**524-0830**
Pennsylvania Avenue, N.W. (7th/9th Sts.)	
U.S. Navy Memorial Museum	**433-2651**
9th and M Streets, Building 76	
U.S. Park Police	**426-6600**
U.S. Passport Office	**783-8200**
U.S. Secret Service	**634-5100**
U.S. Supreme Court	**479-3000**
U.S.S.R. (Embassy of)	**628-7551**
1825 Phelps, N.W.	
Uganda (Embassy of)	**726-7100**
5909 16th Street, N.W.	
Union Station	**484-7540**
United Airlines	**1-800-631-1500**
United Arab Emirates (Embassy of)	**338-6500**
600 New Hampshire Avenue, N.W.	

University Club, The   862-8800
1135 16th Street, N.W.

Upper Volta (Embassy of)   332-5577
2340 Massachusetts Avenue, N.W.

Upstairs Doll House, The   1-301-645-9295
Highway 925, Waldorf, Maryland

Uruguay (Embassy of)   331-1313
1918 F Street, N.W.

U.S. Jet Aviation   892-6200
National Airport

USDA Travel Club, Inc   783-1972
14th Street and Independence Avenue, S.W.

USO

The USO is the organization that Congress chartered to help the members of our Armed Forces in their travels. Washington has a particularily strong organization since this is the center of all military operations. If you are an active member of any branch of the services, all of their facilities are available to you. They will help with any question, request, or problem. If it is entertainment you want, they can frequently arrange free or discount tickets to shows or lectures. They know all about discounts to hotels, tours, and restaurants.The premises of the local organizations usually have comfortable lounges with TVs, libraries, lockers in which to store your personal belongings, and showers.

In Washington there are two locations:

Bob Hope USO Building   783-8117
601 Indiana Avenue, N.W.

USO Center   (Information Booth) 920-2705
National Airport North Terminal   920-6990

V

Valentino   333-8700
The Watergate, 600 New Hampshire Avenue, N.W.

Vatican, The (Embassy of)   333-7121
3339 Massachusetts Avenue, N.W.

Venezuela (Embassy of)   797-3800
2445 Massachusetts Avenue, N.W.

VETERINARIANS

Friendly Hospital for Animals	**363-7300**
4105 Brandywine Street, N.W.	
Kindness Animal Hospital	**949-2511**
2130 University Boulevard, West	
MacArthur Animal Hospital	**337-0120**
4832 MacArthur Boulevard, N.W.	

Viasa Venezuelan Airlines   **1-800-221-2150**

Vietnam Veteran's Memorial
23rd Street at Constitution Avenue, N.W.

Vincenzo   **667-0047**
1606 20th Street, N.W. (Q St./Connecticut Ave.)

Visa Inquiries   **663-1972**

Visitor Information Center   **789-7000**

Vista International Hotel   **429-1700**
1400 M Street Avenue, N.W.   **1-800-HILTONS**

Voice of America, The   **485-6231**
Department of Health & Human Services (North Bldg.)
330 Independence Avenue, S.W.

Voorthuis Opticians, Inc.
4250 Connecticut Avenue, N.W.

W

Waldenbooks   **393-1490**
1700 Pennsylvania Avenue, N.W.

Wallace Wentworth Gallery   **387-7152**
2006 R Street, N.W.

Warehouse Antiques   **1-703-548-2150**
218 North Lee Street, Alexandria, Virginia

Warner Theater   **626-1050**
513 13th Street, N.W.

Washington Area Convention &
    Visitors Bureau   **789-7000**
900 9th Street, N.W. (H St./New York Ave.)

Washington Boat Lines, Inc.   **554-8011**
6th & Water Street, S.W.

Washington Bullets   **773-2255**
Capitol Beltway (exits 15 & 17 east)

Washington Capitals   432-0200
Capitol Beltway (exits 15 & 17 east)

**Washington Dolls' House & Toy
    Museum**   1-301-244-0024
5236 44th Street, N.W. (Jenifer/Harrison Sts.),
Chevy Chase, Maryland

Washington Harbor   342-7366
3000 K Street, N.W. (31st St.)

Washington Hebrew Congregation   362-7100
Massachusetts Avenue and Macomb Street, N.W.

Washington Hilton & Towers, The   483-3000
1919 Connecticut Avenue, N.W.   **1-800-HILTONS**

Washington Monument
14th Street and Constitution Avenue, N.W.

Washington National Airport   685-8000

Washington Park   462-5566
2331 Calvert Street, N.W.

Washington Press Club Foundation   393-0613
National Press Building

Washington Sailing Marina   1-703-548-9027
George Washington Parkway (south of National Airport),
Alexandria, Virginia

Washington Visitor Information Center   789-7000
1455 Pennsylvania Avenue, N.W. (14th/15th Sts.), (Inside
the Willard Collection of Shops)

Watergate Florist, Ltd.   337-2545
2548 Virginia Avenue, N.W.

Watergate Health Club, The   298-4460
2650 Virginia Avenue, N.W.

Watergate Hotel, The   965-2300
2650 Virginia Avenue, N.W.   **1-800-424-2736**

Watergate Salon   333-3488
2532 Virginia Avenue, N.W.

Weather   936-1212

Welty's London Limos   1-301-656-2429
Bethesda, Maryland

Western Union   1-800-325-6000

Westin Hotel, The   429-2400
2401 M Street, N.W.   **1-800-228-3000**

White Flint Mall
11301 Rockville Pike, North Bethesda, Maryland

White House, The. *See*
SIGHTSEEING for more
information   456-1414
1600 Pennsylvania Avenue, N.W.

Why Not   1-703-548-4420
200 King Street, Alexandria, Virginia

Wickel's World of Balloons   449-7460

Willard Room   637-7440
1401 Pennsylvania Avenue, N.W. (14th/15th Sts.)

Willard, The   628-9100
1400 Pennsylvania Avenue, N.W.   1-800-327-0200

Williams-Sonoma   244-4800
Mazza Gallerie, 5300 Wisconsin Avenue, N.W.

WILLIAMSBURG, VIRGINIA

When planning your trip to Washington, if time permits, you'd be well advised to include a few days in Colonial Williamsburg—one of Adele's favorite vacation destinations. Located just 150 miles south of Washington, this completely restored colonial village, spread over 173 acres, includes more than five hundred buildings, including eighty-eight original eighteenth-century structures. Williamsburg's variety is endless: you can learn about eighteenth-century bookbinding and furniture making, visit the homes of those who lived here, be locked in the stocks at the gaol, or go on a shopping spree on Duke of Gloucester Street. Eating hearty fare in the entertaining atmosphere of the four colonial taverns is a refreshing pause from sightseeing. Tie a yard-square napkin around your neck and indulge as the colonials did. Any trip here starts with a stop at the Colonial Williamsburg Visitor Center off U.S. 60 (1-804-229-1000). You can stock up on maps, guidebooks, and information on tours, lodging, and dining. Lodgings range from motels to historic houses and the elegant Williamsburg Inn. (George Washington didn't eat here but Queen Elizabeth II did.) Reserve *well* in advance!

Windows of the East   1-301-654-6444
4747 Elm Street (off Wisconsin Ave.), Bethesda, Maryland

Winston Gallery   333-5414
1204 31st Street, N.W.

Wolf Trap Farm Park   1-703-255-1800
1551 Trap Road, Vienna, Virginia

Wolf Trap Farm's Filene Center   1-703-255-1860
Vienna, Virginia

Women's National Democratic Club   232-7363
1526 New Hampshire Avenue, N.W.

Woodlawn Plantation   1-703-780-4000
9000 Richmond Highway (U.S. 1/Route 235),
Alexandria, Virginia

Woodrow Wilson House, The   387-4062
2340 S Street, N.W.

Woodward & Lothrop   347-5300
11th and F Streets, N.W.

Y

YACHTS

Annapolis Sailing Yacht   1-800-638-5139
Once the property of Walter Cronkite, the 46-foot yacht is
available for cocktail cruises, as well as day or overnight
jaunts. It sleeps ten and includes all the comforts of home,
including a wood-burning fireplace and two bathrooms.

Yale Club of Washington, The   244-7119
4323 Cathedral Avenue, N.W.

Yellow Cab Co.   544-1212

Yemen (Embassy of)   965-4760
600 New Hampshire Avenue, N.W.

Yugoslavia (Embassy of)   462-6566
2410 California Avenue, N.W.

Z

Zaire (Embassy of)   234-7690
1800 New Hampshire Avenue, N.W.

Zambia (Embassy of)   265-9717
2419 Massachusetts Avenue, N.W.

Ziegfeld's   554-5141
1345 Half Street, S.E.

Zimbabwe (Embassy of)   332-7100
2852 McGill Terrace, N.W.

Zip Code Information   682-9595

ZOOS

National Zoological Park 673-4800
3000 Block of Connecticut Avenue
   Open daily except Christmas
   May–September 15th
   Grounds open: 8:00 A.M.–8:00 P.M.
   Buildings open: 9:00 A.M.–6:00 P.M.
   September 16th–April 30th
   Grounds open: 8:00 A.M.–6:00 P.M.
   Buildings open: 9:00 A.M.–4:30 P.M.
   Metro: Woodley Park

A brief trip on Washington's Metro brings you to one of the most popular places in town—the home of the pandas. Adele took a whole roll of photos, the only ones she took in Washington. McDowell wouldn't let her buy the $32 panda sweatshirts so she made him go through the primate house with her. Yuk! Washington has made a major effort to develop a parklike setting where the animals can live and play in comfort. Children and parents alike enjoy watching the elephants, camels, monkeys, and others. We suggest that you call to verify the exact time of the elephant show and sea lion feeding—two extra special events.